Transcendence

Transcendence

My Spiritual Experiences with Pramukh Swamiji

A.P.J. ABDUL KALAM

with

ARUN TIWARI

First published in hardback in India in 2015 by Harper Element
An imprint of HarperCollins *Publishers*

Copyright © A.P.J. Abdul Kalam and Arun Tiwari 2015

P-ISBN: 978-93-5177-405-1
E-ISBN: 978-93-5177-406-8

2 4 6 8 10 9 7 5 3 1

A.P.J. Abdul Kalam and Arun Tiwari assert the moral right
to be identified as the authors of this work.

HarperCollins *Publishers*
A-75, Sector 57, Noida, Uttar Pradesh 201301, India
1 London Bridge Street, London, SE1 9GF, United Kingdom
Hazelton Lanes, 55 Avenue Road, Suite 2900, Toronto, Ontario M5R 3L2
and 1995 Markham Road, Scarborough, Ontario M1B 5M8, Canada
25 Ryde Road, Pymble, Sydney, NSW 2073, Australia
195 Broadway, New York, NY 10007, USA

Typeset in 11/14 Adobe Jenson Pro
by Jojy Philip, New Delhi 110 015

Printed and bound at
Thomson Press (India) Ltd.

To the Righteous People of the World

Contents

Part 3 Fusion of Science and Spirituality

Part 4 Evolution of Creative Leadership

Introduction

I have vivid memories of my childhood in Rameswaram, but one memory particularly stands out, and comes to mind occasionally. As a ten-year-old boy, I recall seeing three contrasting personalities meet from time to time in our home: Pakshi Lakshmana Shastrigal, the Vedic scholar and head priest of the famous Rameswaram temple; Rev. Father Bodal, who built the first church on Rameswaram Island; and my father, who was an imam in the mosque. These three would sit in our courtyard, each with a cup of tea; and they would discuss and find solutions to the various problems facing our community.

Reflecting on this, I can see that my father and his religious counterparts in Rameswaram were expressing a long-standing cultural trait. India has shown a healthy propensity for integrating diverse ideas and reaching a consensus, for thousands of years. And I cannot help but feel that the example of those inter-religious meetings at my family home is most worthy of emulation. Because now, throughout the nation and the world, the need for such frank and genial dialogue among cultures, religions and civilizations is more urgent than ever.

Starting with my father, Jainulabdeen, I have been blessed with some great teachers, who appeared at different stages of my life. My father taught me to view one's role in life as that of an instrument or vessel, through which one takes with one hand and gives with the other. 'There is only one light, and you and I are holes in the lampshade,' he would say. My father lived a simple life as it unfolded before him but never lost sight of the underlying divinity. Throughout my life, I have tried to emulate my father in this regard. My experiences of eight decades have validated the teaching I received from him. I do believe that all human beings carry divinity inside themselves, and that this can lift us out of confusion, misery, melancholy and failure, and indeed guide us when it is contacted.

As a young engineer, I worked with Dr Brahma Prakash. He taught me how tolerance of others' views and opinions is essential in building teams and accomplishing tasks that are beyond the individuals' capacities. He taught me that life is a precious gift, but it comes with responsibility. With this gift, we are expected to use our talents to make the world a better place, to live an ethical and well-balanced life, and to prepare for the spiritual life, which is eternal. Dr Brahma Prakash changed the way I saw the world. He once told me, 'Kalam, if you see this world as mean and rude, it will interfere with your concentration. Negative thinking is similar to carrying twenty bags of luggage on a trip. This baggage will make your trip miserable, and progress will be slow.'

As a project director, I worked with Professor Satish Dhawan, who taught me that a good leader takes the responsibility for the failures of his team, but gives the credit of his success to his colleagues. His academic accomplishments were awesome. He had a Bachelor of Arts in mathematics and a Bachelor of Science in physics, followed by a Master of Arts in mathematics. These were augmented with a Bachelor of Engineering in mechanical engineering, a Master of Science in aerospace engineering and then double PhDs in mathematics and aerospace engineering. When I asked him the secret of his brilliance, he told me: 'Academic brilliance is no different than the brilliance of a mirror. Once dust is removed, the mirror shines and the reflection is clear. We can remove impurities by living pure and ethical lives and serving humanity, and God will shine through us.'

Later, I met Jain muni Acharya Mahapragya, who made me realize the affirmation of a divine life upon earth and an immortal sense in mortal existence. He taught me that our consciousness is the birthplace of our ethics. He said, 'We know something is right when our consciences are clear. Our consciences are our true friends.' Together we wrote *Family and Nation* and articulated two steps to the process of listening to our conscience—to become self-aware so that we can connect to our conscience, and to act on what our conscience says.

I met Pramukh Swamiji, my ultimate teacher, unwittingly. Fate and my curiosity had drawn me to him. Earlier, as principal scientific advisor to the Government of India, I had visited Bhuj to review the rehabilitation work in the aftermath of the earthquake. There, on 15 March 2001, I met Sadhu Brahmaviharidas, a disciple of Pramukh Swamiji. He asked me a startling question which elicited a spiritual response. He asked: 'After the detonation of the first atomic bomb, Robert Oppenheimer remembered the Gita: "Time I am the shatterer of the world". What came to your mind after you detonated India's first atomic bomb?' I was puzzled by this question, and said, 'The energy of God does not shatter, it unifies,' to which he replied, 'Our spiritual leader, Pramukh Swami Maharaj, is a great unifier. He has unified all our energies to regenerate and restore life from the rubble of damage.' I was moved and expressed my desire to meet such a swami. What began as a chance introduction became a divine destiny.

Over several years and multiple meetings with Pramukh Swamiji, I realized that a divine life can have no base unless we recognize the eternal spirit as the inhabitant of this bodily mansion, and integrate all of which the eternal spirit is comprised. That all those living on this planet Earth—around me, away from me, in my country, in other countries; even other species and vegetation and minerals—are all different forms of a great unity. At the most elementary level, all nature is one. Only one noble material weaves constantly different garbs. The nascent convergence of Nano-Bio-Info-Cogno technologies is testimony to this. How can we ensure that this convergence leads to human good and not harm; to the benefit of the marginalized and poor and not to merely an influential few?

With these thoughts on my mind, I travelled to Sarangpur, Gujarat, on 11 March 2014 to see Pramukh Swamiji. This was our latest meeting. We met in a garden inhabited by peacocks, surrounded by beautiful flowers. In an emotionally and spiritually charged atmosphere, Swamiji held my hand for ten minutes. No words were spoken. We looked into each other's eyes in a profound communication of consciousness. It was a great spiritual experience.

I have had a few spiritual experiences even earlier. On 30 September 2001, I survived a helicopter mishap. That night, I had a very vivid dream. I saw myself in a desert on a moonlit night, surrounded by miles of sand. Five great men, namely Emperor Ashoka, Mahatma Gandhi, Albert Einstein, Abraham Lincoln and Caliph Umar, communicated a mission to me for igniting the minds of the young with hope.

On 28 April 2007, in the cave on Philopappos Hill—the place of imprisonment and self-sacrifice of the great soul Socrates—I saw in my mind's eye a powerful streak of lightning. Out of the dark corners of the cave came four apparitions, walking towards me in white robes. Foremost among them was Socrates, who said in a soft voice, 'Thinking is freedom.' Next came Abraham Lincoln who said, 'No human being can be a slave of another.' Then I saw Mahatma Gandhi, who said, 'Eliminate violence in all human missions, let peace prevail.' Finally, I saw Galileo Galilei, who said, 'Truth is beyond human laws.'

But at the garden in Sarangpur with Pramukh Swamiji, there was a difference. On the earlier two occasions, I felt that perhaps my own imagination was at play. This time, Pramukh Swamiji was holding my hand. I became oblivious to the people around us, and was drawn into a kind of timeless silence. I felt that his was the hand of transformation that could bring a change that the world needed today. In these moments, a world vision based on Mother Earth was intuitively communicated to me. Pramukh Swamiji is Gunatit Satpurush, a spiritual person. He has transcended the ephemeral and the modes of nature. I felt as if through Pramukh Swamiji a divine message was transferred to me about something endowed to mankind by God Almighty, but forgotten by humanity.

In a revelatory flash, I realized that the struggle between happiness and unhappiness that had so far been the story of human existence—and the struggle between peace and war that had been the history of the human race—must change. I heard in the silence of his grip on my hand, 'Kalam, go and tell everyone that the power that would lead us to eternal victory amid these struggles is the power of good within us. Communicate to mankind the vision of a harmonious world. This vision would be greater than any other goal ever aspired to by humanity.'

A harmonious world may seem an impossibly utopian vision. But with the guidance of the Divine, and in acknowledging the unity of all creation—and with the helping hand of such transcendent souls as Pramukh Swamiji—the impossible may be achievable. And a harmonious world begins with a harmonious inner world—an unavoidably spiritual quest. For us to ignite our spirituality, we need to look inward and transcend our egos. We need to recognize, connect with and integrate the eternal spirit within.

There are four steps for this: *Search* in the right place, *Remove* the dust, *Open* your inner eye and *See* your destiny waiting for your effort to be realized. Accordingly, I have written this book in four parts. The book starts with my spiritual experiences in the presence of Pramukh Swamiji. The second part reflects on the social work undertaken by the Bochasanwasi Shri Akshar Purushottam Swaminarayan Sanstha (BAPS) under the stewardship of Pramukh Swamiji. The third part shows the way ahead for humanity, with a vision of the fusion of science and spirituality. The fourth part calls for creative leadership, which is essential for the realization of this vision.

The spirit of inclusiveness of BAPS offers a seed to build a glorious crystal of a peaceful and prosperous world, where all civilizations coexist harmoniously and accommodate each other. Pramukh Swamiji has already made an example, by creating a reflective society living through its cultural heritage. He has taken the glory of India to Africa, Europe, America and the Far East in the form of magnificent Swaminarayan temples, strong fellowship of devotees and well-wishers that encompasses millions worldwide. Let it now expand into public dealings—transparent governance and ethical business—based on truth. Driven by the convergence of Bio-Nano-Info-Eco-Cogno technologies, human beings will have unprecedented power. A vision is required to ensure that living conditions at the bottom of the social pyramid will improve across social, political and economic boundaries.

When this book was almost complete, my elder brother A.P.J. Muhammad Muthu Meera Lebbai Maracayer called me from Rameswaram one morning after fajr prayers. Such a call so early in the morning initially worried me, but I was relieved upon hearing his cheerful voice. He asked me, 'Tell me, brother, what is the most important thing you are doing these days?' I had told him about this book. I now expressed my doubt to him: whether it is appropriate for me as a Muslim to write about the leader of another religion.

I have much respect for my brother Maracayer's judgement. He is fourteen years my senior and has lived a very pious life, grounded in Islamic religion and service. He said, 'Kalam, when Prophet Muhammad, *sallallahu 'alayhi wa sallam*, arrived in Medina, there were Jewish and Christian tribes living there. He entered into a treaty with them within a larger framework dealing with inter-Muslim relationships. One of the clauses laid down in the treaty required that each party hold counsel with the other. Mutual relations shall be founded on righteousness; sin is totally excluded.' My brother concluded by asking me to go ahead with the book, and share with everyone details of the pious and virtuous life of Pramukh Swamiji. Thus, the book was finally completed.

I dedicate this book to all the righteous people of the world wherever they are. The Swaminarayan temples and Akshardhams are indeed the sanctuaries of pious and virtuous living. They are abodes of peace and beacons of hope, rescuing people from the bottomless pit of self-indulgence, and, through service, reminding them of their true selves and allowing them to become wholesome human beings. An increasing number of people, particularly in the developed world, are finding freedom from superficial relationships, trivial communications and the constant noise that pervade the modern world, in the counsel and guidance of BAPS saints. May this divine presence increase!

New Delhi   A.P.J. Abdul Kalam
May 2015

Prologue

By the time I reached my home at 10 Rajaji Marg in Delhi after meeting Pramukh Swamiji on 11 March 2014, it was almost midnight. I had my dinner, took a stroll around the 200-year-old arjuna tree in my garden, and went upstairs to retire after a hectic day. My security person gave me a good-night salute, and I bolted my door from inside.

For the last fifty years, I have nurtured a habit of reading a good book, from my sizeable personal library built over five decades, before going to sleep. On this particular night, I randomly searched through my bookshelf. Suddenly, and almost inexplicably, *The Book of Mirdad*, an allegorical book of philosophy written by the Lebanese author Mikhail Naima, came to my hand. It was published in 1954. Though I had it in my library all along, somehow I had never read it.

I sat down on my bed and started reading it.

In the milky mountains, upon the lofty summit known as Altar Peak, stand the spacious and sombre ruins of a monastery once famous as the Ark. Traditions would link it with an antiquity so hoary as the Flood …

I was filled with peace. A strange tranquillity enveloped me. I was not asleep, for I could hear. I was not awake, for I could not move my hand …

'Arise, O happy stranger. You have attained your goal,' I heard a voice say.

'Where am I?' I asked.

'In heaven.'

'And the earth?'

'Is behind you.'

'Who brought me here?'

'He whom you met today.'

'Who are you?'

'I am he.'

'Are you, then, Pramukh Swamiji? But you speak. He did not.'

'But he smiled.'

'Why?'

'To bring a smile to our world. You are the blessed one into whose hands I should deliver the sacred book to publish to the world.'

'What book?'

'The book that would show humanity the way out of the maze of words.'

'Why me?'

'Only you can do it because you see and speak aright; you see nothing but Me and utter nothing but Me.'

'To convey what?'

'That the world has lost its smile and locked itself in the knots of "I" and "Mine". Your world has become a world of barriers and fences and the "I" creates the poles and the barbs that divide them. Humanity is suffering and shredding itself. Kalam, write to break the barriers, overcome the fences and dissolve the divisions created by the "I". Write *Transcendence*.'

PART ONE

EXPERIENCING THE PRESENCE

'Sanctify yourself and you will sanctify society.'

– St Francis of Assisi
Twelfth-century Italian Catholic mendicant

1

Lead India

'A large part of the world received its religious education from India ... In spite of continuous struggle with theological baggage, India has held fast for centuries to the ideals of spirit.'

— Sarvepalli Radhakrishnan
Philosopher and the second president of India

It was a hot summer evening on 30 June 2001 when I met Pramukh Swamiji for the first time. Resplendent in saffron robes, the gentle, fair-complexioned Pramukh Swamiji was radiating divinity. That was the first thought that occurred to me upon seeing him. My friend Y.S. Rajan was with me. We sat down and tried to adjust to Swamiji's powerful and gracious presence with a brief conversation.

I presented to Pramukh Swamiji the ideas of Vision 2020, and said, 'Swamiji, India has had two great visions in modern times. There was a vision for independence in 1857. It took ninety years to get freedom. At that time, the whole nation—young and old—united to achieve freedom. Then in 1950, a republic was envisioned for India to evolve as a nation. Swamiji, what is or what can be such a great vision now? For the last fifty years, India has been a developing country. This means economically it is not strong, socially it is not stable, and its security is insufficient. That is why it is called a developing country. So many people like me are asking:"What should be the next vision for India? How do we transform a developing country into a developed country within the next thirty years?" We have identified five important areas to transform India: education and health care, agriculture, information and communication, infrastructure and critical technology.'

Pramukh Swamiji listened with his eyes fixed on my countenance. He did not speak. I continued, 'Swamiji, our problem is that we may present this to the government, but how do we create people with values to realize such an ambitious vision? What we need is a cadre of value-based citizens. For this you are an expert. We need your advice.'

Pramukh Swamiji smiled. The first words I heard from him were, 'Along with your five areas to transform India, add a sixth one— faith in God and developing people through spirituality. This is very important.' I was taken aback by the clarity, precision and force of his words.

After a pause, Pramukh Swamiji continued, 'We need to first generate a moral and spiritual atmosphere. The present system is suffocating. The climate of crime and corruption is toxic to good thoughts and noble works. This must change. We need to raise people to live by the laws of the scriptures and bear faith in God. For this, we need to rekindle faith in our scriptures and God. Without this, there will be no transformation; nothing will be solved, and you shall not be able to achieve your dream.'

I chose not to interrupt and waited in silence for Pramukh Swamiji's next words. After a while he spoke again. 'Our culture teaches us to learn both para (spiritual) and apara vidya (worldly knowledge). Therefore, together with knowledge of the apara, one should learn the para as well. If one learns this, apara knowledge will become founded on dharma and spirituality. The goal behind God's creation of the universe is that every person, every soul, attains bliss. For this, together with knowledge of His creation, He has given the knowledge of Himself. So, together with this worldly knowledge, knowledge given by God—spirituality—is equally necessary.'

I felt that I was in the Divine Presence. Within Pramukh Swamiji there is a higher presence—the monad, the soul's soul. I felt a strange connection with something that exists in the realm of spirit—the part that is closest to the Divine. There was a light radiating through

Pramukh Swamiji which illuminated my inner self. I felt that I had acquired a sixth sense.

I was taught by my teachers at Schwartz High School in Ramanathapuram that the Divine Presence creates only perfection, and if we call it consistently and earnestly into our lives, we gradually relinquish discord and struggle, and strive for harmony and perfection. All energies that we create will then gradually transform into pure light. This is the giving up of our 'lower will' in the surrender to a 'higher will': the will of God; the will of Divine Presence. Only then can this Presence truly create for us perfect lives.

I realized that, here with Pramukh Swamiji, I was within a transformative moment in my life. I felt as if I was crossing into another realm. So as not to drown in an overwhelming spiritual experience, I said, 'Swamiji, when I first launched a rocket it failed, and I became very depressed and disheartened. At that time I thought about becoming a sannyasi, and giving up everything.'

Pramukh Swamiji said, 'The Srimad Bhagavadgita defines renunciation in a unique way. "One must renounce not the performance of deeds, but renounce the desire for the fruits of those actions." You continued your good deeds selflessly and I am very happy to have you here, my friend.'

Pramukh Swamiji continued, 'Human effort and God's grace move this world. Even failure of the first rocket, which you faced, was for your good; it prodded you to make things better. The way you have worked for the invention of the rocket brought success. God has ultimately given you success.'

I was drawn to Pramukh Swamiji's simplicity. I felt as if I had known him all my life—that I was sitting in the presence of my father and my teachers—in a higher *presence*.

I asked Pramukh Swamiji, 'India was a rich country. Economically it was rich, culturally it was rich. My mind always asks a question: for 3,000 years India has been invaded again and again, but India has never invaded other countries. Why is this?'

Pramukh Swamiji replied, 'It is the virtue of God. A divine quality—not to take what belongs to others, and not to forcibly usurp.

Not to hurt or harass others. We must win over the hearts of others, not their bodies and never their possessions.'

The other sadhus in the room unrolled a big drawing of Akshardham Temple in front of us. This would be constructed on the eastern banks of the River Yamuna in New Delhi, we were told. I was amazed at the grandeur of the plan. Designed in accordance with ancient Vedic texts, it featured a blend of architectural styles from across India. It was to be constructed entirely from Rajasthani pink sandstone and Italian Carrara marble, without any support from steel or concrete, I was informed.

Pramukh Swamiji said, 'People should see this monument and realize that India is not weak, but is an extremely powerful and cultured country. Temples are literally houses of God. They are holy places of worship where individuals make sacred promises with God.'

An hour had passed without anyone realizing. As if emerging from a blissful trance, I stood up to go. Pramukh Swamiji held my hand and said, 'It is good that you have come here today. It has given us much joy. The rishis of the past have also given us science. You too are a rishi. You have achieved such a high post, yet your life is simple.'

Then he said something very inspirational. 'God's blessings are already upon you. I shall pray that your ideas are successfully realized. It was the wish of our guru Yogiji Maharaj[1] to produce spiritually enlightened, skilful and hard-working youths. Go and channel your efforts to ignite the minds of youths all over the world. Lead India!'

Not being clear about what Pramukh Swamiji's words entailed, over the next few days, I performed the prayer of Istikhara[2] several times.

O Almighty, I ask You to show me what is best, through Your knowledge, and I ask You to empower me, through Your power, and I beg You to grant me Your tremendous favour, for You have power, while I am without power, and You have knowledge, while I am without knowledge, and You are the One who knows all things invisible.

I dreamt that I was bathed in a peaceful white light. Hence, with faith in God as the base and *India 2020* as the plan for national prosperity, my life transformed to preside over the nation as the eleventh president of India.

2

You Are Not Who You Think You Are

'Hidden nature is secret God.'

– Sri Aurobindo
Indian nationalist and philosopher

On 30 September 2001, I was flying in a helicopter from Ranchi to Bokaro to attend a Jharkhand State Science and Technology Council meeting. Moments before landing at Bokaro at around 4.30 p.m., the helicopter engine failed and it plummeted to the earth from a height of about 100 metres. All of us on board miraculously survived, and I proceeded with my scheduled programme. But the news of the accident spread across the media. My elder brother called me from Rameswaram to confirm that I was all right.

Pramukh Swamiji's words kept echoing in my mind. 'God's blessings are already upon you. I shall pray that your ideas are successfully realized. It was our guru Yogiji Maharaj's wish to produce such spiritually enlightened, skilful and hard-working youths. Go and channel your efforts to ignite the minds of youths all over the world.' Nothing happens by accident in God's universe or our lives. Where do events like this come from? How do they happen? Why do they happen? Do they have a purpose? What is the force that makes them happen? Was this the time to change the course of my life?

Curiously, these unexpected gifts of guidance are often presented by the universe to influence our thoughts or impact the direction that our lives may take, when we least expect them. Whenever this happens, our free wills are never violated. While we are in our earthly bodies, we always have the choice to react to these events—regardless of their magnitude—the way we see fit.

Upon returning to Delhi, I met Prime Minister Atal Bihari Vajpayee and requested him to relieve me from my duties as principal scientific advisor to the Government of India. He consented, and in November 2001 I moved to the campus of my alma mater, Anna University in Chennai, and resumed my academic pursuits as professor, technology and societal transformation. I became involved in teaching and research tasks, which was something I had always wanted to do. But my official responsibilities never allowed me to teach. Moreover, the divine ordinance to produce spiritually enlightened, skilful and hard-working youths must be fulfilled. I therefore undertook a mission to ignite the young minds for national development, by meeting high school students across the country.

On 10 June 2002, I got a message from Vice Chancellor Dr Kalanidhi's office that a call was waiting for me from the prime minister's office (PMO). This was indeed perplexing, as I had had no contact with any government functionary since I left Delhi in November 2001. When I arrived in the vice chancellor's office, I was connected to the prime minister's office, and after a few minutes, Prime Minister Atal Bihari Vajpayee came on line. He said, 'Dr Kalam, the nation needs you as its Rashtrapati.' I requested him to grant me some time so that I could reflect upon his generous offer and consult my friends and key associates. Vajpayeeji said, 'Please do that. But I need only a "yes" and not a "no".'

By evening, my candidature was announced at a joint press conference addressed by the National Democratic Alliance (NDA) convener, George Fernandes, the parliamentary affairs minister, Pramod Mahajan, the Andhra Pradesh chief minister, Chandrababu Naidu, and the Uttar Pradesh chief minister, Kumari Mayawati. Naiduji described me as 'the best choice'. Mulayam Singh Yadav of the Samajwadi Party (SP) said, 'Dr Kalam is a very good choice for the president's office. He is an able scientist, scholar and eminent person of great fame. He is not the candidate of the BJP (Bharatiya

Janata Party), the RSS (Rashtriya Swayamsevak Sangh), the Shiv
Sena, the Congress or the Samajwadi Party.' I was elected the
eleventh president of India, and the first scientist president of the
republic, by a thumping majority, winning 90 per cent of the votes
polled.

On 25 June 2002, I was sworn in as the eleventh president of India.
My brother, approaching ninety years of age at that time, came from
Rameswaram with his children and grandchildren and a few of my
childhood friends. They all sat in the front row in the majestic central
hall of parliament. Later, my brother would tell me that he had never
imagined, even in his wildest dreams, that he would come to New
Delhi, let alone sit in Parliament House. 'This is the most unexpected
experience in my life. We are truly blessed,' he said.

Reflecting on the unexpected events and blessings that have come
into my life, I can only feel that such divine, mysterious experiences
should truly make us think and wonder what is behind them. And, I
feel, it is imperative to stay aware of what is going on in your life, and
not get enchanted with your own thinking. There are clues, patterns
and phenomena that seem to materialize from nowhere. Watch out
for an unexpected phone call, the finding of an old letter or picture,
actually hearing a voice in your head, having a dream that is related to
your question or a vision that appears while meditating. These are but
a few examples of divine inspiration. Be alert when the unexpected
is unfolding; opportunities knock on the door of a prepared mind,
which has matured through the accumulation of knowledge in certain
areas over a long period of time.

Always keep in mind that, when things go smoothly and fall
into place, you have most likely made the right choices so that
the right event could come into your life. When your decisions or
efforts encounter resistance or roadblocks, seriously re-examine the
choices you have made. There will be signs—guiding events that
will occur in your life. Some years ago I wrote a book with Arun
entitled *Guiding Souls*.[3] I discussed in it my belief, wrought from
own experiences, that such guidance—always true, loving, kind and
in our best interests—is available to all of us.

Guidance can sometimes appear in the midst of calamity. The devastating earthquake of 2001 plunged Gujarat into the gloom of death, destruction and sheer helplessness.[4] Thousands of lives were lost. Hundreds of thousands of people were rendered homeless. Entire livelihoods were destroyed. In these traumatic times of unimaginable suffering, I became involved in rehabilitation and rebuilding efforts, with multiple teams. Just a year later, however, the mindless violence of 2002 dealt us another unexpected blow. Innocents were killed, families were rendered helpless, property built through years of toil was destroyed. The violence was a crippling blow to an already shattered and hurting Gujarat, still struggling to get back on its feet from the natural devastation of the earthquake. I was shaken to the core. Grief, sadness, misery, pain, anguish and agony—these mere words could not capture the absolute emptiness one felt upon witnessing this catastrophe.

On one side was the pain of the victims of the earthquake, and on the other the pain of the victims of the riots. To decisively confront this great turmoil, I chose to go to Gujarat on my first presidential visit outside the capital. Prime Minister Atal Bihari Vajpayee was discomfited by my decision. He asked me, 'Do you consider going to Gujarat at this time essential?' I replied, 'I must go and talk to the people as a president. I consider this my first major task.'

Many apprehensions were expressed to me. Among these were that my visit might be boycotted by the chief minister, that I would get a cold reception, and that there would be agitations from different quarters. But to my great surprise, when I landed at Ahmedabad, not only was the chief minister present, but his whole cabinet—and a large number of legislative assembly members and administrators and some members of the public—were waiting to greet me at the airport. I visited twelve areas: three relief camps and nine riot-hit locations where losses were high. Chief Minister Narendra Modi was with me throughout my visit. In one way, this helped me. As he was with me wherever I went, I was able to suggest to him directly the urgent actions that were required apropos the petitions and complaints I received.

After visiting the relief camps and riot-hit locations, we went to Swaminarayan Mandir on Shahibaug Road to meet Pramukh Swamiji. As we entered the meeting hall, sadhus chanted the Shanti Paath, a mantra for peace, harmony and happiness. Pramukh Swamiji Maharaj warmly welcomed us with garlands. He said, 'It is a great pleasure for us that you have come to the Mandir, especially during this holy month of Shravan.' He spoke to me as a friend, without any burden of my new position. It was as if we were continuing from where we left last time in Delhi a year earlier.

I said, 'Swamiji, since I met you in Delhi last year, my life has been transformed. Many events have taken place. As a scientist, I have travelled extensively, particularly in villages, and met almost a million youths. Now, as the president, I come here again today, both to share with you and seek from you further guidance on bringing peace for the development of society.'

Swamiji said, 'Our society is going through a difficult time, and peace, as you say, has to prevail. There are thousands of victims, both Hindus and Muslims. Right measures need to be taken to alleviate their suffering. Life is sacred, peace is sacred. My vintee (petition) to Rashtrapatiji and Mukhyamantriji is to work for peace and unity of minds. I have only one earnest prayer to God. That never again should such cruelly unfortunate days come in the lives of any other person, society, state or nation.'

I said, 'Swamiji, unity of thought is very important for our country. How can this unity be attained? This unity is the foundation for the country's progress. Swamiji, spiritual organizations have a great effect on the people, and they can bring about this unity. I have a thought in my mind that this great region of Gujarat, which has produced such illustrious leaders as Mahatma Gandhi, who talked of peace, Sardar Vallabhbhai Patel, who unified the kingdoms of India, Vikram Sarabhai, who made such great scientific and technological discoveries—and where spiritual organizations like BAPS have been founded—can itself heal its wounds, and help create unity throughout the country.'

Swamiji kept smiling. He put his hand on my shoulder. I looked into his eyes; they were filled with truthfulness. 'Rashtrapatiji, you are much bigger than what you think. You are a pious soul here on earth to do much bigger work.' When I took his permission to go, he said, 'Give love and compassion to the people of Bhuj. God will shower His grace and will bless you. Because you have sympathy in your heart, you have come all the way to Gujarat to help. May Bhagwan Swaminarayan make you happy. May your health remain good.'

On my way to Bhuj, Pramukh Swamiji's words echoed in my consciousness: 'Kalam, you are not what you think you are. You are born to propagate peace. God knows your past, present and future. He does everything for a reason. Lead the nation without any fear. Don't be afraid of criticism, opposition, or even attacks. Some good will always come out of the bad. Let God be at the core of all your decisions and reasoning. God is the source of all your energy. God is the source of your skill and proficiency. God is the reason behind your accomplishments.'

Before becoming president, as the principal scientific advisor to the Government of India, I had been closely associated with relief activities after the earthquake struck Bhuj a year earlier. Some relief volunteers took me around the camp, explaining the rehabilitation process and showing me its facilities. They had provided water, electricity, rations, sanitation, a community hall and a medical clinic. I was impressed with the technical know-how of the BAPS team, which had designed a complete rehabilitation area where more than 290 families were provided commodious temporary shelter. The ingenious air ventilation system at Swaminarayan Nagar was especially noteworthy.

It was 2.30 p.m., and the ambient temperature was 45 degrees Celsius. Sadhu Brahmaviharidas took me inside a tent house made of tin sheets. It was sweltering outside, but inside the home it was comfortable. Strong cross winds were intelligently harnessed to funnel hot air from the ceiling by making the roof slanted, thereby creating an opening about one foot deep on the upper side of the tent. The hot air rising from the ground was being blown away by the cross wind.

I was overwhelmed by the dedication and the aura of divinity of the sadhus and volunteers who were devoted to this relief and rehabilitation work. Their work was a testament to their proficiency, and a living demonstration of what the Srimad Bhagavadgita calls, 'Yogah karmasu kaushalam', meaning 'Working with proficiency is Yoga'.

And rising to the occasion, the Technology Information, Forecasting and Assessment Council (TIFAC) constructed 500 shelters made of composite boards of jute and coir, and particle boards made of rice husk, with bamboo mat veneers supported on steel channels and angles. They also made more than a hundred fibre-reinforced plastic (FRP) modular toilet units. It was a superb example of how composite materials offer significant advantages over metals in some structural applications. The shelter design had demonstrated the flexibility and efficacy of various combinations of fibre reinforcement and resin materials. Knowledge purposefully applied indeed becomes a divine force.

In retrospect, I realize that I had learned, through Pramukh Swamiji, my true identity. Who am I really? Am I so-and-so with a certain past and a certain body and personality and certain roles, talents, weaknesses, dreams, fears and beliefs? Others may define me in these ways, but that is not who I really am. Who I really am can only be discovered through deeper questioning and exploration, and through a subtler experience of that which is beyond all ideas about myself. It can only be revealed when the mind is quiet and no longer telling me who I am. When all the preconceptions about myself are stilled, what remains is who I really am: consciousness, awareness, stillness, presence, peace, love, and the Divine. You are that which is nameless, and yet has been given a thousand names.

3

Peace Grows When It Is Shared

'Harmony makes small things grow; lack of it makes great
things decay.'

– Sallust
First-century BC Roman senator

On 24 September 2002, at 4.45 p.m., two heavily armed
terrorists arrived in a white car at the Akshardham Temple in
Gandhinagar. They scaled the perimeter fence and opened fire, killing
a woman and a temple volunteer. As they made their way to the main
courtyard, they threw grenades and fired on devotees mercilessly. They
then entered Exhibition Hall 1, killing many more people. Later, they
scaled the walls of the hall and positioned themselves on its rooftop.
When the police units reached the complex, they braved bullets from
the terrorists in their efforts to evacuate the temple visitors.

Eventually, the National Security Guard (NSG) commandos
from Delhi joined the police at 11.30 p.m. Operation Thunderbolt
continued throughout the night and ended with the killing of the two
terrorists at 6.45 a.m. By the end of the attack, thirty-one innocent
pilgrims, devotees and commandos, including one sadhu, had been
killed. More than eighty others were wounded, including twenty-three
police officers. One more seriously injured commando, Surjan Singh
Bhandari, would die after nearly two years of languishing in a coma.

The Akshardham carnage was yet another international tragedy
in which terrorists had taken the lives of innocent men, women and

14

children in a senseless act of violence. Their act of terror was even more acutely felt, since it was perpetrated in the midst of the very place that serves as an inspiration for peace, harmony and tolerance. I called Pramukh Swamiji over the telephone, 'Swamiji, you are not alone. The whole country is with you.' As the president of India, I called it 'a cowardly attack, not only on innocent people, but on the secular national fabric as well'.

Pramukh Swamiji showed magnanimity by not indulging in any blame game or imputing motives. Akshardham was his most priceless, splendid and wonderful creation. Yet he remained calm. His saintliness was touching. His heart bled for the helpless victims of the barbaric act. The attack was meant to stir communal riots and tear apart the fabric of society. But the *sthitaprajna*[5] Pramukh Swamiji defeated these nefarious designs of the terrorists by not reacting to the provocation designed to elicit a backlash. Not only did his hundreds of thousands of disciples venerate him, but also society at large beheld him with the utmost reverence.

Pramukh Swamiji offered his deepest sympathy and prayers for the unfortunate victims and their grieving relatives. He also prayed for the quick recovery of the injured. He even sprinkled holy water and flowers where the two terrorists had died. There was not even a hint of anger in his eyes. He remained calm. Hundreds of people standing there, including sadhus, were astonished by the profound forgiveness of Pramukh Swamiji. His ardent prayers were that in the future, no one should harbour such thoughts of terror, and such tragedies should never afflict any community or any nation, anywhere in the world.

Swamiji encouraged his followers to pray, not punish. Akshardham was reopened to the public on 7 October 2002. Pramukh Swamiji emerged as a true embodiment of the principles of tolerance, patience and forgiveness. I believe that his spiritual calmness and saintliness not only restored peace in Gujarat, but also provided a final seal on the perpetuating cycle of communal violence in the state. When I would later meet Nelson Mandela, I once again saw this power of tolerance, patience and forgiveness.

Akshardham Mandir remains a place of peace, inspiration and harmony. We should be mindful that the temple, the mosque and the church are all part of our history. They are precious monuments of truth. Let us preserve them for posterity. Because when you go to a place of worship, you pray for peace and prosperity, not only for yourself but also for everyone around you. More than places of worship, temples, mosques and churches are all symbols of trust. Mutual trust alone can help us restore peace and develop our country. Let us nurture a purity of mind and heart. And let us never forget the importance of the tenet of peace, which is common to all religions, and is enshrined in places of worship.

As a child, I witnessed the peacemaker role that my father would play in the Rameswaram community. Warring parties—friends, partners, families and neighbours—used to approach him for sulah (meaning peace and peacemaking in Arabic). My Quran teacher taught me that sulah is also the root of the word islah, denoting development and improvement. This term is used to refer to peacemaking. Peacemakers are therefore promoters of good and eliminators of evil. Peace and peacemaking are seen in Islamic tradition as part and parcel of human development. In Islam, peace and making peace are seen as godly acts worthy of praise and reward. Peace is advocated as a divine quality to be pursued in order to achieve the state of felicity that we enjoyed in paradise, man's former dwelling.

Pramukh Swamiji confirmed my childhood learning that everything wants peace. Wild animals—even tigers and eagles—want peace within their groups. Human beings chase after other things—wealth, health, fame and power—only because they ultimately want peace. Even gangs of robbers want peace among themselves; and warmongers want peace with their victory. But the only peace that will fully satisfy us will be the peace of the Divine.

Peace in this world is always partial, fragile and temporary. Still, it is worth pursuing. How do we achieve it? One of Pramukh Swamiji's perspicacious insights is the connection between inner and outer peace. Inner peace comes when our minds and hearts—our ideals and our desires—are in ordered harmony. But sin distorts and destroys that harmony. We achieve inner peace, then, by surrendering our sins at the feet of our guru, for 'the guru is the embodiment of the Divine before us, the guru is our peace'. All the Gunatit gurus in Bhagwan Swaminarayan's succession—Gunatitanand Swami,[6] Bhagatji Maharaj,[7] Shastriji Maharaj,[8] Yogiji Maharaj[9] and Pramukh Swamiji—have been great peacemakers, reconcilers and reformers. They have reconciled the conflicts within people by example, so that they could be at peace and thus bring peace to others.

Pramukh Swamiji's life is an example of how to love peace, have peace and possess peace. He welcomes as many others as he can to share in his peace. The more people who have peace, the greater it becomes. A family house appears smaller as a family grows, whereas the house of peace expands as more people enter it. The most valuable possession you can own is an open heart.

The ideal society, according to the Quran, is Dar as-Salam, literally, 'the house of peace' of which it intones: 'And God Almighty invites to the "abode of peace" and guides whom He pleases into the right path.' Akshardhams are indeed true abodes of peace. The establishment of these abodes of peace on earth entails the establishment of peace in everyday lives, at all levels: personal, social, national and international. Martin Luther King Jr, leader in the African-American civil rights movement, most aptly stated: 'Darkness cannot drive out darkness: only light can do that. Hate cannot drive out hate: only love can do that.'

As a peacemaker, what you can say to someone who does not love peace and wants to quarrel is this, 'Whatever you want to say, however much you hate me, you are still my brother.' You should say this passionately but gently. Say it burning with love, not with temper. This is precisely what Pramukh Swamiji did in Gandhinagar after the terrorist attack. And you must remain aware that patience is the antidote to the restless poison of the ego. Without it, you become a bull in a china shop, blithely destroying your future happiness. In heedless moments, you can trample on the worthiest prospects in your life, only to return to the scene of your folly later in regret.

I believe, after meeting Pramukh Swamiji, that there will surely be an era in which justice, abundance, well-being, security, peace and brotherhood will prevail among humanity. It will be a time in which people will experience love, self-sacrifice, tolerance, compassion, mercy and loyalty. Our physical world is ready and able to accommodate the needs of the spiritually awakened Satpurush.[10] The constraints or demands of our material world are not the real problem; it is our spiritual awareness and philosophical wisdom that is wanting. Akshardhams will defeat the atheistic philosophies and blind beliefs with values and intellect; the world will be saved from wars, conflicts, racial and ethnic hostility, cruelty and injustice. The golden age is before us, not behind us. For this, all religions should promote peace, and above all, eliminate hatred towards people of other faiths and beliefs.

4

Children Are Everyone's Future

'It is easier to build strong children than to repair broken men.'
– Frederick Douglass
Nineteenth-century African-American social reformer

In 2004, Pramukh Swamiji invited me to the Suvarna Bal Mahotsav at Akshardham, Gandhinagar. The celebration was planned as a tribute to Yogiji Maharaj, the founder of BAPS Children's Forum. When I arrived at the Akshardham Mandir on 8 February 2004, orange, green and white balloons filled the sky, and children ecstatically cheered me. Spiritual vigour was reflected in the children's faces. The peace chant by 20,000 children,'Om, dyoho shantih ...' resonated in the air. Overwhelmed with joy, I said, 'You know, Swamiji, I had a great meeting with you in Delhi, and the words of that meeting still echo in my mind, and there is always divine radiation, divine vibration in me. I feel as if you are always near me.' At this glorious function, I felicitated successful entrepreneurs, social workers, police officers, pilots, soldiers, singers, sportsmen and scientists who had made a difference as leaders at the international level. Each one of them had been inspired as a child attending BAPS children's activities. I saw my dream of igniting minds manifesting before me. My eyes welled up with tears. But nothing could have prepared me for what happened next.

After the event concluded, I thanked and bade farewell to Pramukh Swamiji on the stage in front of thousands of children. Sadhu Brahmaviharidas escorted me through the throng to the far side of the complex where my motorcade was waiting. It was a walk of a little over 200 metres. But before entering the car, as I turned to have a look at Akshardham, I was surprised to see Pramukh Swamiji walking behind me, just a few feet away. He had quietly and inconspicuously accompanied me. Taken aback, I asked, 'Swamiji, why did you come so far, all the way to my car?' He replied, 'You have come from so far, all the way from Delhi.' My eyes misted over; I was overcome by his humility. All the way in the flight back to Delhi, I savoured this moment. And from that time, every time the sadhus of BAPS came to Rashtrapati Bhavan, I walked them to the portico.

Upon my return to Delhi, I called my friend Arun, and we planned the writing of our book *You Are Born to Blossom*,[11] to capture the spirit of Pramukh Swamiji's concern for the blossoming of young lives.

Learning is a lifelong process and Pramukh Swamiji is indeed the chancellor of the world's greatest open university, BAPS. Anyone who spends a few moments in his presence will realize that each human being is unique. All human beings are not supposed to be the same, feel the same, think the same, and believe the same things. The key to continued expansion of our universe lies in diversity, not in conformity and coercion. If someone is able to show me that what I think or do is not right, I will happily change. For I seek the truth, by which no one was ever truly harmed. It is the person who continues in his self-deception and ignorance—in spite of hearing the truth— who is harmed. Those who cannot change their minds cannot change anything. These are fundamental truths that should be inculcated in the young, at home and in their formal education, so that they become seekers of truth throughout their lives.

The initial years of one's life are formative and therefore crucial for one's development. Because the truism that our children are our future is so often uttered it has lost its import. The present plus a passing of time is the future. So our present work plus the time in which we do and achieve things together becomes the future world. The present world is being handled, dandled, destroyed and created through this period of time, and what remains will be the future world—good or bad, evolved or mutated. It is easier to build strong children than to repair broken adults. The empires of the future are the empires of the mind. Dream, dream, dream. Dreaming leads to thoughts. Thoughts lead to action.

When we say that today's world is to be the future world, what we mean is, today's people—and the contribution they are making—are going to mould the world, its ways, and its life for the future. Today's people may not remain and survive in the future, but the expectation is that today's children will survive. Naturally, therefore, if the present children are moulded—in their attitudes, in their values, in their ideas and in their ideals—we can expect a better and more organized world tomorrow. And we can achieve our vision for the world that we hope for at this moment.

This future vision may not be realized in our own lifetimes, as change needs a long period of time. Change, though, it will. But what kind of change it will be is determined by the growing generation. Therefore, when we say that today's children are our future, we mean that we must strive now to mould the children to think correctly, to judge carefully, and to have the courage to follow their convictions. Freedom is never more than one generation away from extinction. We do not pass it to our children as an inheritance. It must be fought for, protected and handed over for them to do the same.

Today, India is in a troubled condition because in past generations, its children were neglected. I see this in the tenor of the people of the current generation. There are few visionaries in our country, and even fewer visions. A country without a vision has no future. All the progressive countries in the world are such because their progress is guided by, decided by, thought of and planned by the visionaries of each generation. Pramukh Swamiji relentlessly strives to see that these higher ideals are fostered. He says, 'One little child can change the entire history of humanity.' Through him, I came to know the story of Bhagwan Swaminarayan.

On Ramnavami day, 3 April 1781, a child was born in the family of Hariprasad Pande and his wife Premvati, in Chhapaiya, near Ayodhya. They named the child Ghanshyam. By the age of ten, Ghanshyam had mastered the sacred Hindu texts and joined his father on a trip to

Kashi, now called Varanasi. The king of Kashi had invited Brahmins throughout India there for the occasion of a lunar eclipse, and had hosted them at his palace. At the Gomath Ashram by the Ganga, Ghanshyam's father was asked to chair a spiritual debate. The debate dealt with varying philosophies of dvaita (dual), advaita (non-dual), and other schools of thought that describe worship of God.

Ghanshyam asked his father if he could speak. He then explained to everyone his principle of philosophy, which later became known as 'Swaminarayan Darshan'. In the dvaita philosophy, a devotee worships God while remaining separate from Him, while in advaita the devotee feels a oneness with God. The principle of oneness of God is indeed a celebrated concept in Islam also. In the Swaminarayan philosophy, this oneness is such that God resides within the devotee, and the devotee has a servant–master relationship with God. This was a pivotal moment in young Ghanshyam's life, and an astonishing demonstration of the maturity of his spiritual understanding at this young age. The whole assembly was amazed and accepted Ghanshyam's revelation. This brought deep joy to his parents who, within a few months of this event, peacefully passed away.

On the rainy night of 29 June 1792, Ghanshyam left home, barefooted and clad only in a loincloth. He carried a wooden staff, a handwritten summary of scriptures and a gourd (water pot). Now known as Neelkanth Varni, he survived on alms and fruits that had fallen off trees. He traversed the Himalayan peaks and visited the Kedarnath and Badrinath shrines. He stayed at Badrinath, the spiritual abode of Lord Nara-Narayan, for three months. In February 1793, Neelkanth headed high into the Himalayas to Lake Mansarovar and meditated there for five days. Upon his return to Badrinath, Neelkanth met the young Maharaja Ranjit Singhji, who would later become the king of Punjab and Kashmir. Neelkanth returned to the Gangetic plains, and then headed north again through the Himalayas, towards modern-day Nepal.

In October 1794, in the forests of Nepal, Neelkanth met Gopal Yogi and stayed with him for about a year to master ashtanga (eightfold) yoga. When Gopal Yogi died, Neelkanth travelled across

East Bengal (modern-day Bangladesh) and then to Assam. At the Kamakhya Devi temple in Guwahati, Neelkanth confronted Pibek, a black magician who had terrorized the townspeople, and made him renounce his errant ways. Neelkanth then walked south and stopped at Gangasagar. He stayed at Kapil Muni's ashram in the Sundarbans.

On his way to Jagannath Puri in modern-day Odisha, Neelkanth accepted the devotion of King Rajaram Mukund Dev, of Orissa. On 26 June 1797, the king honoured Neelkanth by seating him on the Jagannath chariot during the annual Rath Yatra. Thereafter, Neelkanth travelled through Tilang, modern-day Telangana, to Venkatachal, modern-day Tirupati, and continued south to Rameswaram.[12] After reaching the southern tip of India at Kanyakumari in October 1798 (during Navratri), Neelkanth headed back north. In all, Neelkanth walked barefoot the length and breadth of India for seven years, one month and eleven days, covering over 8,000 miles (approximately 12,800 kilometres). Finally, his journey concluded at the ashram of Ramanand Swami[13] in the village Loj of the Junagadh kingdom, Gujarat.

When Neelkanth Varni arrived in Loj, Ramanand Swami was in the Kachchha area in north-west Gujarat. Neelkanth Varni stayed at the ashram under Muktanand Swami.[14] On 28 October 1800, Ramanand Swami initiated Neelkanth as Sahajanand Swami and a year later, on 16 November 1801, declared him head of the fellowship. On this occasion, Sahajanand Swami asked Ramanand Swami for two unique boons.

> If your devotee is destined to suffer the sting of one scorpion, may the distress of the stings of millions and millions of scorpions befall on each and every pore of my body, but no pain should afflict your devotee. Further, if a begging bowl is written in your devotee's fate, may that begging bowl come to me, but on no account should your devotee suffer from lack of food or clothing. Please grant me these two boons.

On 31 December 1801, Sahajanand Swami gave his followers the 'Swaminarayan' mantra to chant, and henceforth he became known as

Bhagwan Swaminarayan. Truth seekers from all over flocked to him. Many became dedicated saints, who were instructed by Bhagwan Swaminarayan to travel the countryside to instil purity and spirituality in people's lives. Many thus shed addictions, vices, negative practices and immoral beliefs, and started living positively.

In a single night in the town of Kalavani, Bhagwan Swaminarayan initiated 500 saints as paramhansas (enlightened spiritual teachers). He encouraged spiritual endeavours like continual fasting and strict celibacy. He commanded all to cultivate the highest virtues and to abide by the principles of forbearance and love. Reciprocally, the paramhansas pledged him their lasting devotion.

Bhagwan Swaminarayan passed away at the age of forty-nine on 1 June 1830, in the town of Gadhada. In a short span of twenty-eight years, he had inspired an unparalleled spiritual movement. At the heart of this was the permanent spiritual transformation of all who came in contact with the divine fellowship. His followers were from all walks of life—from regular householders to detached ascetics, from farmers to wealthy kings, from illiterates to erudite scholars and from saints to dacoits—and there was no bar or barrier for his grace. Bhagwan Swaminarayan looked after the personal care, happiness and spiritual progress of all his devotees and hence transformed them.

This life of the child-yogi, Neelkanth Varni, is in itself a timeless story that can inspire the children of our world to rise beyond their circumstances. There is a beautiful poem written by the Lebanese poet Kahlil Gibran:

> Your children are not your children.
> They are the sons and daughters of Life's longing for itself.
> They come through you but not from you,
> And though they are with you yet they belong not to you.

There is little wonder that Pramukh Swamiji takes great interest in the proper grooming of children. He has created Vidyamandirs: value-based rural, urban and international schools for moulding and edifying children; preparing them to face the world of tomorrow and to lead and guide the world of the future. It is a tremendous responsibility. Through Pramukh Swamiji's efforts, many parents now realize they must handle their children more intelligently and lovingly.

Kirtan Patel, a fourteen-year-old boy studying in ninth standard at Girdharnagar-Shahibaug High School, Ahmedabad, attending the Suvarna Bal Mahotsav, asked me, 'President Sir, what was your first thought when you met Pramukh Swami Maharaj for the first time?' This question gave me an opportunity to express my true feelings about Pramukh Swamiji in his presence. This was something that I would not have had the nerve to do otherwise!

I told Kirtan Patel, 'Look Kirtan, Pramukh Swamiji is a great bridge in the vast archipelago of humanity. An archipelago is an island group. Humanity has divided itself into hundreds of islands. These islands are religions. Each island is a beautiful territory, full of flora, fauna and inhabitants, and yet disconnected from the others. Pramukh Swamiji is connecting these different islands by making bridges of love and compassion. When many ask, "How can you mix spirituality and social service?" Pramukh Swamiji asks, "How can you separate the two?"'

Pramukh Swamiji has transformed BAPS into a great global brotherhood. Founded on the pillars of practical spirituality, BAPS today reaches out far and wide to address the spiritual, moral and social challenges and issues that we face in our world. Pramukh Swamiji has built the strength of BAPS on the purity of its nature and purpose.

Under his leadership, BAPS strives to care for the world by caring for societies, families and individuals. This is done by mass motivation and individual attention; through elevating projects for all—irrespective of class, creed, colour or country. Its universal work through a worldwide network is affiliated with the United Nations. Pramukh Swamiji has thus focussed on inspiring a better and happier world.

Today, a million or more committed Swaminarayan followers, many of them living in foreign countries, begin their day with puja and meditation. They lead upright, honest lives, and donate regular hours in serving others. No alcohol, no addictions, no adultery, no meat eating and no impurity of body and mind are their five lifetime vows. Pramukh Swamiji has given a new future to hundreds of thousands of expatriate Indian families, by instilling in their children pure morality and spirituality. It is a value-based educational revolution unprecedented in modern human history, the benefits of which will manifest in ten to fifteen years' time.

5

The Confidence That We Can Do It

'Take up one idea. Make that one idea your life—think of it,
dream of it, live on that idea. Let the brain, muscles, nerves,
every part of your body, be full of that idea, and just leave
every other idea alone. This is the way to success.'

—Swami Vivekananda

On 6 November 2005, Pramukh Swamiji consecrated
Akshardham Temple in Delhi. It has been hailed as the
largest Hindu temple in the world, and one of the seven modern
wonders. I was invited to the inauguration ceremony, along with the
prime minister Manmohan Singh and the leader of the opposition
Lal Krishna Advani. More than 40,000 people were present in the
majestic temple complex. The celebrations, including a traditional
dedication ceremony, patriotic songs and cultural dances with
spectacular lighting were telecast live across the world.

Since 1968, it had been a vision of Yogiji Maharaj, the spiritual
head of BAPS at that time, to build a grand temple on the banks of
the River Yamuna. He shared his vision with two or three devotee
families who resided in New Delhi at the time, and attempts were
made to start the project. Little progress was made, however, because
of the unavailability of land. Yogiji Maharaj passed away in 1971.

Pramukh Swamiji took up the sankalp (solemn vow) of fulfilling
the vision of his guru Yogiji Maharaj and continually inspired his
devotees. A request for land was made to the government authorities,

and several different places were suggested, including Ghaziabad, Gurgaon and Faridabad. Pramukh Swamiji stood firm in following the wishes of Yogiji Maharaj to build a temple on the banks of the Yamuna.

In April 2000, the Delhi Development Authority offered 60 acres of land, and the Uttar Pradesh government offered another 30 acres for the project. Upon receiving the land, Pramukh Swamiji performed puja on the site for the success of the project. Construction of the temple began on 8 November 2000. Designed by Sompuras and BAPS sadhus as conceptualized by Pramukh Swamiji, it took over 7,000 master craftsmen and 4,000 volunteers from all over the world, just two days short of five years to complete this marvellous edifice.

In the tradition of the Bhakti movement, mandirs are erected to provide a means of upholding proper devotion to God on the path towards moksha, or ultimate liberation. BAPS mandirs facilitate devotional commitment to the Akshar Purushottam Upasana, in which followers strive to reach the spiritually perfect state of aksharbrahman (becoming the ideal devotee). They thereby gain the ability to properly worship Purushottam, the Supreme Godhead.

I declared in my speech at the inauguration ceremony of the Akshardham Temple, 'Akshardham has happened at the dawn of the twenty-first century, with the commitment and dedication of one million devotees and volunteers. What has happened today at Akshardham inspires me and gives me the confidence that we can do it. The realization of a developed India is certainly possible before 2020 with millions of ignited minds like yours.'

After the ceremony, I asked Pramukh Swamiji, 'Swamiji, when I see Akshardham and your work, the team spirit and hard work of thousands is visible in this great spiritual centre. How are you able to attract such enthusiastic and spiritual workers? I am dreaming and dreaming of this type of spiritual leadership—purposeful leadership—which is essential for the India 2020 vision: the national economic development mission. Swamiji, you are the embodiment of true spirituality. The divine spirit is incarnate in you. You have so much divine power that I feel that anything is possible in this world. I want to work with you for a better India.'

Pramukh Swamiji said, 'We should work together. I pray that you too have this spiritual energy and may it increase. Your life from the beginning has been very pious. Divine power has worked through you for India.' I suggested erecting a statue of the Tamil saint-poet Thiruvalluvar in the temple complex, and presented to Pramukh Swamiji my poem *The Mother Embraces Her Children*, composed for the occasion:

My journey commenced, in my ancestral home:
Loving families
Multiple cradles,
The civilization of my nation.

My mother nurtured me with love,
My father gave me discipline as strength.
I wanted to be there forever,
But my parents sent me off to grow and excel.

I feel the tender love of my mother here
And the strength of my father's discipline
India can do it
The dawn of civilizational abode—Akshardham.

Pramukh Swamiji heard the poem and looked at me with eyes full of loving compassion. Sadhu Brahmaviharidas, who was translating, added, 'There is a deep need for preserving the values and wisdom of Indian culture among the Indian diaspora. BAPS provides this social, cultural and spiritual sustenance, hence its growth worldwide has been a natural phenomenon. As a consequence of Indian emigration patterns, mandirs have been erected in Africa, Europe, North America, and the Asia-Pacific region. There are over 1,000 mandirs spread over five continents, including around seventy mandirs in North America and twelve mandirs in Europe. Each mandir is a centre of humanitarian activities.'

It was further explained to me that the source of energy in all these mandirs and activities was the spiritual leadership of the guru, who is Akshar incarnate. The personal form of Akshar is present in the form of the gurus. It is through these gurus that Bhagwan Swaminarayan forever remains present on earth. This spiritual lineage began with Gunatitanand Swami and continued through Bhagatji Maharaj, Shastriji Maharaj and Yogiji Maharaj. What Pramukh Swamiji did not say, however— but I understood implicitly—was that I was sitting right in front of the manifest form of Akshar. In Pramukh Swamiji, I felt and experienced the spiritual heritage of over two centuries and the direct energy of Bhagwan Swaminarayan. It was a truly blessed moment of my life. Most edifying for me was that I also realized the importance of the creation of Akshardham; a demonstration of the 'can do' ethos through spirituality. This is most essential for the emerging Indian global community.

Like all great works, the Akshardham project too had its share of difficulties and challenges. Pramukh Swamiji had the patience to persevere for thirty-two years to obtain land. And the stamina to unify and synergize 11,000 craftsmen and volunteers to complete, in five years, a marvel which experts said should have taken fifty years to build! Even the planning, construction and implementation, including financial resources, must have posed formidable challenges. All of these challenges and many more, however, were overcome and transcended in a creative, positive and peaceful way.

I ask you, dear reader, do you persevere in the face of resistance? When confronted with adversity, do you find yourself saying, 'When the going gets tough, the tough get going'? Do you also find yourself saying, 'Where there is a will, there is a way'? Are you one who rises to meet a challenge? Do challenges bring out the best in you? Can you adapt, be resourceful and generally find ways around obstacles in your path? Would you generally describe yourself as a person with a stick-to-it attitude? Are you absolutely unwilling to give up until you have succeeded? When confronted with adversity or difficulty, are you inclined to see problems or solutions? Do you typically say, like Pramukh Swamiji, 'I can do all things through God who strengthens me.' Do you study the lives of great souls who overcame long odds or sailed through extremely difficult circumstances? If you do not, you should perhaps try this; it is inspiring and enlightening.

In my book *Indomitable Spirit*,[15] I caution the youth: 'Success can only come to you by courageous devotion to the task in front of you ... you will be remembered for creating that one page in the history of the nation—whether it is the page of invention, innovation, discovery or fighting injustice.' I quoted from my presidential address to the nation on the eve of the fifty-seventh Republic Day: 'The basis of all systems, social or political, rests upon the goodness of men. No nation is great or good because parliament enacts this or that, but because its people are great and good.' Before 1910, there were no Indian scientists of international repute, but after the First World War, and in particular, between 1920 and 1925—inspired by a nationalist fervour—J.C. Bose, C.V. Raman, Meghnad Saha and Srinivasan Ramanujan emerged as shining stars of the science world. The need for self-expression—the urge to assert oneself—became a dominant motive among the young. It became increasingly apparent that we could prove our mettle before the West, in its realm.

I concluded *Indomitable Spirit* with these words of the Nobel laureate Sir C.V. Raman, from his address to a group of young graduates in 1969: 'I can assert without fear of contradiction that the quality of the Indian mind is equal to the quality of any Teutonic, Nordic or Anglo-Saxon mind. What we lack is perhaps courage, what we lack is perhaps the driving force, which takes one anywhere. We have, I think, developed an inferiority complex.'

India has a vision to become a developed nation by 2020. It is possible only if we achieve a sustained Gross Domestic Product (GDP) growth rate of over 10 per cent for a decade, along with the upliftment of the 22 per cent of our population that is below the poverty line. And if we enjoy a better quality of life in terms of education, health care, employment, infrastructure and security. Technology plays a vital role in realizing this vision.

India today is in a unique position among the nations of the world. India is attracting the attention of all developed countries, because it is the best resource hub of young intelligent minds. The historic status of India, which was dominant during the civilization age, shall return when society has shifted its focus from agriculture to knowledge. Knowledge is of greatest advantage to all of us; it provides an unrivalled opportunity for India to become an economic power and attain developed nation status. The 540-million-strong youth of India have a tremendous responsibility to shape India's future. To realize this potential, thoughtful action is necessary. The life of Pramukh Swamiji is a shining example of the three true steps necessary to succeed in life and fulfil one's potential. These are: (1) aim high, (2) acquire knowledge, and (3) work hard and persevere to overcome problems.

And while emulating Swamiji's greatness may seem unimaginable in many respects, his personification of service to others and self-sacrifice are traits that are indispensable for our country's progress towards developed nation status. The two boons given to Bhagwan Swaminarayan by Ramanand Swami are being fulfilled by Pramukh Swamiji. Whereas his devotee is destined to suffer the sting of one scorpion, he feels the distress of the stings of millions and millions of scorpions on each and every pore of his body, so that no pain should afflict his devotee. If a begging bowl is written in his devotee's fate, that begging bowl comes to him, so that on no account should his devotee suffer from lack of food or clothing.

The life of Pramukh Swamiji is a testimony of perseverance in the face of resistance. When his true devotees are confronted with adversity, they find themselves saying, 'When the going gets tough, the tough get going,' and 'Where there is a will, there is a way.' They rise to meet challenges so that the challenges bring out the best in them. Being resourceful, they adapt to situations, and generally find ways around obstacles in their paths. They are unwilling to give up until they have succeeded. They exemplify the 'I can do all things through Swamiji who strengthens me' spirit. But Pramukh Swamiji would not even listen to this accolade. He would simply say, 'With God all things are possible.'

I have come to appreciate more than ever the need for creating flexible—and even dynamic—organizations like BAPS, so that we can address the wide and assorted variety of human needs in far-flung regions of the planet. Worldwide non-governmental organizations

(NGOs) founded on the principles of integrity, sincerity and humanity—governed selflessly and serving ceaselessly—are the need of the hour. Pramukh Swamiji is indeed the master alchemist, who not only transforms ordinary people into good people, but also amalgamates good people into great organizations.

6

Self-Discipline Is the True Path to Dharma

'The wise discipline themselves; the unwise discipline others.'
— Pramukh Swamiji

In 2006, the phrase 'office of profit' held centre stage in Indian politics. An office of profit means a position that brings to the person holding it some financial gain, advantage or benefit. It may be an office or place of profit if it carries some remuneration, financial advantage or other benefits. The amount of such profit is immaterial. Article 102 (1)(A) of the Indian Constitution bars a member of parliament (MP) or a member of legislative assembly (MLA) from holding any office of profit under the Government of India or the Government of any state, other than an office declared by the parliament by law as not disqualifying its holder. Parliament had earlier exempted certain positions, such as those of ministers and the leader of the opposition, from the purview of this article.

A hornet's nest was stirred up when Smt. Jaya Bachchan was disqualified from the membership of Rajya Sabha on the grounds that she held the position of chairperson of the Uttar Pradesh Film Development Corporation. The matter came all the way to the Supreme Court, which dismissed her challenge to the disqualification order. The Supreme Court held that it was immaterial whether the person actually received any remuneration or pecuniary gains from the office, but that under the relevant provision, the very fact that a person held such a position was valid grounds for disqualification from holding office. Governments, especially coalitions, appeared to be doing everything in their power to retain legislators in their flock, and offering plum positions to legislators had emerged as one method of forestalling their potential dissidence.

The opposition parties smartly turned the fallout from this disqualification against the president of the ruling Congress party, Smt. Sonia Gandhi, as she was the chairperson of the National Advisory Council, which was an office of profit. On 23 March 2006, Smt. Sonia Gandhi resigned from the Lok Sabha and also as chairperson of the National Advisory Council.

With forty-three members from different parties apprehending disqualification from parliament and 200 others from state legislatures facing similar sanction, there was a cross-party consensus that the constitution should be amended. On 17 May 2006, parliament passed a bill seeking to exempt fifty-six posts, including the post of chairperson of the National Advisory Council, from being considered offices of profit and hence attracting disqualification for parliamentarians. The Rajya Sabha approved the bill through a division.

When the Parliament (Prevention of Disqualification) Amendment Bill 2006, popularly known as the Office of Profit Bill came to me for approval, I felt the manner in which exemptions were given was arbitrary. The office of profit concept was developed by the founding fathers of the Constitution, who believed that parliament should and must question the executive. But since ministers and a few members of parliament may also hold executive posts while in parliament, the idea of giving select and careful exemptions to some offices held by them had been devised. The bill contained more than forty exemptions. Most experts advised me that the bill, as it was drafted, subverted the principle behind the original concept of giving careful and select exemptions. I felt the exemptions list in the bill must be purposeful. Why amend the very Constitution of our country merely to accommodate a few politicians who may risk losing their membership of the house?

Removal of every qualification—or, in this case, disqualification— is the basis of concentration of power. It appeared to me that the purity and independence of legislative membership is the target of every political party, so that their people can enjoy more than one position without threat of 'disqualification'. All the political parties were more or less in the same situation as the Congress and the Samajwadi Party. Hence, there was likely to be unprecedented unity and consensus among all the parties in this matter, to protect their present and future political interests. And the political parties that pounced on Smt. Jaya Bachchan and Smt. Sonia Gandhi had no moral authority to reach an agreement to dilute this constitutional ideal.

I had three choices: sign the bill, refuse to sign it, or exercise my right to send back the bill to parliament with a request to make changes to it. I had little choice but to act 'under the advice of the Council of Ministers or the Prime Minister', but under Article 111, the president of India need not 'act under advice' but can take an independent view. I opted for the third choice. I asked parliament to reconsider the bill, and to examine the legality and propriety of the retrospectivity of the bill's provisions. In my view, the bill's focus should have been on evolving criteria for exemption that would be just, fair and reasonable, and applied across all states and Union territories.

I was indeed surprised that the United Progressive Alliance (UPA) government chose to send the bill back to me without any changes. I waited for a good seventeen days for better sense to prevail. But in view of the speculations that I intended to sit over the bill till my tenure ended the following year, or that I would ask for a legal opinion as demanded by the opposition National Democratic Alliance, I eventually signed the bill, after the government set up a Joint Parliamentary Committee to define what constitutes an office of profit as stated in Article 102 of the Constitution. It was 18 August 2006.

During this period, I experienced an intense moral dilemma: should I have signed or should I have resigned? I needed spiritual guidance: an assurance about my decision to sign the bill, to enact legislation which I was convinced was flawed. Pramukh Swamiji arrived in New Delhi on 1 September 2006. I went to see him at Akshardham on 11 September. I was thinking of sharing my predicament with Pramukh

Swamiji, but before I could broach the topic, I found the answer to all my questions in his presence.

While walking with Pramukh Swamiji around the Akshardham Temple, I saw the beautiful Gajendra Pithika, depicting the story of five blind men trying to describe the shape of an elephant. None of these blind men were able to discover the true shape of the elephant. Their descriptions and definitions were partial and incomplete. The parable implies that one's subjective experience can be true, but that such an experience is inherently limited by its failure to account for other truths or a totality of truth. At various times, this ancient parable has provided insight into the relativism, differences and limitations in the expressions of truth. Similarly, the opinions of experts vary because of different perspectives. In my personal dilemma of whether to sign or refuse the bill, I had been flooded and confused by expert opinions—all well-meaning, but partial truths nevertheless. Hence, my decision to follow the Constitution and bow before the supremacy of the parliament was indeed right.

Deeply comforted, and with all the confusion evaporated from my mind, I thanked Pramukh Swamiji by saying, 'Pashyema sharad shatam, jeevema sharad shatam,' a Vedic mantra, meaning, 'May you see a hundred years; may you live a hundred years.' Swamiji smiled and said, 'With me, Rashtrapatiji, you too will have to live a hundred years.' Then he said, 'This spiritual truth is revealed in the Bhagavadgita, "Na jayate mriyate va kadacin ... the soul is eternal; it is never born and never dies."' He very graciously accepted my affection, expressed his love towards me and yet declined my hopeful wishes that he live a hundred-year life.

Pramukh Swamiji uses simple terms and examples to convey complex truths. I asked him, 'How does one connect better to God's consciousness?' Pramukh Swamiji told me, 'You are a rocket scientist. Who would know better than you that as long as there is the pull of gravity, whatever we throw up is always going to come down. But once a rocket is out of the attraction of the Earth's gravity, it will not fall back and will escape into space. Likewise, as long as we are attracted and attached to the comforts of this body, desires of the mind and the material world, we are consigned to the cycle of births and deaths. There will be no escape. But as your worldly desires decrease, you transcend the pull of the world and eventually you connect to God.'

Very early in my life, I learned the virtues of simple living from my father. Later, I found a simple life to be the master key to freedom, self-realization and self-knowledge. I drew inspiration from people who lived simple lives. My own level of simplicity and minimalist living has always remained a work in progress. In my book *Guiding Souls*, I discussed Caliph Umar. This immensely powerful and unimaginably wealthy man lived in a simple mud hut without a door, and walked the streets each evening. He sustained himself on a diet of barley bread or dates; he drank water and preached in a shabby gown that was torn or tattered in twelve places. Self-discipline is the true path to dharma; the right and responsible way of living. Pramukh Swamiji's self-discipline is so perfect that it has become his unconscious second nature.

In Pramukh Swamiji, I see simplicity as a core value, on a par with courage, tolerance, honesty and patience. Perhaps not enough focus is given to simple living when people are young. Youth are misled to believe by thousands of merchants that spending money and obtaining material possessions is the path to happiness. When I see thousands of young devotees engaged in voluntary service at Akshardham, I realize what an incredible gift Akshardhams are to the youth of today, giving them an alternative lifestyle to the one of consumerism, materialism and escapism.

On my way out of the temple in Delhi after speaking with Swamiji, and clear of the issues which had weighed on my mind, I was very pleased to see the statue of the Tamil saint-poet Thiruvalluvar. The statue of this timeless exemplar of spiritual enlightenment and literary prowess was installed in the mandovar, the ornate external wall of the main temple, in accordance with my wish shared with Pramukh Swamiji on the inauguration day. I then realized the attention to detail that Pramukh Swamiji gives. He is a great visionary, but he does not forget the smallest thing. He keeps his word; not just to me, but to everyone. How can he attend to everybody's needs and all the requests that are made of him as he does, yet be so aware of the little things around him? It is because he is so immersed in God and has fully surrendered to Him. I recalled one Thiruvalluvar kural (short Tamil poem) that best captures the greatness of Pramukh Swamiji.

கோளில் பொறியிற் குணமிலவே எண்குணத்தான்
தாளை வணங்காத் தலை

The head that does not bow before the Lord of eight attributes, in prayer,
is like a body with all its senses defunct (Kural 9).

Because Pramukh Swamiji's head is eternally at the feet of God, I find him a perfect embodiment of all the eight Divine attributes: faith, moral excellence, knowledge, self-control, perseverance, godliness, brotherly kindness and love.

7

Nothing Less Than God's Best in Our Lives

'Holiness, not happiness, is the chief end of man.'

— Oswald Chambers
Early twentieth-century Scottish Baptist

It was 11 February 2007. I was taking my morning walk. I had had a beautiful evening the previous day with the ninety-three-year-old eminent writer Khushwant Singh. I went to his house upon hearing that he was unwell. He asked me, 'You are the head of state, why should you waste your time on a pen-pusher?' Khushwant Singh was pleasantly surprised when I told him that I had read the two volumes of his scholarly *History of Sikhs*. He told me, 'President Sahib, when I received your *Ignited Minds* for review, I thought I would tear it to bits, something that I know best. But when I read it, it was a turnaround. I found in you a very good writer. You talked common sense that no one does any more.'

Touched by the sincere appreciation of a scholar-journalist, I was wondering if he would be soon well enough to visit me in Rashtrapati Bhavan; to take a stroll with me in the beautiful Mughal Garden, and meet the deer and peacocks who are the permanent residents here—unlike presidents, who come and go after finishing their five-year terms. My term was to end a few months hence, and I thought it was high time that I invited to Rashtrapati Bhavan some of the fine people who had shaped my thoughts but could not hitherto be with me.

While I was enjoying my walk in the garden, a peacock suddenly appeared in front of me and unfurled its beautiful plumage. It immediately occurred to me that Pramukh Swamiji must visit without any further delay. I wanted to host him in the Rashtrapati Bhavan with his 700 sadhus. I wanted him to sit, talk, walk, meditate; just to spread his aura of goodness where presidents resided. But would he, or would he not come? Even if he declined, I felt that I must invite him. He is above all protocol.

A few hours later, I asked my office to connect me to Pramukh Swamiji. I was told that he was in Mumbai and not well. I sent a message that I would like to speak to him. After about an hour I was connected to him. I was instantly relieved to hear his voice. When I asked about his health, Swamiji said, 'Hearing your voice, I am now healthy and happy. God is also happy.'

I told him, 'Swamiji, do you know why I remember you every day? Because not a day passes without someone coming to me and praising Akshardham. You have revived the heritage of our civilization. No one has been able to do this! Daily, thousands of people from our country visit Akshardham. They all feel proud to be Indian and are inspired to become better human beings. People who come from other countries are also astonished to see the grandeur of Akshardham. You know, not just I, but many throughout the whole nation pray for you.' Swamiji heard my passionate monologue and then said in a soft voice, 'Everything happens as per God's wish.' I lovingly invited him to grace the Rashtrapati Bhavan upon his recovery. Pramukh Swamiji's reply was beyond time and space. He said, 'I am with you in the Rashtrapati Bhavan whenever you remember me.'

Then, in April 2007, I was to address the European parliament on the occasion of the golden jubilee of the European Union. It was a great honour to be invited there. I wanted to convey the message of Pramukh Swamiji. I was, in a sense, disappointed that I was not able to personally meet him to benefit from his advice. But then I realized that we have a divine connectivity, and it is really not important that we sit in front of each other and communicate. Thinking of him is like being with him.

What is the message of Pramukh Swamiji? He is the living head of the Swaminarayan Sampradaya. It is a Bhakti Sampradaya which advocates God within the disciplines of dharma. God is supreme, has a divine form, is the all-doer and is omnipresent. Pramukh Swamiji says that righteousness, right knowledge, detachment and devotion to God are the ways to align with God's will and God's way. A clear alignment brings inner peace, harmony and happiness to the devotee, and a misalignment causes misery, distress and grief. How would I convey this to the gathering of the world's most prominent leaders and statesmen? Would I be able to articulate my thoughts? Would they listen to me?

I addressed the European parliament on 25 April 2007, calling for an evolution of an enlightened society; for evolving a citizenry with a value system, leading to a prosperous and peaceful world. When nations join together to build a cohesive society, it is imperative to ensure that benefits of development encompass all sections of society. The world over, poverty, illiteracy, unemployment and deprivation are fuelling the forces of anger and violence. These forces attach themselves to some real or perceived historical enmity, tyranny, injustice, inequity or ethnic issue. And from religious fundamentalism, virulent extremism erupts worldwide.

In my speech, I said, 'Both India and the European Union have witnessed and are witnessing the unsavoury acts of certain misguided sections of society. We have to jointly address ourselves to the root causes of such phenomena for finding lasting solutions for promoting peace.' While dwelling on the evolution of righteousness and education with a value system, I went a step further in enunciating the views of great souls like Pramukh Swamiji on transforming religion into a spiritual force. He expressed his confidence that different religions could be bridged through spiritual components. I felt as if Pramukh Swamiji was speaking through me when I heard myself saying, 'The spiritual component spreads the values to be inculcated by human beings for promoting a good human life and the welfare of society, while pursuing material life.' The whole parliament gave a standing ovation while the president of the European parliament said, 'They had never heard such a speech.' It was God-inspired!

Earlier, on 29 August 2000, Pramukh Swamiji had emphasized the need of religious unity and spiritual purity in his inaugural address at the Millennium World Peace Summit at the United Nations before almost 2,000 world religious leaders. His words keep echoing in my mind: 'At this hour in human history, we religious leaders should not dream of only One religion in the world, but dream of a world where all religions are One—United. Unity in Diversity is the lesson of life. Flourishing together is the secret of peace …. Let us share this legacy and construct a common platform of values for the rest of mankind to stand on …. Let us teach our followers that religion does not grow by quantity of numbers, but by the quality of spirituality. Vertical depth is much more important than horizontal spread …. Therefore, we should steer our followers away from fanaticism and focus on faith and pure living …. Let us guide ourselves and our followers not just to tolerate but to respect other religions, not just to exist but to co-exist, not just to hail but to help others. We must not progress at the cost of others, but sacrifice a part of ourselves for the good of others.' Pramukh Swamiji's speech was like the Magna Carta of spiritual unity.

I completed my presidential term on 25 July 2007. In my farewell speech to parliament, I enunciated a distinct vision of India which is to be manifest by the year 2020. India is to be a nation—where the rural and urban divide has reduced to a thin line; where there is equitable distribution and adequate access to energy and quality water; where agriculture, industry and the service sector work together in concert; where education with a value system is not denied to any meritorious candidates on account of societal or economic discrimination; which is the best destination for the most talented scholars, scientists and investors; where the best of health care is available to all; where the governance is responsive, transparent and corruption-free; where poverty has been totally eradicated, illiteracy removed and crimes against women and children are absent; where no one in society feels alienated; that is prosperous, healthy, secure, devoid of terrorism, peaceful and happy; that continues with a sustainable growth path, and above all, that is one of the best places to live, and is proud of its creative and effective leadership in parliament, state assemblies and other institutions.

Before my term ended, there was talk in political circles of renominating me; and other such parallel whispers abounded. There were views expressed from some quarters that I must seek a second term as president. The only Indian president who served two terms in office—actually more than two terms; indeed, his tenure exceeded twelve years—was Dr Rajendra Prasad, India's first president. He served from 30 January 1950 to 13 May 1962. While the president's role is apolitical, as it should be in a structure similar to a constitutional monarchy, he is nevertheless part of the political structure. Thus, his election and re-election are political decisions. I phoned Pramukh Swamiji who was in the US at that time. He said, 'Kalam Saheb, do not stand for re-election. Let go! Go and serve the people. By serving selflessly, a person transcends any office, however high it may be.'

On 25 July 2007, as I moved out of Rashtrapati Bhavan with my two old suitcases with which I had moved in five years ago, I felt free like a sadhu. I had always admired the vicharan (spiritual travel) of sadhus. Now, free from the trappings of state protocol and the strictures of security, there was nothing to stop me from travelling: I could go wherever I wanted to go. I resumed my sankalp (solemn vow and intention) of igniting young minds which I had assumed on the night of 30 June 2001 in the presence of Pramukh Swamiji. I had led the Indian state as its president. I would now lead India as an eminent senior citizen. I was surprised by the number of invitations I received and the number of emails that were pouring in. And my house in New Delhi became a pilgrim point for thousands of people visiting Delhi for some work or other. The realization of 'nothing but one God', to be the all-doer and surrendering my actions to his will had become my trajectory.

On 15 October 2008, I completed seventy-seven years of my life. It is not my habit to celebrate my birthday. I live this day every year as any other day, and whenever possible in the best possible oblivion. Towards the evening, I felt an intense desire to speak to Pramukh Swamiji, who was in Gondal. I called Sadhu Brahmaviharidas, 'Please tell Pramukh Swamiji that I am now moving around from one place to another like a sadhu.' Pramukh Swamiji said, 'On the day I met you in 2001, had I not told you that you are a rishi? Ancient rishis had long hair, were great scientists, were not married and worked hard with great values. You are a shining example of simple living and high thinking.'

In his characteristic way, Pramukh Swamiji had rendered me speechless. But I was not in a mood to surrender. I asked, 'Will Pramukh Swamiji certify that I am a sadhu?' Swamiji said, 'Yes. You are a sadhu.' I beamed, 'This certificate from Pramukh Swamiji is like a certificate from the Divine.'

Our connection was getting deeper, and I could sense Pramukh Swamiji's presence even in his absence. In a time so filled with methods and techniques designed to change people—to influence their behaviour, and to make them do new things and think new thoughts—I received this unique gift of being present with Pramukh Swamiji, at all times.

8

Change Alone Is Eternal, Perpetual, Immortal

'You must be the change you wish to see in the world.'

– Mahatma Gandhi

Pramukh Swamiji is a wanderer with a divine purpose. He has visited more than 17,000 villages and sanctified over 750,000 homes. He has led the creation of truly magnificent Akshardhams, but has never permanently stayed anywhere. Throughout his life, he has moved from one place to another—throughout India and the whole world. He has stayed in the homes of his disciples, in their huts, and has mingled with influential leaders and ordinary people alike. I too travel a lot, but he is ten years my senior, and though I had concerns about the capacity of his body to endure the rigours of travel, I also knew that he cannot be made to stay in one place. He is possessed of the cosmic energy, and his life is now beyond any human scheduling or intervention.

I met Pramukh Swamiji on 18 July 2010 at Akshardham, Delhi, and a week later, on 23 July 2010, I visited Akshardham in Gandhinagar. I saw there the enchanting Sat-Chit-Anand Water Show. The show reveals India's ancient secret of inner light through the story of Nachiketa. The story is told in the *Katha Upanishad*. Nachiketa asked Yama, the king of Death, to teach him the mystery of what comes after death. Yama was reluctant to answer this question; he said that this had remained a mystery even to the gods. He asked Nachiketa to request some other boon, and offered many material gains. But Nachiketa replied that material things are fleeting. Yama was secretly pleased with Nachiketa, and elaborated on the nature of the true self, which exists beyond death. The key of the realization is that this self (atma) is pervaded by Paramatma, the supreme Almighty, the Creator and vital force of the universe.

Many technological elements of the Sat-Chit-Anand Water Show make it truly unique in the country, with a 130-foot-wide and 70-foot-high water screen, around 4,000 nozzles, 2,000 lights, more than 100 pumps, a 160-foot-long 'sea-of-fire' (fire spreading on water), along with several fireballs and three powerful lasers—all enhanced by a 7.1 surround sound system. All of this is controlled with extreme precision, with each effect synchronized to within a fraction of a second. I was told that the show has been produced by ECA2, a world-renowned creative agency from France led by Yves Pépin, and supported by 400 professional volunteers, who had given their talent, time, effort and money to make this wonder possible.

I spoke to Pramukh Swamiji, who was in Delhi, on the telephone. I said, 'Thousands of Nachiketas will be created in India due to this water show. I got the idea to write a book while watching this show.' Pramukh Swamiji said, 'We are grateful that you honoured our invitation. I pray for your book, your health and that you are able to serve India.' It is on that day that this book was conceived in my consciousness. Of course, it would take another five years to grow and manifest in its present form.

Whenever I heard about Pramukh Swamiji's health issues, I spoke to him over the telephone. He would always allay my fears, and give his blessings for my health and happiness instead. Gradually, his health declined, and Pramukh Swamiji decided to make Sarangpur his final abode in this life. His dedicated sadhus created the most modern medical facilities to look after him there, and hundreds of thousands of his devotees started visiting Sarangpur just to glimpse Swamiji's great persona.

On 11 March 2014, I too travelled to Sarangpur to meet Pramukh Swamiji with my friend Arun. Y.S. Rajan was already there.

Pramukh Swamiji had stopped eating, hardly drank fluids and was under medical observation. But he was happy and radiant. He exuded peace and enlightenment. I did not see a flicker of pain or sense any complaint in him. He did not speak, but held my hand for more than ten minutes. He gave all three of us a rosary and smiled to the delight of all the sadhus present. I later addressed a gathering of 2,000 sadhus, haribhaktas (devotees) and Vidyamandir students there.

I recollected my visit to the Akshardham Cultural Complex, New Delhi, in November 2005. On that day, I got an answer for the question: How can you integrate spirituality and social service? The answer was that they were indeed inseparable. Those who wished to sincerely serve society must be spiritually pure, and only those who were spiritually pure must sincerely serve society. I then narrated to the assembly an incident that took place more than fifty years earlier and how it led to a great creation.

In 1962, Vikram Sarabhai was searching for a site to establish a space research station in the equatorial region. He visited a number of places. Thumba in Kerala seemed ideal, because it was nearest to the equatorial electrojet (EEJ), a narrow ribbon of an air current flowing eastward during the daytime in the equatorial region of the earth's ionosphere. This would facilitate ionospheric research in the upper atmosphere. But the Pallithura area had many villages and thousands of fishing communities. It was also the location of an ancient St Mary Magdalene Church and the bishop's house.

No politician or bureaucrat would agree to requisition this land for scientific purposes. A resolute Vikram Sarabhai decided to present his case to the bishop of Thiruvananthapuram. At that time, Reverend Father Peter Bernard Pereira was the bishop. Vikram Sarabhai visited his house on a Saturday. The bishop heard him patiently and invited him to attend the Sunday morning service.

The bishop told the congregation, 'My children, I have a famous scientist with me who wants our church and the place where I live for the work of space science research. Dear children, science seeks the truth that enriches human life. The higher level of religion is spirituality. Spiritual preachers like me seek the help of the Almighty to bring peace to human minds. In short, what Vikram is doing and what I am doing are the same—both science and spirituality seek the Almighty's blessings for human prosperity in mind and body. Our abodes and the church will be newly built and given to us. Children, can we give them God's abode, my abode and your abodes for a scientific mission?' There was a pin-drop silence, followed by a hearty 'Amen' from the congregation, which made the whole church resonate.

The bishop of Thiruvananthapuram took the noble decision to dedicate the church for the establishment of the Indian Space Research Organization (ISRO) in recognition of our national scientific goals. I worked in the converted church building that was our design centre. We started rocket assembly and designed a filament winding machine for FRP products. Later, the Thumba Equatorial Rocket Launching Station (TERLS) led to the establishment of Vikram Sarabhai Space Centre (VSSC) and multiple space centres throughout the country.

When I think of that event, I see how enlightened spiritual and scientific leaders can converge in giving reverence to the meaning of human life. The birth of TERLS and then the VSSC gave the country the capability to design, develop and produce sizeable world-class rocket systems. Subsequently, India developed the capacity for launching geosynchronous, sun-synchronous and meteorological spacecraft, communication satellites and remote sensing satellites. These provided instant communication, weather forecasting and the ability to locate water resources for the country. Today, neither Vikram Sarabhai nor Reverend Father Peter Bernard Pereira is with us, but the evidence of their nobility and unity of minds remains, and will continue for generations.

Here, I would like to quote a passage from the book *Satsang*:[16] 'What is left with a person who has given his all? Nothing! But this nothing becomes everything indeed. It becomes an ocean of goodness, of purity and humility, an essence of spirituality that is enough to inspire millions.' Pramukh Swamiji has now reached the supreme state of personhood, which needs no rank, no recognition; not even veneration. Pramukh Swamiji has become the noble soul. He now lives in this awakened state, not moving anywhere, not saying anything, not doing anything, and yet overseeing all that is being planned, created and managed. His life is an example of selfless service and the creation of excellence. In his presence, I have become much more aware of my real self!

Whatever the circumstances of your life demand of you, respond to them in your own individual Pramukh Swamiji–spirited way. Do not waste any time trying to be someone else. We are not here to have someone else's experience. We are here to have our own vivid experience in accordance with the will of God. So do not cling to yesterday, to what happened, to what did not happen. It was all experiential teaching. And do not judge today by yesterday. It is a new class—a new lesson, a new experience. Let us give our best to this today; let us live today to the fullest! Moment after moment, each step is only a step—the journey is indeed eternal.

I do not know when Pramukh Swamiji and I will meet again. His words, however, remain preserved in my memory. We have established a divine bonding, which is forever. How do I summarize Pramukh Swamiji's effect on me? He has indeed transformed me. He is the ultimate stage of the spiritual ascent in my life, which started with my father, was sustained by Dr Brahma Prakash and Prof. Satish Dhawan; now, finally, Pramukh Swamiji has put me in a God-synchronous orbit. No manoeuvres are required any more, as I am placed in my final position in eternity.

In the second part of the book I will capture the work done by Bochasanwasi Shri Akshar Purushottam Swaminarayan Sanstha (BAPS), and attempt to offer the insights and rationale behind the mission of the organization. Swaminarayan Sampradaya is a form of Vaishnavism and a modern sect of Hinduism. Bhagwan Swaminarayan (1781–1830) is the central figure of the organization. BAPS was formally established as an organization on 5 June 1907 by Shastriji Maharaj. It was formed on the founder's doctrinal stand that Swaminarayan had promised to remain manifest in the person of Akshar, a term used to describe his chief devotee and Swaminarayan's abode.

Gunatitanand Swami (1785–1867) is accepted as the first spiritual successor of Bhagwan Swaminarayan, followed by Bhagatji Maharaj

(1829–1897), Shastriji Maharaj (1865–1951) and then Yogiji Maharaj (1892–1971). Pramukh Swami Maharaj is the current guru and spiritual leader of BAPS. He is believed by his followers to be in constant communion with Bhagwan Swaminarayan and, ontologically, the manifestation of Akshar, the eternal abode of Bhagwan Swaminarayan. Under Pramukh Swami Maharaj's leadership, BAPS has rapidly grown into a global Hindu organization, and has witnessed a significant expansion in many measurable parameters. Currently, BAPS encompasses over one million devotees, more than 950 sadhus, 1,100 mandirs, 3,900 centres in multiple continents, over 12,000 weekly assemblies and congregations, and a host of humanitarian and charitable activities. It is indeed a spectacular phenomenon of good works.

PART TWO

SPIRITUALITY IN ACTION

'There is no higher religion than human service. To work for the common good is the greatest creed.'

– Woodrow Wilson
The twenty-eighth president of the United States

9

Portal to the Unseen

'Appearances are a glimpse of the unseen.'

– Anaxagoras
Pre-Socratic Greek philosopher

I was born at the Mosque Street in Rameswaram, in the vicinity of a majestic temple. Rameswara means 'Lord of Rama' in Sanskrit; it is an epithet of Shiva, the presiding deity of the Ramanathaswami temple. Sethu Karai is a place 22 kilometres before the island of Rameswaram, from where Rama is believed to have built a floating stone bridge—Adam's Bridge—that proceeded from Dhanushkodi in Rameswaram to Talaimannar in Sri Lanka. Hundreds and thousands of pilgrims would come to Rameswaram. The entire economy of the island depended on providing them basic services—food and provisions, transport and porter services and boats—and the sale of artefacts such as those made out of seashells.

The head priest of the temple, Pakshi Lakshmana Shastrigal, was a dear friend of my father. Their regularly sitting together, engaged in long conversations, is still a vivid memory. As it was customary in those days to cover one's head whenever going out of the house, my father would wear his skullcap and Shastriji would don a turban. As a small child, I used to wonder how and when the first temple could have been built. Who constructed this huge stone building on this island surrounded by sea? Did Lord Rama actually come here? Did Lord Hanuman really construct the bridge using floating stones? The stone-carved figures in the temple were fascinating. Why were there no images in mosques?

Later, I learnt from my teacher, Siva Subramanian Iyer, that no temples existed during the Vedic age—the era that ended around 500 BC. The practice of fashioning images of deities mentioned in the Vedic mantras might have come into vogue by the end of the Vedic period. My teacher told me that it was widely accepted that, owing to the influence of the cults of devotion, the yajnashala of the Vedic period gradually metamorphosed into temples by the epic period. The earliest temples were built with perishable materials like timber and clay. Cave temples—temples carved out of stone or built with bricks—came later. Heavy stone structures like the Shiva temple in Rameswaram, with ornate architecture and sculpture, belong to a later period still.

Ramanathaswami temple was built in the seventeenth century. Situated close to the sea on the eastern side of the island, this temple is famous for its 1,200 gigantic granite columns. The 54-metre-tall gopuram (gate tower), 1,220 metres of magnificent corridors and the flamboyantly carved columns embellish the temple and elevate its fame. It is indeed a fascinating fact that the water in each of the twenty-two sacred wells in the temple tastes different.

Considering the vast size of this country, it is remarkable that the building of temples has progressed more or less on a set pattern. But in spite of the basic pattern being the same, variations did appear, gradually leading to the evolution of different styles in temple architecture. Broadly speaking, these can be categorized as the northern and the southern styles. The curvilinear towers distinguish the northern style. The southern style features towers in the form of truncated pyramids.

When I met Pramukh Swamiji in 2001, he shared with me the drawings of the Akshardham mandir and complex that would be built in New Delhi. Swamiji explained, 'Akshardham is the heavenly abode of Bhagwan Swaminarayan. It is an imperishable place of everlasting peace and enlightenment.' Every detail of the mandir, exhibitions and environment was laid out before me. I was amazed by the meticulous planning and the underlying messages in its design. I asked, 'What is the one message every visitor should take with them from Akshardham?' The sadhus humbly asked me what should be that singularly important message. I beamed, 'Every Indian should become proud to be an Indian.'

After a few years, when the drawings became a reality, Akshardham truly enhanced the pride and purpose of all pilgrims, and indeed it can make all Indians proud. The sadhus explained that the mandir's pink sandstone represents bhakti, devotion for the Divine, and its white marble symbolizes shuddhi and shanti, purity and peace. Its stunning architecture is well researched, highly authentic and faithful to its ancient heritage. It is filled with traditional patterns and designs, figures and filigree, pillars and porches, and incredible beams and domes. It was hand-carved and erected by no less than 7,000 highly skilled artisans and 4,000 dedicated volunteers. The making of Akshardham in itself is a great revival of art and a unique unifier of human energy and skill.

'Why are temples built? What is the purpose behind them?' I asked Pramukh Swamiji. He explained, 'A temple is the physical manifestation of the unseen.' I reflected upon his short answer and realized that the very nature of human perception is such that whatever is seen and whatever one is involved with—that will be the only truth for him in his experience. Most people are involved, throughout almost the entirety of their lives, with their five sensory organs. And that seems to be the only truth for them—and nothing else. Sensory organs can only perceive that which is physical. And because our perception is limited to the five sensory organs, everything that we know as life is merely the physical: our bodies, our minds, our emotions and our life energies are all physical. When we look up, there seems to be a vast emptiness above, but even there we only recognize the physical. We look at the stars and the moon in the night, and the sun in the day, all of which are physical entities.

A temple or mosque, or any place of worship, is hence a bridge to connect us to a world beyond the physical. Sadhu Brahmaviharidas explained, 'True spiritual places help us to transcend the world of man, connect to God and attain enlightenment. Moreover, regular and sincere prayers can elevate the mind and help one to experience the Divine.' On another occasion, Sadhu Ishwarcharandas explained, 'Atma (soul) is our true self. Akshar exists at an even higher level than our soul. It is the divine essence of our being; the source of all light and life within each of us. When we identify ourselves with Akshar, we are able to directly experience and realize Purushottam, the Supreme Divinity.'

I can see the point that as we open to our divine selves, we can receive their guidance: peace, harmony and illuminating light. We can more easily turn away from the distractions of the physical world, and restore ourselves in the light, love and power of the eternal Divine. Through this connection, we can operate in the world of potential, and manifest our highest path. The Divine will reveal the illusions, desires and attachments that keep us trapped in a lower vibration and on a lesser path. We gain a greater ability to recognize limiting, disharmonious and restricting energies and forms. Not only will this connection reveal these limitations, it indeed enables us to have the power, wisdom and vision to release these energies.

Your divine self is always trying to reach you, to send you the power, illumination, love and wisdom to draw higher forms, thoughts, feelings and situations into your life. Your divine self is wise; it knows all, and is always showing you an easier, better and more joyful way to live. Your divine self is able to break through the limitations of your personality and self-concept, and open you to new ways of living and being. It can be reached by intense prayer. Connecting with the Divine brings a sense of flow, of moving with the current and of being on an upward spiral.

When we wish to assess the scientific knowledge and personality of a scholar, we examine his works and subject them to close scrutiny. Similarly, in order to gauge the talent and ability of an artist, we undertake a study of his creations. In the same manner, we can also perceive the attributes and characteristics of the pure essence of the Creator, from the qualities and orderliness—further, the subtlety and precision—that pervade all phenomena. Thereby, within the limits set by our capacity to know and perceive, we can become acquainted with God's knowledge, wisdom, life and power.

If it were a question of complete and comprehensive knowledge of God, then, of course, we must accept that man's cognition does not extend that far. God's characteristics cannot be placed within given limits; thus whatever comparison or simile we offer for them is bound to be false. For whatever is observable to science and thought in the natural realm is the work of God and the product of His will and command, whereas His essence is not part of nature and does not belong to the category of created things. Hence, man, by way of comparison and analogy, cannot truly grasp the essence of the divine being. By sincere prayers, devotees can only receive guidance.

Whether we enter a temple, mosque or church, with prayer or contemplation of the will, consciousness, knowledge and harmony inherent in the order of being and exemplified in all the various phenomena of life, it becomes abundantly clear that all derives from the will of a Creator. Moreover, these qualities, together with all the other elements of creation that speak of aim, direction and purpose, lead us inevitably to the conclusion that these are verily attributes of the Creator reflected in the mirror of creation.

And although we can witness and garner some understanding of the qualities of the Creator through his works, that which comes to know God and to touch His being is the remarkable power of thought. This is a flash which, deriving from that pre-eternal source, shone on matter and bestowed on it the capacity of acquiring knowledge and advancing towards the truth. It is within this great divine gift that the knowledge of God is manifest. The Holy Quran tells of this so beautifully (Surah Al-Baqarah; Ayat 163–64):

وَإِلَٰهُكُمْ إِلَٰهٌ وَاحِدٌ لَّا إِلَٰهَ إِلَّا هُوَ ٱلرَّحْمَٰنُ ٱلرَّحِيمُ
إِنَّ فِى خَلْقِ ٱلسَّمَٰوَٰتِ وَٱلْأَرْضِ وَٱخْتِلَٰفِ ٱلَّيْلِ وَٱلنَّهَارِ
وَٱلْفُلْكِ ٱلَّتِى تَجْرِى فِى ٱلْبَحْرِ بِمَا يَنفَعُ ٱلنَّاسَ وَمَا أَنزَلَ ٱللَّهُ
مِنَ ٱلسَّمَاءِ مِن مَّاءٍ فَأَحْيَا بِهِ ٱلْأَرْضَ بَعْدَ مَوْتِهَا وَبَثَّ فِيهَا
مِن كُلِّ دَآبَّةٍ وَتَصْرِيفِ ٱلرِّيَٰحِ وَٱلسَّحَابِ ٱلْمُسَخَّرِ
بَيْنَ ٱلسَّمَاءِ وَٱلْأَرْضِ لَآيَٰتٍ لِّقَوْمٍ يَعْقِلُونَ

Your God is but one God. There is no god other than Him,
Compassionate and Merciful, in the creation of the heavens and the
earth, in the alternation of night and day, in the ships that ply the
seas to the benefit of man, in the water sent down from the heavens
to revive the earth after its death, in the different species of animals
scattered across the earth, in the rotation of the winds, in the clouds
that are subordinate to God's command between heaven and earth—
in all of this, there are signs for men who use their intellects.

Places of worship are embodiments of man's intellectual concept
of God and his creation. And just as the Creator's qualities are
indelible in our universe, so too are the attributes of those who build
places of worship in their creations. In the creation of the stunning
Akshardham Temple, I can see the excellence of human intellect,
organizational skills, craftsmanship—and a vision of the Divine. A
place of worship is also a portal to the unseen. Akshardham is perhaps
the finest and most glorious portal to our ancient heritage on earth
and the Divine in heaven.

Akshardham's exquisite structure—reflecting BAPS investment
in a particular form of monumental architecture in Pramukh Swami
Maharaj's time—is reminiscent of temples dating back nearly a
millennium. For the first eighty years of BAPS, its temples were
modest structures; Delhi Akshardham Temple, however, resembles
the intricately carved, tenth-to-twelfth-century western Indian Maru-
Gurjara temples at Dilwara, Modhera and Kiradu. And, like these
medieval temples, it is made of stone without the use of iron or steel.
Pramukh Swamiji has created what few kings could in the long history
of Indian civilization.

When I expressed to Pramukh Swamiji that it is indeed a perfect
place he has built in Akshardham, he said, 'Do not confuse excellence
with perfection. Excellence man can reach, but perfection is God's work.'
In his presence, I felt the nourishment of the celestial forces in man.

10

Warriors of the Light

'Hope is being able to see that there is light despite all of the darkness.'

– Archbishop emeritus Desmond Tutu
South African social rights activist

On 18 September 2004, on my presidential visit to South Africa, I visited Pietermaritzburg, some 70 kilometres inland from the east-coast port of Durban. It was at Pietermaritzburg railway station on 7 June 1893 that Mahatma Gandhi, en route to Johannesburg, was unceremoniously thrown out of a whites-only first-class compartment in the middle of the night, despite the fact that he was holding a valid ticket. A universal hero of human history was born that night. This incident indeed launched a political career that culminated in India getting its freedom.

Indians first came to South Africa as indentured labourers.[17] They struggled to settle and make a living for themselves there; they had to contend with very stringent terms of indenture and the racism of white colonists, who saw them as simply 'units of labour'. The object for which they were brought to South Africa was to supply labour—and that alone. The indentured labourers were barely considered human, and treated as alien. They were expected to perform a certain amount of work for a prescribed period, then return to India. For the five or ten years of their indenture they suffered incredible hardships, including floggings, poor living conditions, separation from family members, and seven days a week of nine-hour working days. Some did indeed choose to return to their places of origin. But most stayed on, making livings out of market gardening and fruit and vegetable vending, before gradually branching out into other occupations.

In 1863, a young man called Abubaker Jhavary, originally from Porbandar on the Kathiawad Peninsula, arrived in Natal via Mauritius. By dint of hard work and business acumen he prospered, and his trade flourished. He was soon exporting dried fish cured by Indians on Salisbury Island in Durban Bay, to India in his own fleet of ships. This set off a new wave of Indian immigration, with the first arrivals in 1869 of so-called 'passenger' Indians—people who paid their own way to Natal. These were mostly from the west coast of India, in particular Mumbai; they were predominantly Gujarati traders who added their rich culture to the already eclectic mix of languages and customs among the Indians in Natal.

These new arrivals soon spread throughout the country, setting up trading stores in remote parts of Zululand and even moving into the Transvaal, or Zuid Afrikaansche Republiek (ZAR). Here, they also flourished, as the gold-mining industry began to expand and sizeable sums of money flowed into the country.

These immigrants were usually young men who arrived alone. As they became more established and their businesses started to prosper, they would build shops with residences either above or behind the shops. When these were ready for occupation, they would return to India to fetch their families. Trade opportunities in East Africa, created by favourable economic and political circumstances, attracted more Indian migrants. Many of them were also compelled to emigrate by economic depressions in Gujarat caused by repeated epidemics, droughts and famines. Gujarati traders and other Indian migrants to East Africa later brought their wives and families, including extended kin.

By 1885, there were sufficient Indians in the country to worry members of the Volksraad (parliament) of the ZAR. As a result of the fears of the whites, Act No. 3 of that year was passed which took away the right of 'Coolies, Arabs and other Asiatics' to own land in the

ZAR. The government also had the right, under this Act, to restrict them 'for purposes of sanitation' to certain areas.

A year after he arrived in South Africa as a twenty-three-year-old barrister, Gandhiji decided to devote himself to serving the Indian community, which was aggrieved by the continuing racial discrimination and humiliation its people were suffering under the white rulers. He was instrumental in the establishment of the Natal Indian Congress in 1894 and the Transvaal British Indian Association in 1903. For over a decade, he prepared numerous petitions and memoranda, led deputations to the authorities, wrote letters to the press and tried to promote public understanding and support—in South Africa, as well as in India and Britain—for the cause of the Indians in South Africa. His professional practice also came to be largely devoted to this cause.

At that time, Gandhiji entertained faith in the fairness of the British and Britain's imperial principles. But it became clear by 1906 that appeals and petitions had proved ineffective, and promises had been broken by government officials. The Transvaal Asiatic Ordinance of 1906, requiring all Indians to register and carry passes, was the last straw. Gandhiji resolved not to submit to this unjust and pernicious measure. The Indian community in the province took a solemn pledge at a large meeting on 31 July 1906 to defy the law. People of all religious persuasions—Hindus, Muslims, Parsis and Christians—and of varied occupations—merchants, hawkers, professionals, workers and indentured labourers—came together in this righteous struggle.

Gandhiji and his colleagues were sentenced to long terms of imprisonment. The strikers were rendered leaderless. The army, police and the employers were ruthless in their attempts to coerce the workers and suppress their strikes. Striking miners were confined in mine compounds turned into prisons and subjected to cruel assaults. Indentured labourers on sugar plantations were beaten and fired at. Several workers were killed. But the strikers remained firm and disciplined. And, of equal significance, they did not deviate from non-violence. John Dube, the first president general of the African National Congress, gave a moving eyewitness account of an incident in which 500 strikers at Phoenix would not move. This was despite whippings, beatings with sticks and rifle butts, horses running amuck in their midst, the torture and killing of their leader and the firing of live rounds. Gandhiji would later recall in *Young India*, 20 April 1921, 'The whole community rose like a surging wave. Without organization, without propaganda, nearly 40,000 people courted imprisonment. Nearly 10,000 were actually imprisoned. A bloodless revolution was effected after strenuous discipline in self-suffering.'[18]

Gandhiji sailed for England in July 1914 en route to India. The twenty-one years which Mohandas Gandhi spent in South Africa were instrumental in transforming him and giving perspective to his philosophy of life. When I later met Nelson Mandela, he told me, 'Mr President, you sent us a barrister, and we returned you a Mahatma.'

But there were many who did not return. They made the African nations their own countries. When these countries eventually became free from their colonial rulers, however, the new establishment and even indigenous people themselves became hostile to these Indians. A poem written by a Kenyan Indian, in a new African nation, comes to my mind. It captures so well the pressure generated by the racial debate over post-independence citizenship, that raged in all three East African countries:

The past has boiled itself over
And we are the steam that must flee.[19]

Nevertheless, Gandhiji's effectiveness in emancipating and reinforcing the dignity of indentured labourers and free migrants alike had far-reaching implications for generations afterwards. The identity and pride which emerged from Gandhiji's campaigns in South Africa was later evident in BAPS missions on the African continent, and sustained African Indians through the tribulations of post-colonial rule. And, like the work of BAPS, the Mahatma's work was God-inspired. Gandhiji consistently talked about the inner voice, and referred to it when exasperated politicians questioned his abrupt decisions. Gandhiji spoke of God as

... a personal God to those who need His personal presence. He is embodied to those who need His touch. He is the purest essence. He simply is to those who have faith. He is in us and yet above and beyond us ... we can feel Him if we will but withdraw ourselves from the senses.[20]

It is my belief that a person's conscience develops at the pace at which his relationship with God develops. And as both develop, the inner voice—which is available to us all—becomes stronger and more reliable as a guide for the actions one plans.

Gandhiji raised the consciousness of expatriate Indians in the African continent from acquiescence to transformation. Harmanbhai Patel was one who embodied this transformation. His father came to East Africa after the construction of the Uganda railway between 1896 and 1901. Railway work started in 1898 from Mombasa. The local people refused to work for the British, perhaps due to their fraught relationship with the previous colonial rulers, the Portuguese. Further inland, the Kamba, Kikuyu and Masai tribes, content with their self-sufficient farms and cattle, were incredulous at the thought of working for wages. The impasse prompted the British East Africa Company—which also ruled the area for a short period—to indenture about 30,000 Indian labourers. Jeevanjee & Co. Ltd of Gujarat provided the company with skilled and unskilled workers.

Once the railway was completed, many of the indentured labourers chose to bring their families over from India and settle in what was then the East Africa Protectorate. The early Asian settlers, hailing mostly from Gujarat, quickly embraced the opportunities to be had in the new British territory. Most settled in the new town of Nairobi, which had been the capital of the British protectorate since 1905. Unlike black Africans, Asians were permitted to reside legally in Nairobi in what was then a burgeoning white settler town.

Owing to the somewhat uncertain social and economic situation in East Africa, women rarely accompanied men on the journey back to Africa. Instead, they would remain in their villages, looking after elders and raising children. Their husbands would make several trips each year to India, to visit their families and establish mercantile connections with the community at large. And, in truth, in the first phase of Gujarati emigration to Africa, their largest trading partner was India, with millions of sterling worth of goods flowing back and forth across the Arabian Sea.

The social and business networks of the earliest emigrants were therefore familial and international. Trust and honour drove the creation of these networks, made all the easier because not all men in an extended family would go to Africa. Those that remained to look after the ancestral businesses would maintain links with their peripatetic relatives, offering not only secure banking but also collateral in the form of real estate. These networks were periodically renewed and strengthened whenever the travellers returned home, either for marriage or to visit their families. Even if the East African Indian couldn't travel to India, he would still strive to maintain relations with the homeland. His house would aim to reproduce the joint-family structure; he would continue to speak Gujarati; he would cherish Indian traditions—and he remained staunchly vegetarian. Charities and foundations were established. India, in other words, remained in their hearts.

This was the state of Indian society in East Africa when Harmanbhai Patel was drawn to the Swaminarayan Sampradaya. The East African Indian lived in a thriving, dynamic and enterprising—albeit somewhat homesick—outpost of Indian culture on the African continent. In 1928, Harmanbhai met Shastriji Maharaj in India, and returned to Africa with some printed pictures of Bhagwan Swaminarayan. These pictures became the nucleus for attracting Indian expatriates, who then started meeting regularly to share spiritual thoughts and feelings in what was called satsang—the brotherhood of the pious.

In 1932, Harmanbhai again visited India. During the days that followed, he was so moved by the divinity of Shastriji Maharaj and the buoyant spirit of the devotees, that he felt there was no point in returning to Africa for the sake of earning a living. How could he give up the priceless, divine company of Shastriji Maharaj? Harmanbhai travelled with Shastriji Maharaj to Rajpur. There, he revealed,

'Swami, I do not wish to return to Africa. People are not inclined towards spirituality there.' But Shastriji Maharaj instructed him to return to East Africa to spread satsang there. Harmanbhai returned a transformed person; he was a man with a mission. Gradually, the message of Swaminarayan Hinduism took root, and the satsang spread across East Africa: in Kenya, Uganda and Tanganyika (now Tanzania).

When some Gujaratis reached Uganda, they discovered an abundance of arable land, fertile with peculiar red and black soils. Immediately recognizing its potential for cultivation, they established thriving agricultural enterprises. They grew cotton, sugar cane, sisal, tea and coffee on a grand scale. By 1938, cotton cultivation alone took up three million acres of land. Uganda was called the 'Kashmir of Africa'. Bountiful returns from agriculture, compared to that in Kenya and Tanganyika, corresponded with a burgeoning of the satsang in Uganda. In 1950, devotees in Kampala, the largest city and capital of Uganda, held an event to celebrate the eighty-fifth birthday of Shastriji Maharaj. People travelled as far as 600 miles for this grand convention.

Nirgundas Swami, a senior disciple-sadhu serving under Shastriji Maharaj, provided spiritual nourishment to the devotees in Africa through his correspondence of long letters—sometimes numbering as much as seventy and 100 pages. The letters elaborated on the faith's creed, devotion and glory. Every word instilled a new power of enthusiasm and commitment. They were circulated through the railway staff or telegraphy, perhaps in a similar spirit to the way that Saint Paul's letters were eagerly circulated among the scattered communities of early Christians. Soon, satsang centres were springing up in other towns and villages. People started celebrating festivals with fanfare and enthusiasm. Gloom and despair were replaced by hope and confidence.[21]

In April 1955, Yogiji Maharaj arrived in Africa for the first time and consecrated the first BAPS temple outside India in Mombasa. Yogiji Maharaj travelled extensively to villages and towns across Africa, inspiring satsang in thousands of aspirants. In October 1959, Yogiji Maharaj made his second visit to East Africa, accompanied by Pramukh Swamiji, Santvallabh Swami and Balmukund Swami. They visited Tanganyika, Uganda, Kenya, Central Africa, Rhodesia, and Nyasaland (now Malawi). During that visit, Yogiji Maharaj consecrated temples at Kampala, Jinja and Tororo. Yogiji Maharaj returned a decade later and opened a temple in Nairobi on 10 February 1970. Then, on 23 January 1971, Yogiji Maharaj departed from this mortal world in Mumbai, passing on the spiritual mantle to Pramukh Swamiji.

Two days later, on 25 January 1971, Idi Amin seized power in Uganda, staging a military coup while President Milton Obote was abroad attending a Commonwealth summit meeting. He promptly declared himself president of Uganda. In August 1972, Amin declared what he termed an 'economic war'. By decree, he expelled some 80,000 Asians—the virtual entirety of whom were Indian—and expropriated their properties and businesses.

Some 30,000, those with British passports, immigrated to the United Kingdom. Others went to Australia, Canada, India, Kenya, Pakistan, Sweden, Tanzania, and the United States. Amin handed the expropriated businesses and properties—including large-scale enterprises and the six well-established BAPS temples in Kampala, Jinja and Tororo—to his supporters.

The value of the Ugandan Indians for the country's economic well-being soon became apparent by their absence. Mismanaged businesses closed and infrastructure collapsed from lack of administration and maintenance. Moreover, the country lost a valuable class of professionals: the Indians comprised a significant proportion of Uganda's doctors, teachers, lawyers and accountants. With shortages of essential commodities and inflation soaring to 1,000 per cent, the already faltering economy disintegrated. The net result of Amin's racist purge was economic and social pandemonium. Uganda eventually spiralled into a violent chaos that claimed as many as 500,000 lives over a period of eight years. Amin's rule of Uganda—and indeed, his very name—has become synonymous with barbarity.[22] Perhaps the only consolation for Uganda's exiled Indians was that they had all but escaped bloodshed.

We can only imagine the anguish of these Indians, many of whose families had lived for generations in Uganda. Deracinated and cast out from their adopted homeland, many began their new lives in refugee dormitories with little more than their faith in God and a suitcase of personal items to sustain them. Their courage and faith in God were to be deciding factors in their fate, however, as they successfully built new lives in foreign lands. The cultural ties which bound them to ancient practices from their motherland had sustained them in their adopted country, and now inspired them in exile.

The strength of their religious culture, and the faith and steadfastness in the face of adversity of Uganda's exiled Indians deeply affected the senior civil servant and chairman of the Uganda Resettlement Board, Sir Charles Cunningham. In his foreword in *Life and Philosophy of Shree Swaminarayan*,[23] Sir Charles singles out faith in God as the prime factor in the rehabilitation of the thousands of Indians who arrived in England as refugees in 1971.

> This ability to draw strength from cultural and religious continuity can help in facing the unpredictable trials of modern life. When nearly thirty thousand people were suddenly expelled from Uganda and had to come, often penniless, to start a new life in Great Britain, their calmness and dignity, their readiness to accept hardship, the uncomplaining way in which so many of them who had known success and prosperity began again at the bottom of the ladder, impressed us greatly. It was evident that they had been sustained by a deep religious faith which had enabled them to accept adversity and to rise above it. They continued to practise that faith, helped by those of the same religion who were already living here, in remote resettlement centres and in the many areas all over the country to which they went ... Many—perhaps most—of those who came here from Uganda were Hindus belonging to the branch of that religion which he [Bhagwan Swaminarayan] founded in the nineteenth century and by whose teachings and precepts their lives are still governed.

As Sir Charles Cunningham noted, a significant proportion of these refugees were staunch BAPS devotees. They gradually rebuilt their lives, and ultimately paid tribute to their faith by helping to construct the first traditional stone mandir in the western hemisphere in 1995: the world-renowned Swaminarayan Mandir in Neasden, London. This mandir hosted a happy ending to the tragedy of the Ugandan Indians. In a turn of fate or with the fruition of faith, in October 1997, twenty-five years after their expropriation by the Ugandan government, President Museveni of Uganda personally returned the four BAPS mandirs in Uganda to Pramukh Swamiji. He performed this deeply symbolic and reconciliatory act in a public ceremony attended by more than 5,000 Indians at the Swaminarayan Mandir in London.

Further, President Museveni invited the Ugandan Indians to resettle in Uganda, assuring them of their safety and security. He subsequently promised restitution and restoration of properties and businesses. It was a deeply healing event for the BAPS members and those who had been banished from Uganda a generation earlier. Responsibility was assumed and reconciliation was achieved. But most importantly, it was an event underpinned by—and indeed, only made possible by—forgiveness.

Forgiving the past and facing the future—in 2010, BAPS joyously celebrated fifty years of satsang in Uganda. I learned from Nelson Mandela that courage was not the absence of fear, but the triumph over it. The brave man is not he who does not feel afraid, but he who conquers that fear. However, Pramukh Swamiji has taught me something more: to overcome fear by forgiving through faith. There are two ways of shining light: by the candle itself or the mirror that reflects it. Pramukh Swamiji is both a lamp of divinity and a mirror of humanity.

11

The Doctor of the Soul

'Happiness resides not in possessions and not in gold, happiness dwells in the soul.'

– Democritus
Pre-Socratic Greek philosopher

I completed my term as the eleventh president of India on 24 July 2007. The press wrote very kindly that I had succeeded in establishing myself as the most popular, outspoken, impartial and far-sighted president. Some even hailed me as an ideal for future generations of Indians, because of my philosophy. I was humbled at the outpouring of such kind and respectful words. For a moment, I missed my parents. They would have been proud to read and hear these accolades, I felt. My father had told me very plainly, 'Abdul, if you surround yourself with the good and righteous, they can only raise you up. If you surround yourself with the ordinary, they will drag you down into the pessimism of mediocrity, and they will keep you there, but only as long as you permit it.' I never permitted that and came thus far listening to the echo of my father's words.

Throughout my term, my main focus was making India a developed country by 2020. I candidly expressed my concerns about the declining standard of politics. I had always been in favour of a strong and self-reliant nation. I spoke against poverty. I advocated value addition in agriculture, the economy and for indigenous armaments, and made significant efforts in these areas. I considered the children of India the future of the country, and always showed my deep concern over the increasing atrocities being perpetrated against them. I always opposed corruption, bribery, political chicanery and communalism.

On 3 July 2007 the Indian parliament hosted a farewell function for me in the central hall. Prior to this event, I had thought:'What do I say there?' Our nation is replete with successful people—including the leaders who would be sitting there at this function—who have achieved much for themselves with little benefit for anyone else. I felt that I needed to speak not merely to these people, but for and on behalf of the Indian people of this generation and the next. For this, I needed to define the future needs of the nation in my speech. And a nation is defined by neither its GDP nor by its social welfare programmes. Rather, a nation is defined by those who have been unified by a cause and a value system, and who are committed to a vision for the type of society they wish to create and bequeath to future generations.

What could India be? I spent many nights reflecting upon this. Finally, I codified a distinct profile of India 2020. And I used the occasion of my farewell function to present this profile, calling on the parliamentarians to work for making India:

1. A nation where the rural and urban divide has reduced to a thin line.
2. A nation where there is an equitable distribution and adequate access to energy and quality water.
3. A nation where agriculture, industry and the service sector work together in concert.
4. A nation where education with a value system is not denied to any meritorious candidates because of societal or economic discrimination.
5. A nation, which is the best destination for the most talented scholars, scientists and investors.
6. A nation where the best of health care is available to all.
7. A nation where the governance is responsive, transparent and corruption-free.
8. A nation where poverty has been totally eradicated, illiteracy

eliminated, crimes against women and children are absent and none in society feels alienated.

9. A nation that is prosperous, healthy, secure, devoid of terrorism, peaceful and happy, and continues with a sustainable growth path.

10. A nation that is one of the best places to live in and is proud of its leadership through creative and effective leadership in parliament, state assemblies and other institutions of the state.

I spoke passionately to the parliamentarians, 'While we have made significant gains in our economic performance, our performance on a range of human development and governance indicators requires significant improvement to achieve the status of a fully developed nation. The future political leadership the world over has to rise to the challenge of sustainability of growth, development, environment enhancement and resources. Honourable members, you have a major role to play in the creation of future leadership for the twenty-first century, in creating missionary zeal among the youth of the nation to promote moral strength, security and prosperity for our people.

'We cannot afford to rest content with past achievements and we have to march in tune with the challenges of the twenty-first century in technology, industry, agriculture, trade, system of governance and leadership style. National leadership has to radiate confidence in our people: that "we can do it". The challenges in realizing the developed India vision 2020 also provide opportunities for innovation in every aspect of governance and legislative actions. As we review the system of governance and legislative processes for the twenty-first century, full advantages and implications of technological revolutions, national and global connectivity, globalization and international cooperation and competition have to be taken into account.'

India celebrated its sixtieth anniversary of freedom on 15 August 2007. PodUniversal, India's first pod magazine, approached me for my views on the 'top ten challenges' of the nation, and how youth can overcome these challenges to realize the vision of a developed India by 2020. I knew from my own experience of working with young scientists and engineers in two large organizations—ISRO and DRDO—that the expansive youthful heart cannot be compressed or constrained for any length of time. There is in youth a purity and fragility of character, which once touched and defiled can never be restored. It is like a delicate fringe in a frostwork, which when torn and broken can never be re-embroidered. The words of Benjamin Disraeli, twice prime minister of England, 'The youth of a nation are the trustees of posterity,' came to my mind. With these thoughts, I formulated a seven-point oath for the youth of India:

1. I realize I have to set a goal in life: to acquire knowledge and work hard to achieve, and when problems occur, I will overcome them.
2. I will work with courage to achieve success in all my tasks and enjoy the success of others.
3. I shall always keep myself, my home and my neighbourhood clean and tidy.
4. I realize righteousness in the heart leads to beauty in character; beauty in character leads to harmony in the home; harmony in the home leads to order in the nation, which in turn leads to peace in the world.
5. I will lead an honest life, free from all corruption and will set an example to others, including my family, for adopting a righteous way of life.
6. I will light the lamp of knowledge in the nation and ensure that it remains lit forever.
7. I realize that whatever work I do, if I do it well, I am contributing to realizing the vision of Developed India 2020.

On 15 October 2007, on my seventy-sixth birthday, I called my elder brother in Rameswaram in the morning and shared some old memories. In the evening, my late sister Zohra's grandson Ghulam visited me, and it suddenly occurred to me that we are all contemporaries, travelling together on spaceship Earth. I shared the analogy with him, and he gave me a very uncomfortable answer. He read for me from the play *Buried Child*,[24] '... you see the way things deteriorate before your very eyes. Everything is running downhill.

It is kind of silly to even think about youth.' Who will help youth emerge out of this pessimism? How can it be done? With these thoughts filling my mind, I boarded the aircraft on my way to the UK and USA a few days later.

On 21 October 2007, I visited Swaminarayan Mandir in Neasden, London. Sadhu Yogvivekdas received me with loving kindness, amidst the chanting of Vedic prayers by young children. The majestic architecture of the temple indeed inspired me. How could this be done in a foreign land? I asked Sadhu Yogvivekdas. He narrated to me a very interesting story that I must share with you.

The roots of the Swaminarayan Hindu Mission in London can be traced back to the early 1950s. London was recovering from the aftermath of World War II. Indians were scarce and scattered. With the blessings of Shastriji Maharaj, Mahendrabhai Patel (popularly known as Barrister), Purushottambhai Patel and other devotees began to meet occasionally for satsang in London. Later, the devotees acquired St John's Baptist Church in Islington, East London, and on 14 June 1970, Yogiji Maharaj consecrated it as a BAPS mandir. To cater for the ever-growing satsang, on 7 July 1991, Pramukh Swamiji laid the foundation stone for a new majestic Shikharbaddh Mandir in Neasden. Work began in November 1992, and in an astonishingly brief period of less than three years, the mandir was inaugurated by Pramukh Swamiji on 20 August 1995.

In the meantime, Sladebrook School across Brentfield Road was also acquired in early 1992, and was refurbished and opened as The Swaminarayan Independent Day School. And so, from a handful of devotees four decades earlier, the BAPS Satsang has grown into a gigantic socio-spiritual organization with youth and children's forums and a women's wing—all reflecting the strength and growth of a benignly powerful, spiritual and philanthropic movement. Through the efforts and blessings of Yogiji Maharaj and Pramukh Swamiji, a dream has turned into a reality.

I was told that on 14 September 1994, when a reporter of the Worldwide Television Channel asked Pramukh Swamiji why he was building a temple in London, Swamiji replied, 'The temple provides for the sentiments and devotion of the devotees. They desired such a place of worship. The temple will satisfy their spiritual thirst and inspire them to greater heights of pure devotion.'

The inquisitive reporter was not satisfied. He asked, 'What is the spiritual importance of a temple?' Pramukh Swamiji explained, 'Every religion believes in the importance of a place of prayer. If a person visits a temple with faith in his heart, he will experience a peaceful mind. The scriptures say that peace is to be found by going to God, listening to the holy teachings of sadhus and by praying. Every religion in its own tradition builds temples and monumental worshipping places. These houses of worship inspire the people.'

It is truly the places of worship that fuel our faith in God, strengthen our society and teach us to trust one another and become trustworthy! Schools will educate the mind, but who will educate the spirit? Hospitals will mend a broken bone, but who will mend broken hope? Cinemas, amusement arcades and discotheques will excite the senses, but where will one go for peace of mind? Pramukh Swamiji further elaborated, 'Places of worship preserve the cleanliness of the soul and keep it from becoming diseased. Some diseases cannot be seen, only experienced. Our scriptures have shown the medicine to be places of worship. All this is not to say that schools and hospitals are not needed. They are. But so are places of worship. Man has both body and soul. Neither should be neglected.'

Indeed, the Swaminarayan Mandir in Neasden is an incredible combination of heaven and earth. It is not just beautiful and spiritual, but is also socially and environmentally friendly. It has been presented the Brent Green Leaf Award in 1995 for its environment-friendly design, and the Most Enterprising Building Award in 1996, presented by the Royal Fine Art Commission. Its creation involved the largest aluminium can recycling project in the UK. Thousands of motivated children, teenagers, youths and adults collected over seven million aluminium cans in just one year! Pramukh Swamiji inspired and involved the new generation with a vision of transformation.

When I boarded my flight to the USA the following day, I had the answer to my question. Youth needs a vision. Youth needs credible guidance. And above all, youth needs an example. Great minds give all three. The vision of a prosperous and peaceful humanity, guidance through the ideals of great institutions like BAPS and the example of impeccable service are the beacons that guide souls from drifting and foundering—however deep and dark the turbulent sea. When I opened *The Kingdom of God Is Within You* by Leo Tolstoy, which I was carrying in my cabin baggage to spend the long trans-Atlantic flight, a brilliant poem appeared in front of me:

Where there is faith, there is love
Where there is love, there is peace
Where there is peace, there is God
And where there is God, there is no need![25]

I believe in God. And I believe the true welfare of human beings is sustained by fulfilling the will of God. Continuing, Tolstoy wrote in *What Men Live By and Other Tales,* 'One may live without father or mother, but one cannot live without God.'[26]

12

A Status Without Parallel

'If you are irritated by every rub, how will your mirror be polished?'

– Rumi
Thirteenth-century Persian poet

In February 2008, I went to Israel to deliver the keynote address at the forty-eighth Annual Conference on Aerospace Sciences. I used this occasion to present World Space Vision 2050 and highlight the need to create a world knowledge platform to achieve this. President Shimon Peres hosted a dinner for me. On 28 February, I visited Jerusalem, one of the oldest cities in the world. It is considered holy to the three major Abrahamic religions—Judaism, Christianity and Islam. But instead of being a peaceful place, this city has endured the worst of human conflict and violence. During its long history, Jerusalem has been destroyed at least twice, besieged twenty-three times, attacked fifty-two times, and captured and recaptured forty-four times.

I walked through the Walled City built in the fifteenth century by Suleiman the Magnificent, the tenth and longest-reigning sultan of the Ottoman Empire. Since the early nineteenth century, the city has been divided into four parts: the Armenian, Christian, Jewish and Muslim quarters. I went to the Mosque of Umar opposite the entrance to the Church of the Holy Sepulchre. Christian-Arab tradition records that, when led to pray at the Church of the Holy Sepulchre—the holiest site for Christians—Caliph Umar refused to pray inside the church so that Muslims would not request conversion of the church to a mosque. He prayed in the open area outside the church, where a mosque was later constructed. Then I walked to Masjid Al Aqsa where Prophet Muhammad, peace be upon him, prayed. I offered namaz in the mosque and sat for a while in contemplation. There, my eyes welled up for no apparent reason. I felt as if my parents were around me, close by. I remembered a story told by my father in my childhood.

During the period of the second Caliph Umar Ibn al-Khattab, the Muslim forces, under the command of Abu Ubaydah, lay siege to Jerusalem in AD 636, after capturing Damascus in the Battle of Yarmuk. The patriarch of the city, Sophronius, stated that he would negotiate only with Caliph Umar, and that nobody would enter Jerusalem before Caliph Umar. Upon hearing this, Caliph Umar proceeded to Jerusalem by camel accompanied only by a servant, though he could easily have made a triumphant entrance to the city bearing standards, with an imposing cavalry which would have made the ground tremble. A kind and just man, Caliph Umar even exchanged turns, alternately riding the camel and leading the beast on foot—like a common camel puller—while the servant rode.[27]

Upon reaching Jerusalem, it was the servant's turn to ride the camel, and as a mark of respect and to ensure that the people see Caliph Umar, he asked the Caliph to ride the camel. Caliph Umar refused, however, entering Jerusalem humbly on foot while his servant rode the camel, surprising and perplexing all who witnessed his arrival—including the patriarch Sophronius. The Christians who watched this event from the walls of Jerusalem were amazed at Caliph Umar's strange simplicity, incredulous that this simple man was the leader of the mighty besieging armies. Impressed by the caliph's humility, and with his fears allayed by Umar's assurances, the patriarch declared to his people that nobody in the world would be able to stand up to people led by such a leader, and surrendered.[28]

Is there any such leader alive today? Reflecting on the many leaders that I have met or read about, none could match the standards of Caliph Umar Ibn al-Khattab. A few months after my trip to Israel, I visited Canada. I gave lectures on 'Canada and India—a Partnership in Global Development' at the University of Waterloo, and on 'Technology in Development for Civil Society' at the University of Toronto. I emphasized that a knowledge society is fundamental for the development of any nation. Technological advances must go hand in hand with social equality, so that the very poor and the rich share the benefits alike. I expounded the concept of Providing Urban Facilities in Rural Areas (PURA) for reaching and teaching the millions that live in the villages of rural India. I talked about the components of a knowledge economy, and proposed a Bio-Nano-IT convergence for progress.

The knowledge economy and a Bio-Nano-IT convergence hold great promise for India's future status as a developed nation. India's success in the burgeoning information technology sector demonstrates that we are in the nascent stages of a revolution. Here, we can harness the vigour, knowledge and aspiration of the world's most youthful society in new and exciting industries that the world could hitherto have barely imagined. I should mention that these industries—and, of course, technological development, a knowledge-based society and rural upliftment—are to a great degree reliant on the stewardship of wise and far-sighted leaders: people with an enlightened vision. And it is almost inconceivable that India would achieve its enormous potential without them.

Moreover, such leaders must be prepared to dedicate themselves to their leadership tasks with humility and spiritual awareness, in the manner of Caliph Umar leading his camel into Jerusalem. And Umar's example in righteously governing this most hotly disputed city— and maintaining peaceful relations amongst the competing religious factions there—is a benchmark for today's inspired leaders.

On 19 April 2008 I visited Swaminarayan Mandir in Toronto. Sadhu Jnanpriyadas welcomed me with a floral garland and tilak, amidst thunderous applause from thousands of Indo-Canadians, both young and old. BAPS trustees guided me and the Attorney General of Ontario, Hon. Chris Bentley, through the Canadian Museum of Cultural Heritage of Indo-Canadians located in the mandir. While going through the museum, I realized the essence of the leadership of Pramukh Swamiji. He can penetrate the mundane and profane that clouds human consciousness and reach the divinity of the human soul. There are no instructions, commands or persuasion, but simple radiance destroying the darkness of ignorance. When I addressed the assembly, I asked everyone present to declare with me:

Where there is righteousness in the heart,
There is beauty in the character.
When there is beauty in the character,
There is harmony in the home.
When there is harmony in the home,
There is order in the nation.
When there is order in the nation,
There is peace in the world.

What is righteousness? What does it mean to be righteous? How is 'righteousness fulfilled' in us? Righteousness is indeed a choice we make in our manner of behaviour as an act of our will. Righteousness is not something that 'falls' upon us simply because we utter some words. Righteousness is cultivated in our lives by our actions. In the Holy Bible we are asked to be clothed in righteousness (Isaiah 59:17, Ephesians 6:13–18). This means we must put it on like a garment. The clothes that one wears do not leap out of the closet on to one's body. One has to make a conscious, deliberate choice to 'put them on'. We need to exercise our powers of choice on a daily basis to put on a garment of righteousness—in our manners, our behaviour and in our conduct in every circumstance in which we find ourselves. But who is this 'I' that would exercise this power? There are so many voices in one's head!

During the year 2003, I visited the Gelug Buddhist monastery at Tawang in Arunachal Pradesh. Arun was with me. It was at an altitude of 3,500 metres. I spent one entire day in the monastery. I found monks of all ages in a state of serenity. Even the laypeople gathered there in large numbers were radiating happiness. Arun asked me, 'What could be the unique feature of this place which brings peace to the people and monks?' When the moment presented itself, I asked the chief monk why peace and happiness were being radiated by everyone in the Tawang villages and the monastery. The chief monk smiled and said after a pause, 'You are the president of India. You will know all about us and the whole nation.' I replied, 'It is very important for me—please give me your thoughtful analysis.'

Before a beautiful golden image of Lord Buddha radiating peace and a smile, the chief monk assembled nearly 100 young and experienced monks. The chief monk and I were sitting in their midst. The chief monk gave a short discourse which I would like to share with you. He said, 'In the present world, we have a problem of distrust and unhappiness transforming into violence. This monastery spreads the message: when you remove "I" and "Me" from your mind, you will eliminate ego; if you get rid of ego, hatred towards fellow human beings will vanish; if the hatred goes out of our minds, the violence in thought and action will disappear; if violence in our minds is taken away, peace springs in human minds. Then peace and peace and peace alone will blossom in society.' I realized the meaning of this beautiful equation for a peaceful life, but the difficult mission for the individual is how to remove the ethos of 'I' and 'Me'.

Many years later, I found the answer in *Sirr ul-Israr*—a great book of Hazrat Shaikh Abdul Qadir al-Jilani—and discussed it in my book *Squaring the Circle*. The 'I' is indeed an internal model to assign oneself an identity. It helps as a reference point to position oneself in the dynamics of life and to make assessments of situations and one's own ability. It is the discriminating, reasoning and causative intelligence. It is ego. And it is the processor of five sensory inputs and a sense in itself. In Islamic tradition, there is ruh, the divine breath; qulb, the emotional heart; sirr, the ego, and nafs, the pleasure-seeking five senses.[29]

By nature, man is innocent; he is inclined to right and predisposed to virtue. This is his true nature, just as it is the nature of a lamb to be gentle and of a horse to be swift. But man is caught in the clutches of selfish desires (hijab-al-nafs, veils or psychic aspects of man's carnal self); customs (hijab-al-rusoom, influences of social, cultural, political and religious environment); and false teachings and superstition (hijab-al-marifat). Any spiritual development starts with purification of the self (tazkiya-e-nafs). This means cleansing the sensual self from its morally hateful, blameworthy and animalistic propensities, and imbuing it with laudable and angelic attributes or qualities. Cleansing of the heart (tazkiya-e-qulb) follows next. This means erasing from the heart its love for the ephemeral world and its worry over grief and sorrow, and establishing in their place an ardent devotion to God alone. Upon completion of these two processes, emptying of the sirr (takhliya-e-sirr) takes place. The thoughts related to positions, status, entitlements, privileges and other vanities must go. If one succeeds in these three, illumination of the spirit (tajliya-e-ruh) automatically happens. The soul is filled with the effulgence of God and the fervour of His love.

Shaikh Abdul Qadir describes twelve special qualities that must be firmly established in the character of a righteous person. He writes:

> As for the two qualities that are from God (Exalted is He), a person who is endowed with them will always be ready to pardon (sattar), always ready to forgive (ghaffar).
>
> As for the two that are from the Prophet (God bless him and give him peace), a person who is endowed with them will be sympathetic (shafiq) and kind (rafiq).
>
> As for the two that are from Abu Bakr (may God be well pleased with him), a person who is endowed with them will be both truthful (sadiq) and charitable (mutasaddiq).
>
> As for the two that are from Umar (may God be well pleased with him), a person who is endowed with them will be active in commanding what is right and fair (ammar) and active in forbidding what is wrong and unfair (nahha).
>
> As for the two that are from Uthman (may God be well pleased with him), a person who is endowed with them will be an active provider of food (mit'am) and one who is devoted to praying (musalli) at night, when the rest of the people are sound asleep.
>
> As for the two that are from Ali (may God be well pleased with him), a person who is endowed with them will be both learned (alim) and courageous (shuja).[30]

If there is a leader of this magnitude and magnanimity amongst us it is Pramukh Swamiji. His response to the inhuman terrorist attack on the Akshardham Temple in Gandhinagar was the epitome of forgiveness. His devotees can vouch for his sympathetic and kind nature, and reflect his loving and peaceful ways. In creating cultural and spiritual centres across the globe by unifying minds and hearts, he has fostered unwavering harmony and truthfulness. Through the creation of value-based schools, hospitals and charities, Pramukh Swamiji has emerged as a true mutasaddiq (the charitable). He has presided over BAPS with a firm and just hand, commanding what is right and fair (ammar) and been active in forbidding what is wrong and unfair.

Pramukh Swamiji often sits in prayer throughout the night for the problems of common people. I have emulated this habit. He attracts to him the best minds of the world—scholars, scientists, thinkers, social workers, businesspersons and leaders—and has selflessly served society in times of disaster: in famines, floods, earthquakes and tsunamis. And even in good times, Pramukh Swamiji strictly adheres to a glorious Swaminarayan tradition that monks and devotees serve all guests food. Pramukh Swamiji is like the Himalayas of humanitarian activities and the Pacific of peace. He is truly peerless.

I wrote this poem on the night of my last meeting with him at Sarangpur:

Your effort, perseverance and contentment
Have granted you a status that has no duplicate.

The suns of the ancients to return in you,
In its orbit up on high, will never cease to radiate.

In the history of saints, Pramukh Swamiji stands out as being unique, in the broad scope of perfection that includes his lineage, his complete development, his piety, his knowledge of religion and adherence to the scriptures, his intimate and direct knowledge of the Divine, and his establishment of Akshardhams—Lord of All the Worlds—in the physical realm.

13

From Within I Rise

'We cannot teach people anything; we can only help them discover it within themselves.'

– Galileo Galilei
Sixteenth-century Italian philosopher

In October 2009, I was invited to deliver an international leadership oration at the annual meeting of the Congress of Neurological Surgeons in New Orleans, Louisiana. Governor Piyush 'Bobby' Jindal was also there. I met Dr James Rutka, a renowned neurosurgeon from Toronto, Canada, and we shared some thoughts on the mind–brain relationship. A lengthy tradition of inquiry in philosophy, religion, psychology and cognitive science has developed an understanding of the mind. But the main question regarding the nature of mind and its relation to the physical brain and nervous system remains unanswered. There are different views on whether the mind is a 'product' of the brain physiology, or whether it is somehow separate from physical existence. There are at least three major philosophical schools of thought: dualism, materialism and idealism. Dualism holds that the mind exists independently of the brain; materialism holds that mental phenomena are identical to neuronal phenomena; and idealism holds that only mental phenomena exist.

The human brain has the same general structure as the brains of other mammals, but has a more developed cortex than any other. Much of the expansion comes from the part of the brain called the cerebral cortex, especially the frontal lobes, which are associated with executive functions such as self-control, planning, reasoning and abstract thought. The portion of the cerebral cortex devoted to vision is also greatly enlarged in humans. Understanding the relationship between the brain and the mind is a great challenge. It is very difficult to imagine how mental phenomena such as thoughts and emotions could be implemented by physical entities such as neurons and synapses, or by any other type of mechanism. Although the human brain represents only 2 per cent of the body's weight, it receives 15 per cent of the cardiac output, 20 per cent of total body oxygen consumption, and 25 per cent of total body glucose utilization. The brain mostly uses glucose for energy, and deprivation of glucose, as can happen with hypoglycaemia in diabetic patients on insulin treatment, can result in loss of consciousness.[31]

What is consciousness? American philosopher Danah Zohar believes that consciousness is the bridge between the classical world and the quantum world. In *The Quantum Self*, he argues that the insights of modern physics can illuminate our understanding of everyday life—our relationships with ourselves, with others, and with the world at large. Zohar gives a model of reality in which the universe itself may possess a type of consciousness, of which human consciousness is merely one expression.

Zohar subscribes to the thesis of Bose-Einstein condensation, which basically reduces mind/body duality to wave/particle duality. Particles are divided into fermions (such as electrons, protons and neutrons) and bosons (photons, gravitons and gluons). Bosons are particles of 'relationship', as they are used to interact. When two systems interact (electricity, gravitation or whatever), they exchange bosons. Fermions are well-defined individual entities, just like large-scale matter is. But bosons can completely merge and become one entity, more like conscious states do. Zohar imagines that such a condensate is the ideal candidate to provide the unity of consciousness.[32]

Japanese-American theoretical physicist Michio Kaku recently offered a new theory of consciousness based on evolution. He defines consciousness as the number of feedback loops required to create a model of one's position in space with relationship to other organisms and finally in relationship to time. He says that even a thermostat has one unit of consciousness. That is, it senses the temperature around it. And then we have a flower. A flower has maybe ten units of consciousness. It has to understand the temperature, the weather, humidity and where gravity is pointing. And then we go to the reptilian brain, which he calls level one consciousness. Reptiles have a very good understanding of their position in space, especially because they have to lunge out to grab prey. Then we have level two consciousnesses— the monkey consciousness. This is the consciousness of emotions and social hierarchies, where we are in relation to the tribe.[33]

And finally, there is our consciousness as humans. We are at level three. We mentally run simulations into the future. Animals apparently do not do this. They do not plan to hibernate. They do not plan the next day's agenda. To the best of our understanding, they have no concept of tomorrow. But our brain is a prediction machine. And so when we look at the evolution from the reptilian brain to the mammalian brain to the prefrontal cortex, we realize that this is the process of understanding our position in space with respect to others—that is emotions—and finally running simulations into the future.

Michio Kaku writes so beautifully:

> The laws of physics, carefully constructed after thousands of years of experimentation, are nothing but the laws of harmony one can write down for strings and membranes. The laws of chemistry are the melodies that one can play on these strings. The universe is a symphony of strings. And the 'Mind of God', which Einstein wrote eloquently about, is cosmic music resonating throughout hyperspace. The entire electromagnetic spectrum—from radar to TV, infrared light, visible light, ultraviolet light, X-rays, microwaves, and gamma rays—is nothing but Maxwell waves, which in turn are vibrating Faraday force fields.[34]

American theoretical physicist and Nobel laureate Steven Weinberg likens consciousness to a radio system. All around us, there are hundreds of different radio waves being broadcast from distant stations. At any given instant, our office or car or living room is full of these radio waves. However, if we turn on a radio, we can listen to only one frequency at a time; the other frequencies have been separated out of their cohesion and are no longer in phase with each other. Each station has a different energy, a different frequency. As a result, our radio can only be turned to one broadcast at a time.[35]

Likewise, in our universe we are 'tuned' into the frequency that corresponds to physical reality. But there are an infinite number of parallel realities coexisting with us in the same room, although we cannot 'tune into' them. Although these worlds are very much alike, each has a different energy. And because each world consists of trillions upon trillions of atoms, this means that the energy difference can be sizeable. Since the frequency of these waves is proportional to their energy, by Planck's law, this means that the waves of each world vibrate at different frequencies and cannot interact any more. For all intents and purposes, the waves of these various worlds do not interact or influence each other.[36]

What if they do? What if a human being possesses or develops the capacity to receive and decipher the waves of these various worlds? For many years, since I met Pramukh Swamiji in 2001, I wondered about his vision, his calmness, and the influence he has over hundreds of thousands of his devotees. Finally, I found the answer in the writings of Michio Kaku and Steven Weinberg. I realized that there is a fourth level of consciousness, wherein the consciousness of the self is transcended and becomes cosmic consciousness. When I see the majestic Akshardham temples, I see within them Pramukh Swamiji's passionate commitment to transcendental values such as beauty, truth, wisdom, justice, charity, fidelity, joy, courage and honour. Everyone who has a heart, knowingly or unknowingly, feels the transcendental beauty and poetry of the Akshardham temples.

I will now elaborate on the level four consciousness that I have observed in Pramukh Swamiji. Imagine that you are a two-dimensional being and that a fence has been created around you and what you want. It would appear as a rectangle. The only way to get what you want is by cutting through the fence, and so everything you study at this level would be about how to move through obstacles and cut through fences.

If you were suddenly given a three-dimensional consciousness, you would look from above at the two dimensional rectangle, and realize that you could simply reach in and take hold of what you want, and that the rectangle or fence was not an obstacle from this higher perspective. But you are still faced with obstacles and hurdles. It is not that things have been delivered on a platter to Pramukh Swamiji. There have been problems, obstacles, resistance, even hostilities—but he never reacted to them. Why? Because he accessed an even higher level of consciousness.

The fourth dimension is a higher dimension of consciousness that comes through the divine connection. We are enveloped in a vast universe of light, consciousness and love. We can reach upward to the higher parts of our being and access this source of inspiration, creative ideas, energy, wisdom, understanding and spiritual vision. With a four-dimensional consciousness, we are in touch with our intuition: an infallible source of guidance and wisdom that leads to rightful action, good choices and decisions, harmonious relationships and a sense of well-being. This is the consciousness that brings us all the resources we need in every moment, and is the source of our abundance. Many blessed souls throughout the history of mankind could expand their consciousness into higher dimensions. Pramukh Swamiji is such a blessed soul.

Expansion of one's consciousness begins with fundamental knowledge—understanding of one's place in the universe, and the interconnectedness of all with the Divine. Imagine that you are a drop in the ocean. If you think you are separate from the ocean, you feel powerless, helpless and unable to tap into the abundance of the ocean that is all around you. If you know that you are a part of the ocean, you have the power of the ocean with you. Through expanding your connections to the ocean, the Divine, you can tap into the unlimited power, abundance and consciousness that is available to you. You will no longer have the identity of a small, helpless drop in the ocean, but instead your identity will be the ocean itself: omnipotent, omnipresent and omniscient.

As you expand your consciousness, through awakening and lifting your awareness above the two-dimensional world of fences—through divine connection or through divine will—you come to know that you are not a small helpless drop in the ocean. You know that you are part of the Divine, that you are loved, that the universe is friendly and that everything is working for you and with you. Any time you have spent in the higher dimensions—contacting the Divine and aligning with the divine will—you will feel this same sense. Even one moment of this contact can bring forth an idea or vision that can change your life—and it will always be for the better.

Pramukh Swamiji has become part of the ocean of consciousness. With his blessings, thousands of his devotees have shifted from their old ways of blocking the true manifestation of their destiny. They have stopped trying to figure everything out; they have ceased trying to control and manipulate the universe into giving them what they want, and put their aspiration and their trust in Pramukh Swamiji. They no longer think that having what they want is dependent upon someone else's power or decisions. They no longer measure their progress or success in traditional cultural terms, but instead by their feeling of righteousness. They have realized that if they do not try to control things mentally, the universe will give to them more bountifully than what they could possibly have envisaged. Pramukh Swamiji has taught four generations of people to rise from within—and their rise has been phenomenal.

14

Walking Over the Waves

'You can't cross the sea merely by standing and staring at the water.'

— Gurudev Rabindranath Tagore

The year 2011 started on an ominous note. On the night of 14 January, at least 102 pilgrims were killed in Kerala's Idukki district at Sabarimala in a stampede. Sabarimala is believed to be the place where King Ayyappan meditated after killing the powerful demoness Mahishi. The temple is situated on a hilltop at an altitude of about 500 metres, and is surrounded by mountains and dense forests. In one of the largest annual pilgrimages in the world, an estimated 100 million devotees visit every year. Most of them follow the 52-kilometre traditional mountainous forest path Ayyappan is believed to have trekked. Men bearing bamboo chairs carry elderly pilgrims to the summit.

A star in the night sky, a flickering light from within the forests in the hills a few kilometres away, and tens of thousands of pilgrims enjoying the bliss of witnessing them afford a sublime experience; this is the allure of the Sabarimala pilgrimage. The night of 14 January 2011 was no different, with the twin spectacles of the star and the light—known as Makara Jyoti and Makara Vilakku respectively—keeping the milling crowds enthralled. But this time, as the crowds surged downhill from the vantage point at Pullumedu near Vandiperiyar after viewing the star-and-light spectacle—which pilgrims deem to be a veritable heaven-and-earth combination—a killer stampede occurred.

I was saddened, and pondered for many nights without sleep why such mishaps occur and how they can be avoided. One of my distant relatives died on 12 January five years ago, along with at least 346 other pilgrims, in a stampede during the ritual ramy al-jamarat on the last day of the Hajj in Mina. He was old and lived a pious life; he used his lifetime savings to go to Mecca—and died there. Why do bad things happen to good people? Is there an answer? Any explanation? Is there any closure to this perennial quest?

In April 2011, I was invited to the Fermi National Accelerator Laboratory (called 'Fermilab'), in Illinois, near Chicago. Fermilab is a US Department of Energy national laboratory specializing in high-energy particle physics. Enrico Fermi was an Italian physicist, best known for his work on the first nuclear reactor, called Chicago Pile-1, and for his contributions to the development of quantum theory. With the Sabarimala stampede incident still on my mind, I picked up a poetry book of young poet David Whyte at the airport, to read during my long flight; to find the answer I was seeking.

David Whyte looked at the great questions of human life through the eyes of the pilgrim: someone passing through relatively quickly; someone dependent on friendship, hospitality and help from friends and strangers alike; someone for whom the nature of the destination changes step by step as it approaches, and someone who is subject to the vagaries of wind and weather along the way.

> To empty your bags; to sort this and to leave that;
> To promise what you needed to promise all along,
> And to abandon the shoes that had brought you here
> Right at the water's edge, not because you had given up
> But because now, you would find a different way to tread,
> And because, through it all, part of you could still walk on,
> No matter how, over the waves.[37]

The metaphor of walking over the waves led me into deep contemplation. I was born in the vicinity of the sea, and spent innumerable evenings watching the waves from the shore. Even as an adult, when I was working in Thumba, the sea would beckon me, and

I spent many hours gazing at its swell. I was awed by its vastness and the incessant movement of waves. In the night, when stars—millions of them—were shining above, and waves after waves—millions of them— were arriving and receding, this great show of energy and order made me realize how small a human being is in the great scheme of things.

Spiritual teachers often describe the 'I' (or ego) as a constriction of consciousness. This is a particularly apt description of the inner landscape, since whenever we are identified with our own personal drama to the exclusion of the larger cosmos around and inside us, our consciousness is indeed constricted to a very narrow focus. When the cabin staff dimmed the lights in the aeroplane—while we were crossing the Atlantic Ocean en route to Chicago—I felt as if I was sitting at the seashore, and a new meaning of the 'walking over the waves' metaphor occurred to me.[38]

What do the waves symbolize? Are they not the petty concerns which normally dominate our internal narrative? Rushing for work in the morning, feeling subsumed under mountains of obligations and commitments, dealing with people who lack not only skills but also understanding, and once again trying and once more failing. What goes on in the head is like living in a prison. We are all locked behind the bars of comparison, jealousy and deficiency. Is it possible to find liberation and freedom? I did not have to resign myself to living in a madhouse for the rest of my life.

The secret of coming out of this prison, of overcoming the ego, is having the clarity to realize that it is only an illusion. The Torah says that the ego is like a giant man holding a battleaxe who is standing in front of you at a crossroads. The fool is frightened and runs for his life. The wise person looks closely and sees that the giant has no feet; he walks right past him.

That is the ego: all bark, no bite. If you can recognize the ego as a giant mirage, you will be able to see through it and increase the frequency with which you experience life through the soul. If the ego is the mud on the lens of the soul, then this clarity is the water that washes it away. It begins with the awareness of the true nature of human experience: you are a soul, but you experience life through the senses of the body. This is indeed the 'walking over the waves'. I fell into a deep sleep and woke up only after the aircraft landed in Chicago. It was 24 April. I decided to spend my evening at the exquisite Swaminarayan temple at Bartlett, on the outskirts of the city.

Sadhu Vivekmurtidas welcomed me there. It was a beautiful atmosphere: in the temple gardens adorned by flowers and lights, 1,500 Indian-American children chanted Vedic mantras. How could this all be possible in a foreign land renowned for its fast-paced life and the individualistic orientation of its citizens? I was told that in 1970, Yogiji Maharaj blessed K.C. Patel, who was leaving for America, and asked him to hold regular satsang assemblies. 'Do not just work as a migrant worker, but inspire the whole of America,' Yogiji Maharaj said. Then, through the ceaseless inspiration and the epic efforts of Pramukh Swamiji during his visits in 1974, 1977 and 1980, the satsang community witnessed spectacular growth.

Sadhu Atmaswarupdas once shared with me that in 1980, Pramukh Swamiji tirelessly travelled from house to house across America in order to satisfy the wishes of the devotees, disregarding his health and personal needs. He placed the devotees first and himself last. Eventually, during this tour, his vision deteriorated to such an extent that he could not see his own slippers. His worsening cataracts could have resulted in blindness; he needed to undergo emergency eye surgery. This was scheduled in Boston under the eminent ophthalmologist Dr Hutchinson. When devotees in London came to know this, they requested that he have the operation in London, so that the much larger following in the United Kingdom could avail themselves of Pramukh Swamiji's darshan during his recuperation. Not to dissatisfy any group of devotees, Pramukh Swamiji agreed to have one eye operated on in Boston, and the other in London. Unmindfulness of his personal comfort—and his willingness to share even his eyes in accordance with the wishes of the devotees—exemplifies Pramukh Swamiji's extraordinarily selfless nature.

The following day in Chicago, Pier Oddone, Peruvian-American particle physicist and director of Fermilab, took me 330 feet underground to the Main Injector Neutrino Oscillation Search

(MINOS), and explained the Main Injector Experiment for v-A, or MINERvA, a neutrino scattering experiment that was being conducted there. Later in the day, I spoke on 'World Knowledge Platform: Synergizing Core Competencies of Multiple Nations'. I highlighted several ways that modern-day technologies make it possible to learn from the past, to improve the present quality of life and to pave the way for future societal improvements. I explained that the challenges confronting our society today require the best minds from many parts of the world to come together and engage in multidisciplinary and multinational collaborations.

Expanding on my uplifting experience at the Swaminarayan temple the previous evening, where I had witnessed a delightful local demonstration of spiritual dedication, far removed from its cultural wellspring, I said,

> Humanity is devoting more and more attention to climate change, energy, water, disease, economic turbulence and terrorism, which are all of concern to the entire world and the solutions for which are beyond any individual nations or group of nations. In all areas of technology development, which will bring benefit to society at large, we need to think globally and act locally.

In today's knowledge economy, the exchange of ideas has become the new means of industrial progress. The advent of social networks and mobile technology is shifting employers' competitive edge from hiring workers who gather knowledge to hiring workers who communicate it. When every company, every city, every country and every individual are increasingly interconnected, business and government leaders must look beyond their own biases to discern real patterns and anticipate events. And they must look beyond their own needs in addressing another salient challenge of our times, which is work culture: how to change entrenched work practices— of both employers and employees—evolved around selfishness. It is here that I see the historic relevance of Pramukh Swamiji's mission, which provides higher purpose and direction in faraway places. It helps people to float atop the waves of mundane selfishness, to create universal centres of selfless service.

15

Living in the Witness of God

'Sir, my concern is not whether God is on our side; my greatest concern is to be on God's side, for God is always right.'

– Abraham Lincoln
The sixteenth president of the United States

The frightening memories of December 1964 are still vivid in my mind. Just before the midnight of 22 December, Dhanushkodi Passenger train no. 653, carrying 110 passengers and five railway staff, was only a few hundred yards from Dhanushkodi railway station when it was hit by a massive wave caused by a super-cyclonic storm. The whole train was washed away, killing all people on board. The storm surge—a veritable wall of water—engulfed most of the surrounding island, devastating the entire town. On a short work visit to Rameswaram at the time, I witnessed the surging waters stop just short of the majestic Ramanathaswami temple, where many people had taken refuge from the fury of the storm. Naval vessels sent for the relief and rescue of marooned people reported bloated bodies floating around the eastern end of Dhanushkodi.

There was a train service up to Dhanushkodi called the Boat Mail from Egmore station in Chennai. The train would halt at a pier on the south-eastern side of Dhanushkodi township, where a waiting steamer would transport passengers to Sri Lanka across the Palk Strait. The train line and pier were never restored, and the service never resumed after the mishap. Following this disaster, the Government of Tamil

Nadu declared Dhanushkodi unfit for habitation. In December 2004, when I visited this area as the president of India, I was told that just before the arrival of the tsunami, the sea around Dhanushkodi receded about 500 metres from the shoreline, exposing the submerged part of the erstwhile township for a short while.

Rameswaram is the closest land point in India to Sri Lanka. Throughout history, people have regularly ferried across the 50-kilometre-wide Palk Strait that separates the two lands. According to the *Mahavamsa*—a historical book written in the Pali language on the kings of Sri Lanka—the ancestors of the Sinhalese came from Lata Rashtra, which comprises the modern state of West Bengal and some portions of the states of Jharkhand and Bihar. Tamils were present and actively involved in trade along the southern coast of Sri Lanka, during all periods of history. Anuradhapura, the ancient Sinhalese capital situated in the modern-day North Central Province, is heralded as an ancient cosmopolitan citadel with diverse populations.[39] It supported a sizeable Tamil population, and was ruled from time to time by Tamil kings.

Since Sri Lanka gained independence from Britain in 1948, relations between the majority Sinhalese and minority Tamil communities have been marred by simmering discord, boiling over into episodes of deadly violence. Rioting against the Tamils in 1956, 1958, 1977 and 1981—and a pogrom in July 1983—led to the formation and strengthening of militant groups advocating independence for Tamils. The ensuing civil war resulted in the death of more than 100,000 people and the disappearance of thousands of others. The civil war ended in 2009, but misgivings remain.[40]

In January 2012, I was invited by the Government of Sri Lanka to launch the Trilingual Sri Lanka initiative. Language is never a simple issue of communication. In contemporary social and political practice everywhere, language has a role and significance far beyond its utilitarian purpose. In this, Sri Lanka is no exception. At this time, Sri Lanka has ended an immensely destructive military conflict that had as much to do with a crisis of identity linked with language, as to ethnicity and contested notions of binary nationalism and competing interpretations of history. In this context, this is a crucial time to seriously consider the politico-developmental aspect of language in envisioning the future of the country.

To promote the Sinhala and Tamil languages, both Tamil and Sinhala politicians espoused the idea of swabhasha during the colonial period in the early twentieth century. So, contrary to popular contemporary belief, the politics of language in Sri Lanka have not always been a reflection of inter-ethnic rivalry. In its initial stages, the demand for swabhasha carried overtones of class dissatisfaction, even though the blurred outlines of Sinhala nationalist aspirations were also discernible. But these aspirations were not clearly articulated, and did not receive popular support at this stage. Demand for swabhasha was essentially a protest against the privileges enjoyed by the English-educated elite—in securing government positions, in commerce and in society at large—which were denied to the masses educated in the local languages.

The precedence given to the Sinhala language in the 1950s and 1960s, and the gradual phasing out of English—which served as the link language between Sinhalese and Tamil speakers—further exacerbated the ethnic tensions that led to the bloody thirty-year civil conflict in Sri Lanka.

After the end of this decades-long internecine strife, there are government-sponsored efforts afoot to encourage people to speak both languages—Sinhala and Tamil—and to promote English as a common or 'link' language. Towards that goal, President Mahinda Rajapakse named 2012 the 'Year of Trilingualism', launching a ten-year plan to make Sri Lanka a nation of three official languages: Sinhala, Tamil and English. I shared with President Rajapakse some not-so-well-known words from one of the greatest political leaders of our time, Nelson Mandela: 'If you talk to a man in a language he has learned in school, it goes to his head. If you talk to him in a language that he has heard from his mother, it goes to his heart.'

On 22 January 2012, I visited the headquarters of Sarvodaya Shramadana Movement, the largest people's organization in Sri Lanka. Sarvodaya, formally known as Lanka Jatika Sarvodaya Shramadana

Sangamaya, is developed around a set of coherent philosophical tenets drawn from Buddhism and Gandhian thought, and has been operational for almost fifty years. The founder of the Sarvodaya Shramadana Movement, Dr A.T. Ariyaratne, won the Gandhi Peace Prize in 1996 and the Niwano Peace Prize in 1992, for his work in peacemaking and village development.

On 23 January 2012, I visited Jaffna Hindu College, which was established in 1890 in the wake of a spiritual revival inspired by the valiant efforts of Srila Siri Arumuga Navalar. It was founded to provide education in English-medium with a Hindu environment, as all the English-medium schools in Jaffna at that time were Christian missionary schools. I saw in the prayer hall my picture displayed on the wall, along with the portraits of Swami Vivekananda and Mahatma Gandhi. When I asked about the correlation between the portraits, I was told that Swami Vivekananda visited Jaffna Hindu College on 24 January 1897, and Mahatma Gandhi came there on 27 November 1927, and that my visit there was considered a threefold blessing. I wished, that day, that Pramukh Swamiji had accompanied me to bestow his own blessings on this august institution.

Educational institutions such as Jaffna Hindu College—of all different faiths—are founded on the premise of combining academic and spiritual education. The latter necessarily entails a moral education, because spirituality cannot exist without a moral core. And a moral education is imperative for the development of youth, for man is naturally and ineluctably a moral being; many of his perfect attributes are attained through moral values. Without morality, grave problems face man—especially in the social dimension—and hence he can in no way achieve lasting happiness. A man may only be a man in the truest sense of the word when he is aware of the boundaries of morality and doesn't encroach on them. Because having a sense of morality is indeed the defining characteristic between humankind and the animal kingdom, and it is only through morality that we have a sense of humanity and spirituality.

But in addition to man's natural moral disposition, other material needs such as eating, sleeping and other necessary desires, are deep-rooted in human nature. Since man lives in a material world, he has greater tendencies to material desires. And where there is a conflict between his material and moral and spiritual desires, he finds himself in a dilemma; choosing the moral or spiritual path may seem rather difficult.

Hence, if man's moral education isn't considered earnestly, it will fail to be of consequence and thus, in the constant conflict between the moral values (transcendental aspects) of human life, often the animal aspects prevail. Moral education is not an easy task. It cannot be accomplished by merely dispensing snippets of advice or prescribing superficial remedies. It must be laid on a solid foundation.

It is a pity that we live in a world where morality and moral values are not intrinsic to our societies. Although everyone advocates moral values, it is evident that our age is one of moral decadence and the death of human values. In pondering the fate of societies throughout history where morality was neglected, as it was thought to be a peripheral concern, we may clearly see that one of the pillars of prosperity for a society is moral education. Therefore, families should not view the moral education of their children and adolescents as a perfunctory or even dispensable aspect of their upbringing. For, education should never focus solely on academic pursuits. One might be specialized in a field of knowledge or technology, but this does not make him a real human being. Humanity is valued in terms of moral standards. And families that don't pay due attention to the moral education of their children are truly neglecting their most fundamental duty. The moral education of a child must be considered sacrosanct.

The best method of education is by imparting behavioural patterns. That is, parents should behave in such a way as to imbue in their children acceptable, decent morality, sowing the seeds of moral values in their minds. Enlightened behaviour of parents fosters a spiritual and moral atmosphere at home. Children who grow up in an atmosphere where morality and spirituality prevail will be predisposed towards righteousness. In a nutshell, children have an innate predisposition to moral values, and, thus inspired, children will be inclined towards righteousness.

Conversely, if a father or mother always solves his/her problems aggressively, for example, and with a bad temper, the children will gradually get accustomed to such behaviour. At school, they will be prone to quarrelling with their schoolmates and grown-ups; they will become quick-tempered and unruly, causing themselves and their parents much trouble. To reform their ways and habits then is no easy task. Parents should know that providing a wrongful example is visiting their sins upon their children.

If, however, there is sincerity, understanding and decent behaviour at home, and family problems are encountered with tolerance and open-mindedness, the children will follow suit. If backbiting is prevalent in the household, how can we expect children to hate this immoral habit? Our behaviour affects children far more than our words. If children don't hear any backbiting on the part of their parents, they seldom tend to indulge in it themselves. Such is also the case with other negative traits such as lying and jealousy—it is largely a matter of children emulating what they witness in their families. Therefore, if we are to attach great importance to the moral education of our children, we have to attach greater importance to our own moral education.

My mother once told me that one day a mother asked Prophet Muhammad, peace be upon him, to tell her little child not to eat too many dates. The Prophet asked the woman to come next day with the child. She came as she was told, and the Prophet advised the child to stop eating too many dates. The woman asked the Prophet why he didn't advise the child the day before. The Prophet answered that he himself had eaten dates on that day. In fact, the Prophet never preached what he had not practised himself.

It is thus worth remembering the dictum 'practise what you preach', and noting that if parents act in a way other than what they say, children lose confidence in them and don't wholeheartedly embrace their advice. Or, this becomes a lesson in hypocrisy and multiple personality—which is, in fact, no personality. We should always remain aware, with moral education, that children pay more attention to what they see than to what they hear. Hence, to avoid mental confusion for children, there should be consistency between what they see and what they hear.

Good morals become second nature to man if he practises what he learns from moral education. From early childhood, parents should try to form good habits in their children through practice, because the first habits that are formed in man are the lasting ones. In the pre-elementary school period of development, moral education is received simply through forming good habits, for children don't yet have such mental faculties necessary to assimilate moral rules and standards. But in elementary school, children are apt to receive moral education directly.

As children grow up, they should be given opportunities to practise certain good acts repeatedly so that good habits may be inculcated in them. These good habits will be assets in their future.

How to influence moral values among students and how and when moral values should be taught are indeed momentous questions for schools. These questions have even more gravity and urgency for schools beset by the gamut of behavioural problems among their students. Sometimes, we can ascribe delinquency to the influence of modern times or the effect of improper care by parents. Or it may be an effect of change in society or a turbulent family environment. Regardless of the cause of delinquency, it is clear that a well-considered moral education can forestall it.

Pramukh Swamiji has recognized moral education as a critical need for children. He has continued to nourish children's activities begun by Yogiji Maharaj. He takes a special interest, spares personal time and encourages volunteers to help develop children through moral values, personal discipline and spiritual traditions. Worldwide, BAPS conducts over 6,800 weekly assemblies, specially catering to these needs for over 250,000 children of all ages: from infants to pre-teens. In addition to excelling in their personal lives, these children actively and proudly contribute to social projects. In many BAPS centres, children participate in paper recycling projects. In England, as already mentioned, the children of BAPS were involved in a record-breaking aluminium can recycling project.

But probably the most noteworthy of all children's initiatives are the de-addiction campaigns conducted by BAPS children in India. I personally invited, to the Rashtrapati Bhavan on 5 July 2007, the sadhus and child leaders who had helped to plan, manage and conduct this incredibly effective programme, and felicitated them. The statistics of this programme were staggering, and its impact long-lasting. During school vacations, select boys and girls were specially tutored in the hazards of addictions. They visited cancer patients and were motivated to reach out to friends, relatives, neighbourhoods and the public at large. In just twenty days, 23,000 BAPS children and 5,000 leaders had contacted over 2.1 million addicts, of whom 630,000 pledged to give up their addictions to smoking, tobacco, alcohol, drugs, gambling and other vices; this accounted for an annual saving of over 344 crore rupees, along with a priceless saving of human misery! The de-addiction campaigns reinstilled my belief in the future of our nation through empowerment.

Upon meeting the children involved in the programme, I asked them, 'How does one become great like Pramukh Swamiji?' The children were at a loss and looked at each other, puzzled. I smiled and asked them to repeat after me, 'If I have a beautiful mind, I will have beautiful thoughts; if I have beautiful thoughts, I will have a beautiful life; if I have a beautiful life, I will become a great soul like Pramukh Swamiji.' Testing the children further, I questioned, 'Convincing people to leave their addictions is difficult. If somebody refused to leave his addiction, how did you deal with him?' The children explained, 'President sir, we tried to convince such people by showing them the specially printed photographic booklet and logically explaining the scientific basis of the harmful consequences of their habits.'

I was delighted with the children's presentation and conviction, and further questioned, 'Why do people go back to their addictions? Even if you have freed them, why do they go back?' The children tried to reply and finally resigned, asking me to tell them. I narrated a story. 'Remember, there are two people sitting on everyone's shoulders. On the right sits the angel and on the left sits Satan. Now, when Satan wins, people go back to addictions, and when the angel wins people are freed from addictions. So how do you make the angel win?' The BAPS children replied in a flurry of answers ... hard work ... confidence ... good thoughts ... prayer .... Then they asked me, 'Please tell us, how can we make the angel win?'

I elaborated, 'Remember, every time you do good deeds, the angel wins and every time you do bad deeds Satan wins. Knowledge makes the angel free; it makes him powerful. Ignorance makes Satan free; it makes him powerful. Knowledge makes you a better person and a greater person. The satanic forces lead one to indulge in alcohol, drugs and other addictions and to do bad things. And the angelic forces lead one towards an addiction-free life, truth, love, non-violence and other virtues. You children were able to free people from addictions because you convinced them that by increasing the strength of angelic forces, people could overcome the satanic forces. You were instrumental in enhancing the angelic forces in individuals and giving them the strength to get rid of addictions and bad habits.'

I finally asked the children to repeat after me: 'Confidence leads to creativity; creativity leads to knowledge; knowledge leads to thinking; thinking makes one great.' I once again congratulated the children, 'All you children have done wonderful work. By freeing so many people from addictions what have you learned?' The children replied, 'We will never ever keep addictions in our lives. We will never allow our parents or relatives to keep addictions. And we will free our friends and others from addictions.' I was very happy with the answer and stood up for a group photograph. I shared a secret with them, 'Come, I will teach you another secret. Everybody should smile, because every time we smile the angel wins and every time we sulk Satan wins. So always wear a smile and always make other people smile. And you children should always be happy, because you have a greater force than the angel and Satan: the force of Pramukh Swamiji; his blessings are always upon you and all of us. So always keep smiling.'

Then turning to the sadhus I sent a heartfelt message: 'Please tell Pramukh Swamiji that he is doing a wonderful service for our people. He has a beautiful mind, a beautiful heart. Ask him to shower his blessings upon me.'

Pramukh Swamiji has enhanced the worth of children's education by establishing Vidyamandirs: academic schools with value-based education. BAPS has built and runs over 100 schools, hostels, research centres and institutions. I recall personally composing a handwritten message for the inauguration of one such international school, BAPS Swaminarayan Vidyamandir at Raisan, near Ahmedabad on 28 June 2006.

Dear Students of BAPS School,

Courage

Courage to Think different,
Courage to Invent,
Courage to discover The Impossible,
Courage to Combat the problems and Succeed,
Are the Unique qualities of youth.

I, the youth of my nation,
will work and work with Courage
For prosperity of my nation.

26-6-06   Greetings
*   A.P.J. Abdul Kalam*

Dear Students of BAPS School,

Courage
Courage to think different,
Courage to invent,
Courage to discover the impossible,
Courage to combat the problems and succeed,

Are the unique qualities of youth.
I, the youth of my nation,
Will work and work with Courage
For prosperity of my nation.

26-6-06   Greeting
                                                            A.P.J. Abdul Kalam

And Pramukh Swamiji wrote, for this occasion, these profound words for the children of the world: 'Beloved Children, Whatever is written, if not read; whatever is read, if not contemplated; whatever is contemplated, if not practised in life, then what is the point of writing?

HIS DIVINE HOLINESS
PRAMUKH SWAMI MAHARAJ
(SWAMI NARAYANSWARUPDAS)

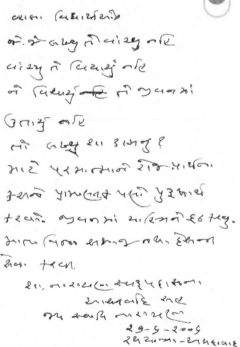

B.A.P.S. Swaminarayan Sanstha, Shahibaug Road, Ahmedabad - 380 004. Gujarat. India
e-mail: swamishri@baps.org • www.baps.org

So, pray daily to God and sincerely work hard. Strengthen good character in your life. And serve your parents, society and country.'

On 15 June 2012, Pramukh Swamiji underwent a medical procedure to receive a cardiac pacemaker. I called Swamiji in the hospital and said, 'God bless you. I pray for your good health.' As if to allay my fears, Swamiji himself gave me an update on his health. Out of concern for his health and various other reasons, Pramukh Swamiji's travel to Jaffna Hindu College did not materialize. Later, upon learning about this predicament, Pramukh Swamiji made special prayers for the peace and prosperity of the people of Sri Lanka.

On 22 December 2012, I inaugurated the World Confluence of Humanity, Power and Spirituality in Kolkata. I decided to present there a road map with four characteristics for the birth of world-enlightened citizens, expounding on dharma. I had learnt from Pramukh Swamiji the four characteristics of the satpurush, namely, one who controls the actions of the senses and mind but is not subdued by them; one who only performs activities related to God; one who staunchly observes the five vows: nishkam (overcoming lust and worldly desires), nirlobh (overcoming greed), niswad (overcoming taste), nisneh (overcoming worldly attachments) and nirman (overcoming ego); and one who transcends the body, mind and sense and is in constant communion with God.

The Holy Quran tells (Surah Al-Ra'd, Aayat 13: 28):

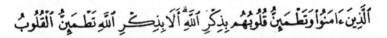

Indeed, in the remembrance of Allah do hearts find satisfaction.

I declared in the conference that a satpurush is indeed an enlightened citizen who is in charge of his senses and mind, who performs all his actions with God at the centre, who observes a strict moral code and worships God. People should be able to see in us something of God. The way we act, speak, look and even think should reflect God and God's ways.

16

To Give and Forgive Is Divine

'The weak can never forgive. Forgiveness is the attribute of the strong.'

– Mahatma Gandhi

In November 2012 I visited the China Academy of Space Technology (CAST). The Academy was founded in 1968; it is the main spacecraft development and production facility in China. CAST successfully launched China's first satellite *Dong Fang Hong* (Red East I), on 24 April 1970. India launched its first Rohini Satellite on 18 July 1980. I met a large number of Chinese scholars at Beijing Forum, a Chinese-government-backed intellectual body. Prof. Zhu Shanlu, chairman of Peking University, invited me to teach the subject of my choice at his institution once a year, and to stay as long as I wish. The subject could be science and technology or humanities.

The Chinese culture is one of the world's oldest. Most of its social values are derived from Confucianism and Taoism. The concept of reincarnation is widely accepted, and one's conduct is tempered by a belief in the connection between this life, the afterlife and the next incarnation. Along with a belief in the holy, there is a recognition of the existence of evil. Elders, seniors, extended families and particularly parents, are to be respected, heeded and looked after. Respect continues even after their deaths. Chinese people believe in three realms— heaven, the living and the deceased—existing side by side. Heaven is a place for saints or rested souls and hell for the criminal deceased.

In this context, I remember Pramukh Swamiji and his message of universal goodness, wherein everyone has an equal opportunity to rise to heaven.

On 30 July 2013, I visited the Andhra Mahila Sabha, a premier women's organization in the country with more than forty units. These units focus on education, health care, empowerment and old age care—particularly the care of aged women. The organization provides training and education to women and children, and enables them to harness their services for building the nation. It reaches out, giving free treatment to the needy and dedicating itself to the rehabilitation and integration of disabled children. The Sabha spreads literacy among women and counsels them on matrimonial and property matters. It conducts training for teachers and trainers of teachers, and instructs in various mass media of communication. Additionally, it provides shelter and food at affordable rates to needy senior citizens, who desire to live the remaining years of their lives respectably.

The roots of the Sabha, though not the Sabha itself, reach back more than a century. There was a rise in political and cultural awareness among the people of Hyderabad state towards the end of the nineteenth century. The culture and language of the overwhelming majority of the people living in the state were suppressed by the Nizam at this time. Therefore, the natural desire for education and cultural development—and promotion and development of their mother tongue—were inevitably linked with the struggle against the Nizam's rule.

Durgabai Deshmukh founded the Andhra Mahila Sabha. She is hailed as the 'Mother of Social Service in India'. A woman of simple living and high thinking—a freedom fighter, lawyer, social worker and politician—she was a member of the Constituent Assembly of India and the Planning Commission of India. She married C.D. Deshmukh, the first Indian governor of the Reserve Bank of India, and finance minister in India's Central cabinet in the years 1950–56. Responding to the pressing needs of society, Durgabai started a number of successful institutions, and exhibited great self-sacrifice and vision. When her worldly journey ended in 1981, she left Andhra Mahila Sabha with a rich legacy of the eternal values cherished by everyone.

I used the opportunity of my visit to the Andhra Mahila Sabha to emphasize the divinity of womanhood. I said, 'On the planet Earth, womanhood is indeed the Almighty's gift. I would like to narrate a story on human creation. God wanted to create the best of His creation. He worked for millions of years, designing and evolving the image of His creation. He went on looking at the image; He improved and improved it and finally decided to give it life. He looked at the galaxies, the oceans and beheld His own creation—man. As soon as man received life, two things happened. First, he opened his eyes and smiled. God was happy. The second, he opened his mouth and said, "Almighty, thank you". God was very happy. He was so delighted to see His creation and felt that His creation did the two right things.' This innate gratitude in man must be expressed for the manifold gifts women bring to our world—in giving life, in working for their families and in binding the very fabric of society. This is more relevant now than perhaps at any other time in history, given the challenges faced by women in contemporary India.

What are the three most important issues facing Indian women today? We had a good discussion at the Andhra Mahila Sabha, and what emerged out of it was the dual role of Indian women: earning money and yet carrying out the traditional role of homemaker. What is the solution? A Gujarati member of the sabha said that Pramukh Swamiji had solved this problem very effectively in Gujarat by setting up a process of holding regular ghar sabhas (family assemblies), and that Andhra Mahila Sabha should adopt his model. Later, when I received a delegation of Akshardham sadhus, I requested them to brief me about the ghar sabha initiative of Pramukh Swamiji.

The homemaker has the ultimate career. All other careers exist for one purpose only, and that is to support this ultimate career. Management of discords amongst family members lies at the heart of homemaking. No matter how wise and intelligent people may be, there can always be discord at home, between father and son, husband and wife, mother-in-law and daughter-in-law, and brothers and sisters.

People want things to go their way. That is the root cause of family discord. Only love can remove the discord. Young American author Jonathan Safran Foer writes so beautifully in his novel *Everything Is Illuminated*, 'One day you will do things for me that you hate. That is what it means to be family.'[41]

It is the ego that is at play in all quarrels—and especially in family quarrels. Even if one is not at fault, one has to forgive and forget. One should also cultivate equanimity—composure, calmness and level-headedness—otherwise there will be no peace. Pramukh Swamiji says that only correct understanding leads to happiness. If one has it, even the poorest feel happy, and without it even the rich feel ill at ease. So, when will familial understanding eventuate? When a family eats together and prays together! Pramukh Swamiji gave this togetherness the title of ghar sabha and declared it a cure for all discords.

Having personally read and replied to more than 700,000 letters, Pramukh Swamiji possesses a profound understanding of personal and family issues. Once, Pramukh Swamiji was answering letters from his devotees, which were as usual filled with personal and family problems. Someone sitting nearby, observing that Swamiji still had a large pile of letters to read and reply to, placed his hand on the pile and enquired, 'Swamiji, what can be done to prevent these problems and lessen these letters?' Pramukh Swamiji gave a very insightful answer, 'If every family meets together, eats together and prays together daily, such problems would not arise.' These words blossomed into one of the most important and successful BAPS initiatives: the ghar sabha. In this daily family gathering, the members pray, read scriptures, discuss values and amicably settle any differences.

Pramukh Swamiji has articulated five principles which promote family unity: meet each other; praise and appreciate each other; recognize and acknowledge the talents and virtues of your family members, particularly encouraging children by appreciating them; help each other; and, above all, exercise forgiveness. One should forgive others for their mistakes, errors or omissions. When you forgive, you in no way change the past—but you surely change the future. The truth is, unless you let go—you forgive yourself, you forgive the situation and you realize that the situation is over—you cannot move forward. The bond that links your true family is not one of blood, but of respect and joy in each other's lives. In the modern world, rarely do members of one family grow up under the same roof. Families are made in the heart. The only time family becomes null is when those ties in the heart are cut. If you cut those ties, those people are not your family. If you make those ties, those people are your family. And if you hate those ties, those people will still be your family because whatever you hate will always be with you.

> I may not always be with you
> But when we are far apart
> Remember you will be with me
> Right inside my heart.

On 10 December 2013, I was in Chennai. I called Pramukh Swamiji by telephone and wished him well on his ninety-third birthday. He was resting at Sarangpur. The next day when I addressed Kendriya Vidyalaya students and teachers on the occasion of the golden jubilee celebrations of Kendriya Vidyalaya Sangathan, I shared with them the glorious spiritual leadership of Pramukh Swamiji, and how he had transformed human lives with his loving kindness. I particularly mentioned the true story of Kukad and Odarka villages in the Saurashtra region.

A centuries-old dispute over land between these villages had evolved into a gory and seemingly endless feud involving forty-four surrounding villages (eleven supporting Kukad and thirty-three supporting Odarka). With each succeeding generation, violence intensified as men from both warring factions were killed and cremated on the outskirts of the villages. Hatred prevailed to the extent that apaiya (refusal to drink water) had been declared. Villagers refused to even drink water from the wells of their enemies. For both parties, the conflict engendered total ostracization and threatened complete annihilation. All efforts made over a period of 200 years by successive rulers—British authorities, the maharaja of Bhavnagar Krishnakumar Sinhji and the Gujarat state government—had proved futile.

Over a decade, I have enjoyed many discussions
with Pramukh Swamiji, in person and over the phone,
establishing a close, lifelong friendship.
These interactions have opened new windows
to my inner world and new horizons
of the outer world.

(Swaminarayan Akshardham,
New Delhi, 6 November 2005)

When I last met
Pramukh Swamiji in Sarangpur,
he was 94, frail, weak and silent.
He lovingly and firmly
held my hand and smiled.
This gave birth to the beginning and
ending of this book,
Transcendence.

(Sarangpur, Gujarat,
11 March 2014)

Pramukh Swamiji graces a
satsang assembly of 5,000 devotees.

(BAPS Swaminarayan Mandir, London,
25 April 2004)

In my first meeting with Pramukh Swamiji, when I presented the plans for India 2020, his first words were, 'Along with your five areas to transform India, add a sixth one—faith in God...'

...And he guided me
to develop people through
spirituality.
His simplicity, integrity and
clarity inspired me.

(Dr Kalam and Y.S. Rajan with Pramukh Swamiji
and BAPS swamis in New Delhi,
30 June 2001)

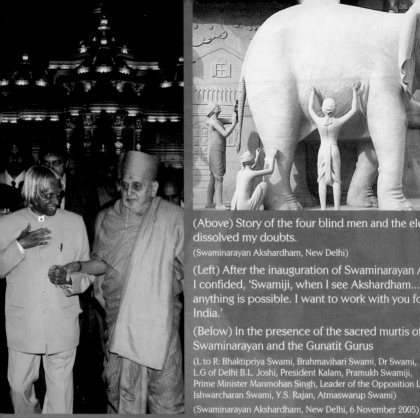

(Above) Story of the four blind men and the elephant dissolved my doubts.

(Swaminarayan Akshardham, New Delhi)

(Left) After the inauguration of Swaminarayan Akshardham I confided, 'Swamiji, when I see Akshardham... I feel that anything is possible. I want to work with you for a better India.'

(Below) In the presence of the sacred murtis of Bhagwan Swaminarayan and the Gunatit Gurus

(L to R: Bhaktipriya Swami, Brahmavihari Swami, Dr Swami, L.G of Delhi B.L. Joshi, President Kalam, Pramukh Swamiji, Prime Minister Manmohan Singh, Leader of the Opposition L.K. Advani, Ishwarcharan Swami, Y.S. Rajan, Atmaswarup Swami)

(Swaminarayan Akshardham, New Delhi, 6 November 2005)

During the Suvarna Bal Mahotsav, we walked amidst a sea of 20,000 BAPS children. I was overjoyed when one brave child asked me what I liked most about Pramukh Swamiji.

(Swaminarayan Akshardham, Gandhinagar, Gujarat, 8 February 2004)

I was overwhelmed
to meet the children
at the BAPS
Swaminarayan
Mandir in Neasden,
London.

(21 October 2007)

I personally felicitated the BAPS De-Addiction Campaign:
23,000 children contacted 2.1 milion people and freed
630,000 addicts.

(Rashtrapati Bhavan, New Delhi, 5 July 2007)

At the BAPS Swaminarayan Mandir in Chicago, I realized the crucial role a mandir can play in creating tomorrow's leaders.

(24 April 2011)

After the Gujarat earthquake and riots, on my first visit as President, Pramukh Swamiji gave blessings for development and social harmony.

(BAPS Swaminarayan Mandir, Ahmedabad, 13 August 2002)

I addressed the
European Parliament, calling for
an evolution of an enlightened society.
I felt as if Pramukh Swamiji
was speaking through me when I
emphasized the need of a spiritual
component for promoting a good
human life.

(European Parliament, Strasbourg,
25 April 2007)

Pramukh Swamiji addressed the
Millennium World Peace Summit:
'At this hour in human history,
we religious leaders should
not dream of only One religion
in the world, but dream of a world
where all religions are One – United.
Unity in Diversity is the lesson of life.
Flourishing together
is the secret of peace.'
(United Nations, New York, 29 August 2000)

BAPS's core philosophy of Akshar-Purushottam represented by Bhagwan Swaminarayan (R) and his first spiritual successor, Gunatitanand Swami (L).

One child can change the world – the inspiring journey of the child-yogi Neelkanth (Bhagwan Swaminarayan) has been beautifully documented in the film *Neelkanth Yatra*.

Gunatit Gurus: Young Pramukh Swamiji standing behind his gurus Shastriji Maharaj (R) and Yogiji Maharaj (L).

In the 1980s, Pramukh Swamiji transformed the life of Ramsang Bapu of Odarka, one of the most brutal members of the warring communities. This led to a cascading effect of goodness winning over evil. Pramukh Swamiji personally visited the region and met the village chiefs, convincing them to think beyond the past and focus on the future. On 12 April 1990, Pramukh Swamiji gathered the hardened Kshatriyas and their leaders from all the warring villages. For the first time in 200 years, they met without weapons and sat under one roof. Pramukh Swamiji collected water from the wells of the villages in one ceremonial pot. He performed its puja and offered it to God; and personally served this holy water to each leader, thus dissolving their hardened apaiya pledge.

Finally, he blessed everyone with these words, 'Today, you have come together to overcome this age-old conflict. With a generous heart and open mind the dispute has been resolved. To give up animosity is a great act. For a small piece of land, a big dispute arises. Despite knowing this, we cannot give it up. This is ignorance. A true saint removes the "I and mine" and replaces it with "ours". Even your ancestors will rejoice. They will be liberated. When we unite, their souls find peace. Today is an age of unity. With it lies progress. Only by forgetting and forgiving will there be progress. All of you have come closer to one another, and closer to God.'

It was the first time the Kshatriyas had seen each other smiling, laughing and happy. Pramukh Swamiji gave life to the Vedic concept of ajatashatru—one with no enemies.

In May 2014, I went to Edinburgh and addressed the Scottish parliament. I was fascinated by the rich landscape with magnificent historic buildings, all scrupulously maintained and preserved. The kingdom of Scotland was merged with the kingdom of England in 1707 to form the kingdom of Great Britain. For the next three hundred years, Scotland was directly governed by the parliament of the United Kingdom at Westminster; the lack of a Scottish parliament remained an impediment for the fulfilment of Scottish national identity. In September 1997, a referendum was put to the Scottish electorate, securing a majority in favour of the establishment of a new devolved Scottish parliament with tax-varying powers, in Edinburgh. An election was held on 6 May 1999, and on 1 July of that year power was transferred from Westminster to the new parliament.

On 15 May 2014, Edinburgh University conferred upon me an honorary degree. Professor Sir Timothy O'Shea, principal of the university, lauded my contributions to science and technology, and my commitment to helping transform India into a developed nation by 2020. The university was considered a principal intellectual centre during the Age of Enlightenment, for which Edinburgh was given the epithet 'the Athens of the north'. Alumni of the university include some of the major figures of modern history, including the physicist James Clerk Maxwell, naturalist Charles Darwin, philosopher David Hume, mathematician Thomas Bayes, surgeon Joseph Lister, signatories of the American Declaration of Independence John Witherspoon and Benjamin Rush, inventor Alexander Graham Bell, the first president of Tanzania Julius Nyerere and a host of famous authors including Sir Arthur Conan Doyle, Robert Louis Stevenson, J.M. Barrie and Sir Walter Scott. That this venerable institution honoured me was indeed a blessing. The third verse of the Sermon on the Mount, in the Holy Bible says, 'Blessed are the meek: for they shall inherit the earth.' While receiving my honorary degree, I closed my eyes and remembered Pramukh Swamiji, my inner inspiration.

The first part of this book recounted my experience with spirituality. The second part described this spirituality in action. Now, in the third part of the book, I would like to symbolically express my oneness with Pramukh Swamiji by exploring the essential oneness of science and spirituality. I will examine a number of deeply spiritual eminent scientists and thinkers, sharing the stories of Pythagoras, Galileo Galilei, Albert Einstein, Gregor Mendel, Baruch Spinoza, Srinivas Ramanujan, Jagdish Chandra Bose, Subrahmanyan Chandrasekhar and Francis Collins. In doing so, I will highlight the confluence of spiritual belief and scientific inquiry. I will also discuss the emerging Gaia philosophy, named after Gaia, the Greek goddess of the earth. Gaia is an inclusive term for theories propounding the concept that living organisms on a planet will affect the nature of their environment in order to make the environment more suitable for life. This set of theories holds that all organisms on a life-giving planet regulate the biosphere to the benefit of the whole.

PART THREE

FUSION OF SCIENCE AND SPIRITUALITY

'Science is not only compatible with spirituality; it is a profound source of spirituality.'

– Carl Sagan
Astronomer and author

17

In Contemplation of the Beauty of Creation

'The creation of a thousand forests is in one acorn.'

– Ralph Waldo Emerson
Nineteenth-century American poet

The dialogue between science and religion is amongst humanity's oldest and most controversial, drawing each era's great thinkers into some of history's most heated debates. The modern friction between science and religion stretches from Galileo's famous letter to the exchanges of today's leading intellects. And yet we are seeing that, for all its capacity for ignorance, religion might well have some valuable lessons for secular thought, and the two need not be regarded as opposites.

Since I first met Pramukh Swamiji in 2001, I have explored the relationship between the scientific and the spiritual. I have found that true science and true spirituality are not merely compatible; they can be one and the same. What is the source of life? We don't even know what an atom is—whether it is a wave or a particle—or if it is both. We don't really have any idea of what these fundamental building blocks of the universe are. That is the reason we speak of the Divine. There is a transcendent energy source. When the physicist observes subatomic particles, he's seeing a trace of this energy on the screen. These traces come and go and come and go, and we come and go—all of life comes and goes. That energy is the aspiring energy of all things. Mystic worship addresses this.

From Ptolemy the Greco-Egyptian writer of second-century Alexandria, to Richard Dawkins in the present time, we can see the intense spiritual elevation that science is capable of inspiring. Ptolemy wrote:

> I know that I am mortal by nature and ephemeral, but when I trace at my pleasure the windings to and fro of the heavenly bodies, I no longer touch earth with my feet. I stand in the presence of Zeus himself and take my fill of ambrosia.[42]

And Richard Dawkins writes:

> A universe with a God would look quite different from a universe without one. A physics, a biology where there is a God is bound to look different. So the most basic claims of religion are scientific. Religion is a scientific theory.[43]

In the rest of this book, I will be sharing with you my thought processes in this regard, that have evolved over the years of my fellowship with Pramukh Swamiji.

'Spirit' comes from the Latin word *spirare*, meaning 'to breathe'. What we breathe is air, which is unquestionably matter, however thin. Despite usage to the contrary, there is no necessary implication in the word 'spiritual' that we are talking of anything outside the realm of science. Science is not only compatible with spirituality—it is an essential source of spirituality. Some philosophers believe that modern quantum theory can indeed define consciousness and where religion and spirituality meet. When we recognize our minuscule presence in an immensity of light years and in the passage of aeons; when we grasp the intricacy, beauty and subtlety of life; only then is that soaring feeling—that sense of elation and humility combined—surely spiritual. So are our emotions in the presence of great art or music or literature, or our acts of exemplary selfless courage such as those of Mahatma Gandhi or Nelson Mandela. The notion that science and spirituality are somehow mutually exclusive does a disservice to both.

Let us go back 600 years. The Black Death, one of the most devastating pandemics in human history, was ravaging the world.

Originating in or near China, the killing disease spread via the Silk Road or by ship, reducing the world's population from an estimated 450 million to some 350 million. The aftermath of the plague created a series of religious, social and economic upheavals which had profound effects on the course of human history.[44]

The devastation caused by the Black Death in Florence eventually resulted in a shift in the world view of people in fourteenth-century Italy. Italy was particularly badly affected by the plague, and it has been speculated that the pervasiveness of death at this time and its familiarity caused thinkers to dwell more on their lives on earth, rather than on spirituality and the afterlife.[45]

The publication in 1543 of Nicolaus Copernicus's *On the Revolutions of the Heavenly Spheres* and Andreas Vesalius's *On the Fabric of the Human Body* marked the beginning of a scientific revolution. A new view of nature emerged, replacing the ancient views that had dominated intellectual discourse for almost 2,000 years. Galen's treatment of the venous and arterial systems as two separate systems, for example, with William Harvey's pioneering discovery that blood circulated from the arteries to the veins 'impelled in a circle, and … in a state of ceaseless motion', revolutionized the medical understanding of the times.[46]

Perhaps the most stellar of all the revolutionary scientific thinkers of this era was Galileo. Galileo Galilei was born in Pisa, then part of the Duchy of Florence, Italy, in 1564. Galileo seriously contemplated entering the priesthood as a young man, but instead enrolled at the University of Pisa for a medical degree to appease his father. In 1581, while he was studying medicine, he noticed a chandelier swinging in a breeze, in larger and smaller arcs. He surmised, by gauging the speed of its movement with his heartbeat, that the chandelier took the same amount of time to swing back and forth, regardless of how far it was swinging. This, it seems, was the beginning of his fascination with the motion of celestial bodies.

Until that time, Galileo had deliberately been discouraged from studying mathematics, simply because a physician earned a good deal more than a mathematician at that time. But upon accidentally attending a lecture on geometry, he talked his reluctant father into letting him study mathematics and natural philosophy instead of medicine. Inspired by the artistic tradition of the city and the works of the Renaissance artists—and perhaps in imbibing the pervasive ethos of the Renaissance—Galileo cultivated an aesthetic sense. In 1589, Galileo was appointed to the chair of mathematics at the University of Pisa.

In the Catholic world of Galileo's time, the majority of educated people subscribed to the Aristotelian geocentric view: that the earth was the centre of the universe and that all heavenly bodies revolved around the earth. Biblical references—Psalm 93:1, 96:10, and 1 Chronicles 16:30—include text stating, 'the world is firmly established, it cannot be moved'. In the same manner, Psalm 104:5 declares: 'The Lord set the earth on its foundations; it can never be moved.' Further, Ecclesiastes 1:5 states that 'the sun rises and sets and returns to its place'. Galileo, however, inspired by the earlier work of Copernicus, propounded a heliocentric view of the earth and other planets orbiting the sun.

In 1616, Pope Paul V ordered Galileo to abandon his heliocentric Copernican opinions. Further, he was commanded not to hold, teach, or defend the heliocentric theory in any way whatever—either orally or in writing. For sixteen years, Galileo wavered between what he believed and what he was asked to believe; but he eventually decided to put in writing what he thought was right.

And for his resulting book expounding the heliocentric theory, *Dialogue Concerning the Two Chief World Systems*, Galileo was to pay dearly. In a colossal blunder, and with an astounding lack of tact, Galileo lampooned his supporter Pope Urban VIII by mouthing the pope's geocentric views in the book with a buffoon character named 'Simplicio'. Galileo was subsequently declared 'vehemently suspect of heresy' at the Inquisitional trial in 1633. Specifically, he was found guilty of having held the heretical opinions that the sun lies motionless at the centre of the universe, that the earth is not at its centre and moves, and that one may hold and defend an opinion as probable after it has been declared contrary to holy scripture. He was required to 'abjure, curse and detest' those opinions. He was sentenced to house arrest, under which he remained for the rest of his life.[47]

Galileo was one of the first modern thinkers to clearly state that the laws of nature are mathematical. He made original contributions to the science of motion through an innovative combination of experimentation and mathematics. He famously wrote in his book *The Assayer*:

> Philosophy is written in this grand book—I mean the universe—which stands continually open to our gaze, but it cannot be understood unless one first learns to comprehend the language and interpret the characters in which it is written. It is written in the language of mathematics, and its characters are triangles, circles, and other geometrical figures, without which it is humanly impossible to understand a single word of it; without these, one is wandering around in a dark labyrinth.[48]

Four hundred years after Galileo Galilei invented the first telescope, his legacy endures. His invention, and his thought, continue to influence how the world views science and how science views the world—and, of course, the universe. Today's telescopes have led to the discovery of at least 100 billion galaxies in the universe. This poses a provocative cosmological question: 'If the purpose of the universe is that human beings could live there, why would God create so many galaxies? Clearly one would be more than enough to support our solar system. Yet there are countless galaxies distributed in strange ways and evolving all the time.' So the question we are faced with in cosmology is how to explain the vastness and purpose of the universe.

Galileo's legacy is a call to go beyond what can be observed. The questions about the immensity of the universe, its origin and its end, do not admit only one answer of a scientific character. Whoever looks at the cosmos following Galileo's lesson will not be able to stop only with that which he observes with a telescope; he will have to ask himself about the meaning and end to which the whole of creation is oriented. In this context, philosophy and theology have an important role in preparing the way for further knowledge.

Galileo valued scripture. He stressed that the Bible should not be taken literally or as an instrument for proving science. By doing so, he hoped this view might foster reconciliation between faith and science. Unfortunately, Galileo's detractors took the opposite view and saw his efforts as an attempt to interfere in theology. Galileo's point on literalism taught something very relevant to the coming generations. Through the Bible one can come to appreciate the aesthetics of creation. Man can never present himself in creation just by studying it from a physical standpoint. As we study the universe, symbolic language and resorts to aesthetic and poetic emotions overwhelm us.[49]

From primal belief during the Stone Age, to the Vedic Age, through the so-called 'Axial Age' of the Buddha, Confucius, Plato, and Zoroaster, to modern Christian missionaries and the rise of Islam, belief has been reified by culture. Thus we reach the fundamental question: Does God exist? That is, have we discovered God? Or have we invented him? Are there so many similarities among the great religions because God is really the product of universal wish-fulfilment? Did humans everywhere create supernatural beings out of their need for comfort in the face of existential tragedy and to find purpose and significance in life? Or have people in many places, to a greater or lesser degree, actually gained glimpses of God?

People who are unable to understand perfectly both scripture and science far outnumber those who do understand them perfectly. The former, glancing superficially through the scriptures, could easily arrogate to themselves the authority to decide upon every question of physics on the strength of some word which they have misunderstood, and which was consciously employed by the sacred authors for some different purpose. And the smaller number of understanding men could not dam up the furious torrent of such people. These people would gain the most followers, simply because it is much more pleasant to gain a reputation for wisdom without effort or study, than to consume oneself tirelessly in the most laborious disciplines.

It is necessary for the scriptures, in order to be accommodated to the understanding of every man, to speak many things, which appear to differ from the absolute truth so far as the bare meaning of the words is concerned. But Nature, on the other hand, is inexorable and immutable; she never transgresses the laws imposed upon her, or cares a whit whether her abstruse reasons and methods of operation are understandable to men. For that reason, nothing physical which sense and experience sets before our eyes, or which reasonable demonstrations prove to us, ought to be called into question—much less condemned—upon the testimony of passages in the religious books. These passages may, in truth, have some different meaning within their words. For the scriptures are not chained in every expression to conditions as strict as those which govern all physical effects; nor is God any less excellently revealed in Nature's actions than in the sacred statements of the scriptures.

18

Religions Are the Signposts of God

'Just as a candle cannot burn without fire, men cannot live
without a spiritual life.'

– Buddha

Pythagoras lived some 2,500 years ago on Samos, the Greek island
in the eastern Aegean Sea that separates the mainlands of Greece
and Turkey. Pythagoras travelled extensively. He wandered in various
kingdoms in Egypt, Arabia and Persia for the purpose of collecting all
available knowledge, and especially to learn information concerning
the secret or mystic cults of the gods. Pythagoras made influential
contributions to philosophy and religion in the late sixth century BC.
He is revered as a great mathematician, mystic and scientist, and is
best known for the theorem which bears his name.[50]

Pythagoras is regarded as the first person to apply the term *cosmos*
to the order of the universe. 'A complex and orderly system, such as
our universe; the opposite of chaos,' he said. One of the most famous
discoveries of Pythagoras was that the chief musical intervals are
expressible in simple mathematical ratios between the first four integers.
Pythagoras declared that 'all nature consists of harmony arising out of
numbers'. 'All nature' is all of space–time and everything that exists
therein, including all planets, stars, galaxies, the contents of intergalactic
space, the smallest subatomic particles, and all matter and energy—in
short, it is everything. Pythagorean ideas exercised a marked influence
on Plato, and through him, all of Western philosophy.[51]

The most distinct testament of the ancient Hindu view of the cosmos is the eleventh chapter of the Bhagavadgita. The poem itself was created in relatively modern times—around six to eight centuries ago. But this chapter contains the oldest cosmological concepts available to us, expressed in a language comprehensible to us without resorting to precarious interpretations. One might say that here we encounter the ancient Vedic precepts in a form expressed for our purposes in later times.

> Shri Krishna: See me then, O son of Earth,
> As one in the plurality of forms
> As a more heavenly Nature, various
> And countless as the stars of heaven are ...
>
> Regard as a unitary Whole
> The whole world, with all its forms.
> It is my body. I myself its spirit:
> And everything that is, is all in me ...
>
> Shocked with wonder Arjuna sank down,
> Shivering; then with devotion
> Bowing his head, he folded his hands,
> And spoke thus to the Lord of the Universe ...
>
> Arjuna: I see you now: with many arms,
> With countless breasts to nourish
> Everything in the world, and many eyes;
> With no beginning, middle, or end ...
> Without beginning, middle, or end,
> Infinite in power; incessant in activity.[52]

Islamic scripture about the universe is similarly profound and arcane—and correspondingly poetic. The Isra and Miraj are the two parts of a night journey or Shob-e-Miraz that, according to Islamic tradition, Prophet Muhammad, peace be upon him, took during a single night around the year AD 621. It has been described as both a physical and spiritual journey. A brief sketch of the story is in Sura 17, Al-Isra of the Quran, and other details come from the Hadith, supplemental writings about the life of the Prophet.

They moved for five hundred thousand light-years within the radius of the first paradise. The buraq (heavenly beast) moved faster than the speed of light, for each of its steps could reach wherever his sight did. The entire distances they travelled were filled with angels whose number is known only to the Creator, praising Him and glorifying Him with all kinds of praises.

Prophet Muhammad, peace be upon him, sitting on the buraq and accompanied by the angel Gabriel, ascended seven layers towards infinity, and met all earlier prophets and angels. Finally, a stage came when the angel Gabriel told the Prophet that beyond that no one had ever gone. 'Muhammad!' Gabriel said, 'You now have to step down from the buraq and move to a place which no one has entered before you.'

Muhammad (peace be upon him) then moved through one veil after another until he passed through one thousand veils. Finally he opened the Veil of Oneness. He found himself like a lamp suspended in the middle of a divine air. He saw a magnificent, great and unutterable matter. He asked his Rabb (Lord) to give him firmness and strength. He felt that a drop of that presence was put on his tongue and he found it cooler than ice and sweeter than honey. Nothing on earth and the seven paradises tasted like it. With this drop, Allah put into Muhammad's heart the knowledge of the First and the Last, the heavenly and the earthly. All this was revealed to him in one instant shorter than the fastest second. He was ordered to move forward. As he moved he found himself elevated on a throne that can never be described, now or later. Three additional drops were given to him: one on his shoulder consisting in majesty, one in his heart consisting in mercy, and an additional one on his tongue which consisted in eloquence. Then a voice came from that presence, which no created being had heard before: 'Muhammad! I have made you the intercessor for everyone.'

At that moment Muhammad (peace be upon him) felt his mind enraptured and taken away and replaced with an astonishing secret. He was placed in the fields of Allah's Eternity and Endlessness. In the first he found no beginning and in the second he found no end. Then

Allah revealed to Him: 'My end is in My beginning and My beginning is in My end.' Then Muhammad (peace be upon him) knew that all doors were absolutely closed except those that led to Allah, that Allah cannot be described within the confine of a place in speech, and that Allah encompasses the everywhere of all places.

This is a secret that no tongue can be stirred to express, no door opened to reveal, and no answer can define. He is the Guide to Himself and the Rabb (Lord) of His own description. He is the Beauty of all beauty and the speech by which to describe Himself belongs to Him alone.[53]

For many centuries, the universe remained a wonderful enigma. Philosophers, writers and poets saw their own fancies and fantasies in the infinity around them. At the beginning of last century, Albert Einstein took a hard look at the universe. He wrote:

A human being is a part of the whole called by us universe, a part limited in time and space. He experiences himself, his thoughts and feeling as something separated from the rest, a kind of optical delusion of his consciousness. This delusion is a kind of prison for us, restricting us to our personal desires and to affection for a few persons nearest to us. Our task must be to free ourselves from this prison by widening our circle of compassion to embrace all living creatures and the whole of nature in its beauty.[54]

In 1930, Einstein composed a kind of creed entitled 'What I Believe', at the conclusion of which he wrote, 'To sense that behind everything that can be experienced there is something that our minds cannot grasp, whose beauty and sublimity reaches us only indirectly: this is religiousness. In this sense ... I am a devoutly religious man.' In response to a young girl who had asked him whether he believed in God, he wrote, 'Everyone who is seriously involved in the pursuit of science becomes convinced that a spirit is manifest in the laws of the universe—a spirit vastly superior to that of man.' And during a talk at Union Theological Seminary on the relationship between religion and science, Einstein declared: 'The situation may be expressed by an image: science without religion is lame, religion without science is blind.'[55]

These reflections of Einstein—and he made many more like them throughout his career—bring the German physicist close to the position of a rather influential German theologian. In his 1968 book *Introduction to Christianity*, Joseph Ratzinger, who would later become Pope Benedict XVI, offered this simple but penetrating argument for God's existence: the universal intelligibility of nature, which is the presupposition of all science, can only be explained through recourse to an infinite and creative mind which has thought the world into being. No scientist, Ratzinger said, could even begin to work unless and until he assumed that the aspect of nature he was investigating was knowable, intelligible and marked by form. But this fundamentally mystical assumption rests upon the conviction that whatever he comes to know through his scientific work is simply an act of rethinking or recognizing what a far greater mind has already conceived.[56]

Ratzinger argued for the essential sameness of religion and science, since both involve an intuition of God's existence and intelligence. Had not most of modern physical sciences emerged out of the universities of the Christian West? Modernity has indeed emerged out of—and in stark opposition to—repressive, obscurantist and superstitious Christianity. There is a deep congruity between the disciplines that search for objective truth and the religion that says, 'In the beginning was the Word.'[57]

Given the many other things which he said about belief, perhaps it would suffice to say that Ratzinger was reacting against primitive and superstitious forms of religion, just as St Paul was when he said that we must put away childish things when we have come of age spiritually. A person can be a genius in one field of endeavour and remain naive, even inept, in another. Few would dispute that Einstein was the greatest theoretical physicist of the last century, but this is no guarantee that he had even an adequate appreciation of sacred scripture. The 'stories' of the religious books have been the object of sophisticated interpretation. Masters such as Sankara, St Augustine and Imam Gazali have uncovered the complexity and multivalence of the symbolism of their scriptures, and have delighted in showing the literary artistry that lies below its sometimes deceptively simple surface. American anthropologist Clifford Geertz said this so well:

> A religion is a system of symbols which acts to establish powerful, pervasive, and long-lasting moods in men by formulating conceptions of a general order of existence and clothing those conceptions with such an aura of factuality that the moods and motivations seem uniquely realistic.[58]

One of the things that is most unique about India's culture is the way in which the holy, the spiritual and the everyday are so intrinsically linked.

19

Mind Is the Matrix of All Matter

'To the mind that is still, the whole universe surrenders.'

– Lao Tzu
Philosopher and poet of ancient China

If you were God, with limitless resources and power, how might you go about creating a world for your children? Surely you would want to create a world over which you could keep a watchful eye; a world where you could hear your children's cries and respond as necessary. You would not be likely to send your children away, out of sight and out of mind, because first, you would want them close at hand, and second, there is no other in whose care you could or would entrust them.

Or would you like to empower them with free will and send them away so that they could exercise their will and judgement, without in any way affecting your plans for their future? Would you create a world where they could experience the joy and pain of life and grow in wisdom, maturity and strength of character; where they could learn what it means to love and to be loved, to inflict pain and to be hurt— and to choose between these alternatives?

Or would you like to create a world where your children could be ultimately safe, no matter what happens? To accomplish this, you might consider letting your children romp in the image of a world, like in some sort of a computer simulation or interactive video game, wherein you keep playing at different levels and are welcome to return every time after you lose.

If your answer is the third option, you have understood correctly the concept of maya. In the Puranas and Vaishnava theology, maya is described as one of the powers of Vishnu, a manifested form of Supreme God. It became associated with sleep; and Vishnu's maya is sleep, which envelops the world. In Tamil literature of the Sangam period, Krishna is found as mayon, with other attributed names such as Mal, Tirumal, Perumal and Mayavan. In the Tamil classics, the feminine form of the word māyol is Durga; she is endowed with unlimited creative energy and the great powers of Vishnu, and is hence Vishnu-Maya. As Mahamaya, she clouds the knowledge of the young child, bestowing individual ego and ideas of ownership on him; screening him from wisdom and involving him in the pleasures and pain of the transactional world.

The transactional world is created out of concrete objects and people. A false reality is superimposed on the various names and forms. A matrix is created and we live trapped in it, forgetting that it is indeed unreal. This world, which we think we see, is maya or an appearance: like a computer simulation, a video game. It has no permanent reality—it is only a passing show. Our bodies, which are made of the same material—the five elements—are also perishable. But we are not solely these bodies. Our reality is something far greater, since we are actually a part of the divine consciousness that is 'breathed' into our perishable bodies. This breath is imperishable and eternal and untouched by the changes of the body, which take place in the world of space–time.

The moment we demarcate ourselves as belonging to a specified place and time, we separate ourselves from our roots and thus bring suffering on ourselves. We are the creators of time and space. When we bring energy to conscious awareness, through the act of perception, we create separate objects that exist in space through a measured continuum called time. By creating time and space we create our own separateness.[59]

Although the powers of understanding of human senses are limited to three spatial dimensions, the scope of our universe is not limited to three dimensions. Many of the natural phenomena happening within our universe transcend the three-dimensional scene. Therefore, the mechanisms of operation of the brain and consciousness cannot be understood in terms of chemicals and electrical charges in human cells. Consciousness is not confined within the human skull. How then do we understand consciousness?

German theoretical physicist Max Planck was the first to observe that the electron behaves differently when being observed by a human. When the electron is not being observed, the electron behaves like a wave, but when an observing instrument is placed in the experiment, the electron behaves like a particle. Max Planck hypothesized that an electron will change its behaviour or reality depending on whether or not the electron is being observed: it is as if the electron is aware that it is being observed. This awareness is very similar, if not the same, as human awareness and may be related to the same consciousness. We see what we want to see!

Max Planck is best known as the originator of quantum theory, for which he won the Nobel Prize in physics in 1918. Just as Albert Einstein's theory of relativity revolutionized the understanding of space and time, the quantum theory revolutionized human understanding of atomic and subatomic processes. Together they constitute the fundamental theories of twentieth-century physics.

Planck came from a traditional, intellectual family. His paternal great-grandfather and grandfather were both theology professors; his father was a law professor. The legend is that when Planck's physics professor advised him against going into physics, saying, 'in this field, almost everything is already discovered, and all that remains is to fill a few holes', Planck replied that he did not wish to discover new things, but only to understand the known fundamentals of the field.[60]

Planck regarded the scientist as a man of imagination and faith: 'faith' interpreted as being similar to 'having a working hypothesis'. For example, the causality principle is not true or false—it is an act of faith. He also said:

> Both religion and science require a belief in God. For believers,
> God is in the beginning, and for physicists God is at the end of all

considerations ... To the former He is the foundation, to the latter, the crown of the edifice of every generalized world view.[61]

Like Einstein's theory of relativity, quantum physics reveals the universe to be a single gigantic field of energy in which matter is just a 'slowed down' form of energy. Further, quantum physics explains that matter or energy does not exist with any certainty in definite places, but rather shows 'tendencies' to exist. Even more intriguing is the notion that the existence of an observer is fundamental to the existence of the universe—a concept known as 'the observer effect'—implying that the universe is a product of consciousness: the mind of God.

The greatest thing that Max Planck and his quantum physics did for the spiritually minded person was to show that the world—as the senses tell us and as the Newtonian scientists had been telling us— is not a solid thing. Physicists went to the heart of matter and were astounded by what they saw. Matter was not solid at all as our senses tell us but merely energy in motion. In fact, matter is composed of subatomic particles that have no design or shape and do not follow any standard order. Sometimes they behave like waves and sometimes like particles. And sometimes they behave like both, as well as many things at the same time. Hence these physicists actually proved maya in a scientific way.[62]

Towards the end of his illustrious scientific career, Planck also looked very closely at the problem of free will, and gave a rough version of the logical opposition between determinism and blind chance in the standard argument against free will. He declared, 'Our own consciousness tells us that our wills are free. And the information, that which consciousness directly gives us, is the last and highest exercise of our powers of understanding.'

Let us ask for a moment whether the human will is free, or whether it is determined in a strictly causal way. If we assume the law of strict dynamic causality as existing throughout the universe, how can we logically exclude the human will from its operation? What do we then mean when we say that the human will is free? Let us put it this way: a man is always given the chance of choosing between at least two options when it comes to a question of taking a decision. The law of causality cannot lay down any line of action for him and it cannot relieve him from the rule of moral responsibility for his own doings. For the sanction of moral responsibility comes to him from another law, which has nothing to do with the law of causality. His own conscience is the tribunal of that law of moral responsibility, and there he will always hear its promptings and its sanctions when he is willing to listen.

It is a dangerous act of self-delusion if one attempts to get rid of an unpleasant moral obligation, by claiming that human action is the inevitable result of an inexorable law of nature. The human being who looks upon his own future as preordained by fate, or the nation that believes in a prophecy which states that its decline is inexorably decreed by a law of nature, merely exemplifies a lack of willpower to struggle and win through.

Another important thing that Max Planck discovered was that subatomic particles had no meaning in isolation, but only in relationship with everything else. At its elemental level, which is the quantum level, he saw that matter could not be chopped up into intelligible units, but was completely indivisible. If we want to understand the universe, we will have to see it as a dynamic web of interconnectedness. Human beings are a coalescence of energy in a field of energy, which is connected to every other thing in this universe. This energy field is the central engine of our being. We can never be estranged from the other aspects of this universe since we are all bound fundamentally to this field.[63]

Since we are totally connected with everything and every creature in this universe, it is most foolish for each of us to strive to better ourselves without regard to what happens to others. Human suffering stems from this very fact; that we have cut ourselves off from our roots and have condemned ourselves to a life of isolation. This was not how nature meant us to be. Modern physics has thus given us a correct evaluation of our place in the world. The human consciousness, as our scriptures have always told us, is a crucial factor in making up this universe. Subatomic particles settle down from their constant erratic movements and take on solid shapes only when we observe them. On the quantum level, all living beings—including human beings—are packets of quantum energy constantly exchanging information with an inexhaustible field of energy. Pramukh Swamiji calls this field of energy 'chitta'. Information about all aspects of life is relayed through the interchange of information on the quantum level.

As a child, I would watch, for many hours in the evenings, birds hovering over the sea in beautiful formations. They would be winging their way across the sky and then suddenly all of them would veer to a different course, as if at some hidden signal. The same phenomenon can be noticed in fish. I assumed that these birds and fish had a novel method of communicating with each other by some radar or some sound signal which we cannot hear, but now experiments on the quantum field prove that they are all in touch with this field and receive their orders simultaneously from it.

The functions of our minds, like thinking, feeling, etc., draw information from the quantum field, which is pulsing simultaneously through our bodies and brains. The physical, mental and behavioural changes of all human beings, wherever they are, follow a roughly twenty-four-hour cycle. They sleep and arise responding to light and darkness in their environments. In fact, similar circadian rhythms are found in most living things, including animals, plants and many tiny microbes. We resonate with the universe.

Every breath we take is part of the universal breath, and every breath we give out is our contribution to universal life. The 'breath'—the life force—is the same in everything and everyone and is spread everywhere simultaneously. Our lives can only become perfect if we participate in this great interchange with the universe. Max Planck said:

> As a man who has devoted his whole life to the most clear-headed science, to the study of matter, I can tell you as a result of my research about atoms this much: There is no matter as such. All matter originates and exists only by virtue of a force, which brings the particle of an atom to vibration and holds this most minute solar system of the atom together. We must assume behind this force the existence of a conscious and intelligent mind. This mind is the matrix of all matter.

20

Growing into Highly Evolved Physical and Spiritual Beings

'The purpose of our journey on this precious Earth is now to align our personalities with our souls. It is to create harmony, cooperation, sharing, and reverence for Life. It is to grow spiritually. This is our new evolutionary pathway.'

– Gary Zukav
Spiritual teacher and author

During my lifetime, I have seen deoxyribonucleic acid (DNA) discovered and the human genome deciphered. And it is quite possible that genetics and computers will merge within a decade. Organic computers could be realized from biological substances that can function like a semiconductor. It is school-level knowledge today that our own genomes carry the story of evolution, written in DNA— the language of molecular genetics—and the narrative is unmistakable. A doctor will matter-of-factly tell a patient that his genes had already loaded the gun and his lifestyle just pulled the trigger. From inheritance of property and fortune by birth to a preprogrammed end of life, the story of genetics is a very fascinating one.[64]

The founder of the modern science of genetics was not a scientist, leave alone a world-renowned scientist of his day. Nor was he particularly modern; he was born in 1822 in what is now part of the Czech Republic. The Augustinian monk Gregor Mendel, the first known person to trace the characteristics of successive generations of living things, joined a monastery at an early age and taught natural science to high-school students.

Mendel's attraction to research was based on his love of nature. He was not only interested in plants, but also in meteorology and theories of evolution. Mendel often wondered how plants obtained atypical characteristics. On one of his frequent walks around the monastery, he found an atypical variety of an ornamental plant. He took it and planted it next to the typical variety. He grew their progeny side by side to see if there would be any approximation of the traits passed on to the next generation. He found that the plants' respective offspring retained the essential traits of the parents, and therefore were not influenced by the environment. This simple observation gave birth to the idea of heredity.[65]

The first heredity law, which is the law of segregation, is entirely based on Mendel's observations regarding the breeding of plants. It states that genes (units of heredity) are in pairs, and the paired gene becomes divided when the cell is divided. Each paired gene is present in both halves of the egg or sperm. When Mendel's theories were integrated with the chromosome theory of inheritance by evolutionary biologist Thomas Hunt Morgan in 1915, they became the core of classical genetics. Morgan would win the Nobel Prize in 1933 for discoveries elucidating the role that the chromosome plays in heredity.

Gregor Mendel's life shows that a devoutly religious person, who has devoted his life to his beliefs, can also be interested in science and contribute to scientific discovery in a profound way. While it can be safely assumed that Mendel was a learned man, had a penchant for detail, and was patient and persistent by nature, he also had a heart for people. He could be easily overwhelmed by his empathy for others.

Mendel's work was rejected at first in the scientific community, and was not widely accepted until after he died. During his own lifetime, most biologists held the idea that all characteristics were passed to the next generation through blending inheritance, in which the traits from each parent are averaged together. Instances of this phenomenon are now explained by the action of multiple genes with quantitative effects. People interested in the history of science should be told— and told most emphatically—that the laws of genetics were discovered by a creationist who understood the Genesis statement, 'Let them bring forth ... after their kind.'[66]

In 2007, during my visit to the US, I came to know of American developmental biologist Bruce Harold Lipton's work in promoting the idea that genes and DNA can be organized by a person's beliefs. I was presented his book *The Biology of Belief*.[67] Until recently, conventional science has held that genes control life, a concept known as genetic determinism. Bruce Lipton propagated, through his book and his research, the exciting new field of epigenetics, which reveals a completely different truth. Genes do not control life. It is the environment, and more specifically, our perception of the environment that controls gene activity. In the end, it comes down to a simple case of 'mind over matter' in controlling the fate of our lives.

Bruce Lipton's research on cloned stem cells, spread over forty years, revealed the mechanisms by which perceptions created in the mind control the lives and fate of the fifty trillion living cells that comprise our bodies. Thought processes cause the brain to release information-containing neurochemical and vibration signals that are sent to the cells. Signals sent by the brain are translated into biological responses in the cell through the action of protein 'perception' switches built into the cell's membrane. The membrane proteins that 'read' and respond to these environmental signals are called receptors.

Bruce Lipton writes in his *The Biology of Belief*,

> It was through my study of membrane receptors that I was led to an awareness that would radically transform my life. Though I sought science as an alternate to accepting spiritual truths, lessons learned from my stem cell cultures revealed that life was not an issue of science *or* spirituality; it was an amalgam of science *and* spirituality. Every thought we're thinking, every movement we make, everything around us is basically energy. Therefore, thoughts and intentions are very powerful when it comes to forming the reality we live in. Those who have been following my research on this website know that there are very dark forces trying hard to manipulate us into negativity.

When I applied these insights to the life and works of Pramukh Swamiji, I realized that the process of 'waking up' is indeed a very personal experience. A guru triggers awakening with energy, as Bruce Lipton understands energy. And this awakening, when it occurs, is as inevitable and natural as parents passing their genes on to children, in the way that Gregor Mendel explained. Once we become aware of existence through our guru—and that our true nature and the world we thought to be real is anything but what we've been told—there's no turning back.

It is by no means necessary, however, to take the lonely path of a monastic life thereafter. One can live and work in this world as an awakened professional. Through BAPS, it is happening for all walks of life. Whether it is a corporate employee who wakes up to the scam being perpetrated on humanity and pulls out of 'the matrix', or a normal taxpaying worker who realizes he is contributing to a military-industrial machine hell-bent on control and world domination, it is all awakening.

It is important that the innate spiritual nature of human beings, whether we call it social liberty or the freedom to create and manifest as we truly are, is not suppressed. It is imperative for good people to know that they are working for bad people, powers and programmes—wittingly and unwittingly. This will help them to change and improve our existing structure. I see Swaminarayan sadhus and devotees as good people performing wonderful services within their overarching societal programme, believing it can be changed constructively.

It is essential, though, to address the overarching, deceitful and destructive powers and mechanisms at play in our world. These are attempting to lower humanity to a weakened and subservient state, through health degradation, dumbed-down education, mindless 'bread and circuses', electronic media, depraved violence and sex-oriented entertainment. When I see people from various walks of life coming to do service in Swaminarayan temples, I can see an intrinsic awareness and a conscious response to the corrupted material world, elevating them regardless of the current toxic social and physical world.

The beauty of gaining a new spiritual perspective is that it puts negative influences in our environments in their place. We discover new ways to perceive our true indomitable spirit, which gives tremendous peace and confidence, in spite of what we are currently facing. It has been said that most people only embrace real change when the pain of remaining the same drives them to it, or fate leaves them no choice. In the book *Target 3 Billion*, I pointed out that while many people in the developed world are programmed for luxury, major portions of the rest of the world have been engaged in some fairly significant change, because the pain of the status quo has become intolerable.

And the status quo of our inner lives may actually be a form of escapism. We are born with an incredible intelligence, the ability to feel things intensely, and to create amazing works of art. Yet ironically, the very things that make us human make us vulnerable to losing our connection with ourselves and with the universe in which we live. Our minds create a substitute universe within which we seem to exist, and we mistakenly focus on this universe of impressions about ourselves: what we like and dislike; what we feel; who we think is good or bad, and so on.

All these things give us a sense of personal identity. They make us think that we are something unique, independent and apart from all else around us. Our thoughts, ideas and opinions shape us into what we imagine ourselves to be as human beings. And from there, we live our lives. Alone and isolated, we become commanders of ourselves, without the vision to see beyond the confines of our personal universe. We are cut off—like a fortress.

With such an attitude and limited awareness, we become impenetrable to anybody. We denounce the wisdom of others when it does not fit into the emotional framework of our lives. We choose to agree only with opinions of others who share our personal values and feelings about things, rather than investigate directly and objectively into the nature and basis of our views. And in this state of ignorance, we become subservient; we are at the mercy of the popular status quo. Our true selves become ever more lost the further we proceed in this manner, and the prospect and task of recovering ourselves become ever more distant and difficult.

Unfortunately, there is no way to perceive this reality until we are lucky enough to get a glimpse of it directly, with the help of a great teacher—one who would open a window in the fortress. And even then, we have to take what we see seriously enough: it needs to matter to us if we are going to change our world views and escape our samsaric (indefinitely ignorant and miserable) condition. So strong and ingrained are our self-created belief structures, that they blind us from seeing past them. They obscure the truth, however clearly and directly it is presented to us. The expedient methods taught by the Gunatit sadhus are very effective in treating these worldly illnesses. Each of these methods, however, requires a firm faith, an unwavering resolution and dedicated practice in order to give satisfying results. If you are strong in faith, you will achieve the same perfection of Purushottam. The Swaminarayan community is assisting in the shift of human consciousness, from that of an enslaved species to that of a liberated one. And it is indeed helping to determine our path right now: for individuals, for nations and for the entire planet.

21

The Highest Virtue Is the Intellectual Love of God

'God is a metaphor for that which transcends all levels of intellectual thought. It is as simple as that.'

– Joseph Campbell
Mythologist and author

If a stone falls from a height on someone's head and kills him, it may be inferred that the stone fell in order to kill the man. For if it did not fall to that end, God willing it, how could so many circumstances have concurred by chance? Perhaps it happened because the wind was blowing hard and the man was walking that way. But we can persist: why was the wind blowing hard at that time? Why was the man walking in that place at that time? If you answer again that the wind arose then because on the preceding day, while the weather was still calm, the sea began to toss, and that the man had been invited by a friend, we can press on—for there is no end to the questions which can be asked: but why was the sea tossing? Why was the man invited at just that time? And we may not stop asking for the causes of causes until we take refuge in the will of God.

Baruch Spinoza called this manner of imputing every phenomenon to the will of God 'the sanctuary of ignorance'. He wrote:

One who seeks the true causes of miracles, and is eager, like an educated man, to understand natural things, not to wonder at them, like a simpleton, is generally considered and denounced as an impious heretic by those whom the people honour as interpreters of nature and the Gods. For they know that if ignorance is taken away, then foolish wonder, the only means they have of arguing and defending their authority is also taken away.[68]

The breadth and importance of Spinoza's work was not fully realized until years after his death. Baruch Spinoza was a Dutch philosopher. While laying the intellectual groundwork for the modern conceptions of the self and the universe, Spinoza lived an outwardly simple life as a lens grinder, turning down rewards and honours throughout his life, including prestigious teaching positions. He gave the family inheritance to his sister. His philosophical accomplishments and moral character prompted the later French philosopher Gilles Deleuze to name him 'the "prince" of philosophers'.

Spinoza argued that God exists and is abstract and impersonal. He contended that everything that exists in the universe is one reality, and there is only one set of rules governing the whole of the reality which surrounds us and of which we are part. Spinoza viewed God and Nature as two names for the same reality. He believed God or Nature to be a single, fundamental substance; 'that which stands beneath' rather than 'matter', and that this is the basis of the universe; and all lesser 'entities' are actually modes or modifications of this basis. Further, he believed that all things are determined by Nature to exist and cause effects, and that the complex chain of cause and effect is understood only in part.

Spinoza was a thoroughgoing determinist who held that absolutely everything that happens occurs through the operation of necessity. For him, even human behaviour is fully determined, with freedom being our capacity to know that we are determined and to understand why we act as we do. So freedom is not the possibility to say 'no' to what happens to us, but the possibility to say 'yes' and fully understand why things should necessarily happen that way. By forming more 'adequate' ideas about what we do and our emotions or affections, we become the adequate cause of our effects, internal or external, which entails an increase in activity, versus passivity.[69]

Spinoza also held that everything must necessarily happen the way that it does. Therefore, humans have no free will. They believe, however, that their will is free. This illusionary perception of freedom stems from our human consciousness, experience and indifference to prior natural causes. Humans think they are free but they 'dream with their eyes open'. For Spinoza, our actions are guided entirely by natural impulses. He famously stated, 'Men are conscious of their desire and unaware of the causes by which their desires are determined.' Spinoza's determinism is ever more illuminated in his famous quote in *Ethics*:

> The infant believes that it is by free will that it seeks the breast; the angry boy believes that by free will he wishes vengeance; the timid man thinks it is with free will he seeks flight; the drunkard believes that by a free command of his mind he speaks the things which when sober he wishes he had left unsaid ... All believe that they speak by a free command of the mind, whilst, in truth, they have no power to restrain the impulse which they have to speak.[70]

For Spinoza, 'blame' and 'praise' are non-existent human ideals existing only in the mind, because we are so acclimatized to human consciousness interlinking with our experience that we have a false ideal of choice predicated upon this. In the universe, anything that happens comes from the essential nature of objects, or of God/Nature. According to Spinoza, reality is perfection. If circumstances are seen as unfortunate, it is only because of our inadequate conception of reality. While components of the chain of cause and effect are not beyond the understanding of human reason, human grasp of the infinitely complex whole is limited because of the limits of science to empirically take account of the whole sequence.

Spinoza also asserted that sense perception, though practical and useful for rhetoric, is inadequate for discovering universal truths. And Spinoza's mathematical and logical approach to metaphysics, and therefore ethics, concluded that emotion is formed from inadequate understanding. His concept of *conatus* states that human beings' natural inclination is to strive towards preserving an essential being, and to assert that virtue/human power is defined by success in this preservation of being by the guidance of reason as one's central ethical doctrine. According to Spinoza, the highest virtue is the intellectual love or knowledge of God/Nature/the Universe.

In the final part of *Ethics*, his concern with the meaning of 'true blessedness', and his explanation of how emotions must be detached from external cause and so be mastered, foreshadow psychological techniques developed in the 1900s. His concept of three types of knowledge—opinion, reason and intuition—and his assertion that intuitive knowledge provides the greatest satisfaction of mind, lead to his proposition that the more we are conscious of ourselves and Nature/Universe, the more perfect and blessed we are (in reality); that only intuitive knowledge is eternal. His unique contribution to understanding the workings of the mind is extraordinary—even during this time of radical philosophical development—in that his views provide a bridge between religions' mystical past and the psychology of the present day. Given Spinoza's insistence on a completely ordered world where 'necessity' reigns, good and evil have no absolute meaning. The world as it exists looks imperfect only because of our limited perception.[71]

The attraction of Spinoza's philosophy to late eighteenth-century Europeans was that it provided an alternative to materialism, atheism, and deism; it engendered believing in the existence of God on purely rational grounds. Three of Spinoza's ideas strongly appealed to them:

1. the unity of all that exists;
2. the regularity of all that happens;
3. the identity of spirit and nature.

Many authors have discussed similarities between Spinoza's philosophy and Eastern philosophical traditions. The nineteenth-century German Sanskritist Theodor Goldstücker was one of the early figures to notice the similarities between Spinoza's religious conceptions and the Vedanta tradition of India, writing that Spinoza's thought was:

...a western system of philosophy which occupies a foremost rank amongst the philosophies of all nations and ages, and which is so exact a representation of the ideas of the Vedanta, that we might have suspected its founder to have borrowed the fundamental principles of his system from the Hindus, did his biography not satisfy us that he was wholly unacquainted with their doctrines ... We mean the philosophy of Spinoza, a man whose very life is a picture of that moral purity and intellectual indifference to the transitory charms of this world, which is the constant longing of the true Vedanta philosopher ... comparing the fundamental ideas of both we should have no difficulty in proving that, had Spinoza been a Hindu, his system would in all probability mark a last phase of the Vedanta philosophy.[72]

Max Müller, in his lectures, noted the striking similarities between Vedanta and the system of Spinoza, saying that 'the Brahman, as conceived in the Upanishads and defined by Sankara, is clearly the same as Spinoza's "Substantia"'. Helena Blavatsky, a founder of the Theosophical Society, also compared Spinoza's religious thought to Vedanta, writing in an unfinished essay:

As to Spinoza's Deity—natura naturans—conceived in his attributes simply and alone; and the same Deity—as natura naturata or as conceived in the endless series of modifications or correlations, the direct outflowing results from the properties of these attributes, it is the Vedantic Deity pure and simple.[73]

When an author sent the book *There Is No God* to Einstein, Einstein replied that the book did not deal with the notion of God, but only with that of a personal God. He suggested that the book should be titled *There Is No Personal God*. He added further:

We followers of Spinoza see our God in the wonderful order and lawfulness of all that exists and in its soul as it reveals itself in man and animal. It is a different question whether belief in a personal God should be contested. Freud endorsed this view in his latest publication. I myself would never engage in such a task. For such a belief seems to me to lack of any transcendental outlook of life, and I wonder whether one can ever successfully render to the majority of mankind a more sublime means in order to satisfy its metaphysical needs.[74]

Baruch Spinoza was a master integrator of science and spirituality. He wrote:

> Whatever is, is in God, and nothing can be or be conceived without God. In nature there is nothing contingent, but all things have been determined from the necessity of the divine nature to exist and produce an effect in a certain way. Things could have been produced by God in no other way, and in no other order than they have been produced.[75]

I understood the meaning of Gunatit more thoroughly after studying Spinoza. A Gunatit sadhu is one who has realized that God is not some goal-oriented planner who then judges things by how well they conform to his purposes. Things happen only because of guna and its laws. God is beyond gunas—Gunatit. And a Gunatit has no end set before it. All things proceed by a certain eternal necessity of guna.

22

A Dimension As Vast As Space and As Timeless As Infinity

'That deep emotional conviction of the presence of a superior reasoning power, which is revealed in the incomprehensible universe, forms my idea of God.'

– Albert Einstein

There are many methods and belief systems that can teach us to improve our lives by doing something special with our minds. Whether it is through religious beliefs, peaceful meditations or positive human thinking, there is widespread interest in the idea that our minds can help us. Some systems teach us to peacefully contemplate thoughts, some to actively exercise thoughts, and some to clear out our thoughts and meditate on nothing at all. Many of these can be helpful.

Every mental cause and effect relationship could be considered to involve seeds of thought. In the progression of thoughts from other-worldly to concrete, each successive level can prompt the next. We will be looking to examine the earliest and most abstract seeds of thought. To think beyond images is to enter a mental realm of spiritual abstractions, of words and thoughts that may be seen only as the faintest of wisps in the mind's eye. This is where we can go to find the fundamental seeds of goodness. For the spiritual and infinite ideas to dawn on us, we have to reach beyond human beliefs and beyond finite images.

When spiritual seeds germinate mentally, they emit spiritual energy—they emit light. Thus, one gets to see new spiritual ideas as they appear just at the point of conception. Not only does this enable you to improve the beliefs that make up your sense of things, it also enables you to do it with wonder. Earlier in this book, I talked about Pythagoras, and discussed how his ideas provided the bedrock on which the entire Western philosophy was later built. It is similarly evident throughout human history that great ideas have emerged when the time was right. And cognizant of the context in which they emerged, these ideas have constituted knowledge that was essential for humanity to move on for the common good at that juncture. Mathematics is one case in point.

Perhaps another such idea was of infinite existence. In 1584, the Italian philosopher and astronomer Giordano Bruno proposed an unbounded universe in *On the Infinite Universe and Worlds*. In a statement that was revolutionary in his time, and may still seem so for some in our times, he wrote: 'Innumerable suns exist; innumerable earths revolve around these suns in a manner similar to the way the seven planets revolve around our sun. Living beings inhabit these worlds.'[76] And mathematics can be seen to be infinite. Hungarian mathematician Paul Erdos said that man can learn everything about physics and biology, but definitely not about mathematics, because mathematics is itself infinite. I discussed mathematics in detail in my book *Squaring the Circle*.

How could some people think radically and develop ideas that changed the course of human thought? Nineteenth-century Danish philosopher Sören Kierkegaard compared geniuses to thunderstorms: they go against the wind, they terrify people, and they cleanse the air. Srinivasa Ramanujan was one such thunderstorm. With almost no formal training in pure mathematics, Ramanujan made extraordinary contributions to mathematical analysis, number theory, infinite series and continued fractions.

Living in Erode, which is located on the banks of River Kaveri, about 400 kilometres south-west of Chennai, Ramanujan had no access to the larger mathematical community, which was centred in Europe at that time. He developed his own mathematical research in isolation. He was hailed a natural genius by the English mathematician G.H. Hardy, in the same league as the mathematicians such as Swiss mathematician and physicist Leonhard Euler and German mathematician Carl Friedrich Gauss. Science writer Robert Kanigel wrote a biography of Ramanujan, dubbing him 'The Man Who Knew Infinity'.

Ramanujan has been described as a religiously orthodox person with a somewhat shy and quiet disposition; he was a dignified man with pleasant manners. He lived an austere life while at Cambridge and never compromised his vegetarianism. Ramanujan credited his brilliance to his family goddess, Mahalakshmi of Namakkal. He looked to her for inspiration in his work, and claimed to dream of drops of blood that symbolized her male consort, Narasimha, after which he would receive visions of scrolls of complex mathematical content unfolding before his eyes. He often said, 'An equation for me has no meaning, unless it represents a thought of God.'

What we can learn from Ramanujan's life is that human beliefs about spiritual aspects mirror or shadow, to a limited degree, aspects of absolute or ultimate spiritual truths. Like the shadow of a man's hand that we might mistake for the real hand, human religious beliefs often have a ring of truth to them. Upon examination, however, like shadows, human beliefs will be found to be missing some dimensions when compared to their infinite originals. Nevertheless, powerful human beliefs can sometimes strike us as absolute truths. When deeper beliefs are revealed to us as we progress spiritually, we can often attach great meaning to them. It is not hard to get so wedded to an improved belief that we feel like holding on to it forever. But even the most inspired human beliefs are transitory and need to be examined and regenerated.

In daily life, we can reliably apply spiritual action at four levels— obedience, belief, understanding and knowledge. Each individual will tend to favour one specific level of action based on his or her relative stage of spiritual practice. Our individual beliefs establish the context within which we will perceive spiritual efficacy and exercise spiritual action. When a number of these levels have been brought into play, they will tend to act in series. Learning about these four levels provides a basis for understanding the patterns in which human religious beliefs form. We can also understand the stages of universal and individual spiritual evolution and the different ways individuals perceive spiritual issues.

Obedience, as a type of spiritual action, is the relationship between word and action. But the question can arise: obedience to what? This is something we have to discover. Obedience, as a type of spiritual action, first occurs to us when we relate to our spiritual ideal as a lawgiver, when we follow spiritual precepts, or when we perceive specific spiritual imperatives. Even if we are erroneous in our interpretations, a sincere desire to be obedient to good sometimes has the spiritual power to influence matters for the better.

Obedience can sometimes be exercised as an entirely internal activity. An internal commitment or resolution to obey, unaccompanied by an outward opportunity, can sometimes be as much an act of obedience—as far as the spiritual world is concerned—as an outward act. Even the desire or will to be obedient can sometimes energize the spiritual force of obedience. One thing that distinguishes obedience from the next level of spiritual action is that there may be no obvious association between our behaviour and an immediately positive outcome. And actions associated with obedience may sometimes appear to involve sacrifice.

We should remain aware, though, that obedience to any command is perilous. Obedience to good commands will unfailingly engender goodness. But the consequences of unmindful obedience range from the benign to the calamitous.

The degree to which obedience can truly be fruitful depends on identifying the proper authority, discerning directions with clarity and carrying out actions successfully. In practice, I feel that discerning directions with clarity is the most challenging of these. Without valid authority, however, the concept of obedience is at best questionable. In this sense, obedience is dependent on relationship. And although there is no necessity for authority to be vested in a person, it is hard to imagine learning spiritual obedience without having mastered human obedience.

For those of a more advanced spiritual wisdom, true authority could be experienced as awareness of spiritual law or spiritual principles, the infinite word, an infinite identity or pure inspiration. In any event, a command needs to be evaluated to see if it comes from a reliable authority. And real authority for the spiritual seeker has very little to do with what other people say or think.

The second level of spiritual action involves our beliefs. Beliefs are conclusions that we accept about our world. Our beliefs significantly comprise our sense of reality; they largely determine how we perceive and feel about our world. Beliefs form as we accept conclusions about what is true and what is real. They predispose us to expectations about outcome. Where obedience may manifest as an almost automatic response to a command, beliefs involve us in considered actions. When we imbibe beliefs in goodness that go beyond appearances, it gives us our trust and faith.

To regenerate beliefs, we must possess sound spiritual principles and reason based on those principles. To improve or expand our beliefs through spiritual understanding, we should think expansively based on the spiritual principles pertinent to the matters at hand. Thinking based on spiritual principles introduces us to the idea of science. True science involves cognition derived from established principles and conclusions of understanding that are validated in experience. Those who base their thinking on spiritual principles— and have their conclusions demonstrated in practical life—will experience their spiritual pursuits as being spiritually scientific. Their pursuits are perceived thus because of the manner in which they are conducted—and they proffer a true sense of knowing.

And when something is known or understood, this understanding is often accompanied by a brief glimmer in the mind, not unlike a faint inner visual experience; an instance of seeing: Aha! Newly understood ideas are often comprehended by being glimpsed momentarily in the mind. Since one believes what one sees—and especially when one sees one's understood thoughts—the mental seeing that results from the spiritual process of understanding can bring beliefs into accord with already established conclusions: the things seen. For this reason, an enlightened way of developing or enhancing your beliefs is to understand and perceive the operation of spiritual principles through basing your thinking on them.

The fourth level of rational spiritual action involves knowledge. Knowledge is a level of knowing that is deeper than understanding. Knowledge is not theoretical. It is an embodied sense of knowing and being. Spiritual knowledge expands and evolves as we identify with our spiritual principles, understand them, embody them, and allow them to be infinite. By acting on our best thoughts, we eliminate any sense of separation between their source and our true identity. At the level of spiritual knowledge, the source of our principles is not separate from the spiritual mind and the ego and the will that we reflect. We are open to knowledge when we are willing to recognize spiritual laws as our laws, spiritual beliefs as our beliefs, spiritual sense as our sensations, and infinite identity as our identity. We begin to encounter true knowledge when we let our spiritual principles be infinite. This level of comprehension goes beyond simply understanding the principles involved. The principles are part of what we call our identity.

Spiritual knowledge does not necessarily come from experience, but it never comes without it. Understanding and experience can work together to form knowledge. If I do not understand something, however, and then I experience it, I may still lack both understanding and knowledge. And much knowledge may appear to be beyond conceivable material experience. Look at the sky. We are not alone. The whole universe is friendly to us and conspires only to give the best to those who dream and work.

23

The Unique Throb of Life in All Creation

'Our prime purpose in this life is to help others. And if you cannot help them, at least do not hurt them.'

– Dalai Lama

I was standing near the pond at Akshardham Temple in Delhi. Pramukh Swamiji pointed towards a beautiful lotus flower and said, 'Rashtrapatiji, as a lotus flower is born in water, grows in water and rises out of water to stand above it unsoiled, so you, born in the world, raised in the world and having overcome the world, live unsoiled by the world.' I was overwhelmed with the simple adoration of Swamiji's words, which held more import for me than any other appreciation or award I had received. The lotus flower is an ancient divine symbol in India: its unfolding petals suggest the expansion of the soul; the growth of its pure beauty from the mud of its origin is a heavenly inspired metaphor.

The designer of the first helicopter and writer, Arthur Middleton Young, famously wrote, 'God sleeps in the minerals, awakens in plants, walks in animals, and thinks in man.'[77] The ground we walk on, the plants and creatures, the clouds above constantly dissolving into new formations—each gift of nature possesses its own radiant energy, bound together by cosmic harmony. In this chapter, I will discuss Sir J.C. Bose, who is best known for his ingenuity and perspicacity in the field of microwave physics, and was perhaps the first scientist in the world to understand the unique throb of life in all creation. As goes one popular song:

Can you throb to the pulse of life?
Can you let your heart pump you down long red tunnels?
Can you let your heart become the central pump house for all
    human feeling?[78]

Sir J.C. Bose turned his attention to the world of plants in the early days of the twentieth century, merging the boundaries of what had been quite separate disciplines—botany and physics—and establishing a nascent field of biophysics. In lectures at the Royal Institution and the Royal Society, he drew analogies between semiconducting electric responses in metals, plants and muscles. He declared:

Humans, animals and plants are members of a continuum of existence,
and this includes the inorganic world. There is no sharp demarcation
between the realms of the living and non-living. Life did not emerge
from lifeless matter. Rather, matter has life-like properties.[79]

Comparing his research on properties of semiconducting metals and plants, Bose reached a radical conclusion:

How can we draw a line of demarcation and say, 'here the physical
process ends and there the physiological begins'? No such barrier
exists. The responsive processes in life have been foreshadowed in
non-life. Every plant, and even the organ of every plant, is excitable
and responds to stimulus by electric response. At the source of both
the inner and outer lives is the same Mahashakti who powers the
living and the non-living, the atom and the universe.[80]

Sir J.C. Bose confirmed for me that that all science is philosophically informed. I knew, of course, that trees and plants had roots, and their stems, bark, branches and foliage reached up towards light. But I was coming to realize that the real attraction was light itself.

The evidence so far suggests that life on earth started as a single breakthrough cell after hundreds of millions of years of chemical evolution. This ancestor cell divided and diversified over the course of billions of years into the fantastic variety of organisms that we know today. We know that these had a common origin, because all cells use the same type of ribonucleic acid (RNA) and DNA molecules for their genetic material—indeed, a few genetic sequences are present in all living organisms. 'All the organic beings that have ever lived on this earth may be descended from one primordial form,' wrote Charles Darwin in *The Origin of Species*. In a real sense, all life on earth may be related as siblings and cousins, just as all humans appear to descend from a single mother.

Some of the first recognizable life forms on earth were algae, a family of simple organisms. Dutch tradesman and scientist Anton van Leeuwenhoek was the first person who observed algae growing like 'little animals'. This was in 1678. He declared: 'All life functions take place inside of cells, making them the smallest unit of life.' Two hundred years later, German botanist Matthias Schleiden and his zoologist colleague Theodore Schwann claimed: 'All living things are made up of cells.' Finally, German physician Rudolf Virchow concluded that according to his observations, it was possible 'for cells to arise only from pre-existing cells'.

Forms of algae were not only some of the first organisms. They were also crucial to establishing conditions for more advanced forms of life on earth. The primitive earth's atmosphere was probably like that of Venus and Mars: more than 95 per cent carbon dioxide, with around 3 per cent nitrogen. There would have been traces of other gases, but no free oxygen. In these conditions, only anaerobic bacteria could survive—bacteria that require no oxygen. When the cyanobacteria—blue-green algae—emerged, they completely changed the earth's atmosphere. In their respiration process, and using solar energy for photosynthesis, the blue-green algae consumed carbon dioxide and released oxygen. Eventually, free oxygen began to accumulate in the atmosphere. The ozone layer, which shields life from damaging ultraviolet radiation, was formed. The blue-green algae altered the planet far more drastically than we have done so far. Because of the continuing presence of life, earth's atmosphere is now quite different from that of the other planets. It is 77 per cent nitrogen, 21 per cent oxygen, 1 per cent water vapour, and 1 per cent argon. Carbon dioxide makes up about 550 parts per million (ppm).[81]

In addition to producing life-giving oxygen, the blue-green algae helped to regulate temperatures on the planet. Scientifically speaking, the earth was at first hot, from the energy of the collisions that formed it. As the planet cooled, the carbon dioxide and methane released by the earliest bacteria acted as greenhouse gases, keeping temperatures high enough for life. But then the sun gradually began to increase its output. The blue-green algae mitigated the effect of the powerful sun: they consumed carbon dioxide and gave off oxygen. Carbon dioxide and methane levels in the atmosphere dropped, reducing the greenhouse effect, so the earth's temperature did not rise substantially. Life also kept the water it needed on earth. Hydrogen—the major component of water—is a light gas; it would have evaporated out to space without living processes to bind it, leaving the planet as arid as Mars.

Life even altered geology. Free oxygen combined with iron in the sea and on land, creating iron oxides and other mineral deposits. The skeletal remains of sea creatures, deposited as ocean-floor sediments, became chalk and limestone. Other organic remains became coal and oil. Together, life and non-life on earth created what British environmentalist James Lovelock has called Gaia, after the Greek goddess of earth. Gaia was the great mother of all: creator and giver of birth to the earth and all the heavenly gods; the Titans and the giants were born to her.

James Lovelock conceptualized Gaia as an integrated system linking together plants, animals, bacteria, rocks, oceans and the atmosphere in a unity that shapes the planet and maintains life on earth. Even the major elements of life—carbon, oxygen and nitrogen—pass, in turn, through air, plant and animal life, soil, water and the earth's crust, in cycles lasting hundreds of millions of years. We are one with the planet and with all life.

Seen as a system, Gaia is not a single organism but a community: a living, breathing community of all living beings evolving in harmony with their non-living environment. She is crafted, like a statue, by a mixture of creativity and discipline. As in evolution, the creativity comes from genetic mutation and sexual reproduction; the discipline comes from natural selection adapting organisms to their environment.

There are limits to Gaia's powers. She cannot keep at bay the chills and fevers of glacial and interglacial periods. She could not cope with a massive increase in the sun's size, which will happen when the sun becomes a red giant in a few billion years' time. She might not survive a massive meteoric impact on the earth or the explosion of a nearby supernova. And she may not be able to endure the damage we are inflicting on her.

Gaia nurtures life in general—not any particular form of life. In the past 600 million years, she has presided over five major mass extinctions, which saw many kinds of animals like dinosaurs and ammonites disappear. The Permian extinction wiped out between 75 and 90 per cent of all species. But life went on, and the niches left by extinct species filled with new families of living creatures.

Gaia functioned well as long as she functioned autonomously and automatically. She had no mind, no planetary brain. She worked by the creativity of matter and life, weaving webs of interdependence. It was when she acquired a brain, in the shape of human intelligence and technology, that things began to go wrong.

Humans do not have the science or wisdom to control Gaia. But we do have science and technology powerful enough to inflict serious damage on her. Already we are making a disturbing impact on most ecosystems, and on three of Gaia's four major zones: the biosphere, the hydrosphere and the atmosphere. In the long term, the impact of our actions will also feed through to the lithosphere and alter the earth's geology. So we are not Gaia's mind in any wonderful, mystical sense; we are not guiding her on to new heights she could never reach without us. We are a very dysfunctional sort of mind. Like the mind of a heavy-drinking, drug-abusing, chain-smoking glutton, we harm ourselves and our 'body', Gaia, by overconsuming and polluting.

Since the invention of agriculture, we have been destroying local ecosystems and biodiversity. But it is only in the twentieth century that we have begun to interfere in some of the most basic elements of the Gaia process. About half a century ago, we began using chlorofluorocarbons (CFCs), chemicals that were believed to be totally harmless. It was only in 1985 that we discovered that they were destroying the protective ozone layer. This is increasing human skin cancer. It may also be reducing the yield of crops. And it may be adversely affecting the growth of plankton, a crucial source of food to many large aquatic organisms, and through that causing detriment to oceanic ecosystems and processes.

Even more detrimentally, we are disrupting Gaia's mechanisms for temperature control—especially by increasing the levels of carbon dioxide and methane in the atmosphere. Coal and oil were formed from plant remains millions of years ago. By mining and burning them as our main energy source, we are increasing carbon dioxide in the atmosphere, from a pre-industrial level of 280 parts per million (ppm), to 360 ppm in 1995 and 550 parts per million in 2015. Our 1,300 million cattle, our 250 million hectares of irrigated fields—and our countless rubbish heaps—have more than doubled methane in the atmosphere from a natural level of 700 parts per billion (ppb) to 1,600 ppb in 1995 and 1800 ppb in 2015.

Projections by the Intergovernmental Panel on Climate Change (IPCC) suggest that global temperatures may rise between one degree Celsius and four degrees Celsius by the end of the next century, based on present trends. This change will raise sea levels. It will shift ecological zones, change rainfall patterns, and produce massive disruptions in agriculture. As always, Gaia will do her best to cope. Even in the worst case scenario, life in some lowly form will probably endure. But many plant and animal species, unable to adapt quickly enough, will perish. We may be one of them. There was a poet, who once wrote:

> You cannot pluck a little flower
> Without the shaking of a star.[82]

All life is one. There is one common consciousness, which links the life of all beings into one great cosmic unity. There will be consequences whenever we damage one thing or violate another thing. British environmental writer Paul Harrison beautifully expressed our urgent need to change:

When our era was young, we believed as children believe. Now we are adults, it is time to put away childish things. It is time to adopt a religion that embraces the space age, and that supports our love of nature and our efforts to preserve the earth.[83]

Mark Hopkins—chairman of the executive committee, National Space Society, USA—and I have long shared humanity's dream of all nations living together in prosperity and peace. We envision a world moving forward, through global collaboration in space, to meet the challenges that now face our planet earth. We are conscious that all nations have to strive to make our planet liveable again. This, after centuries of devastation of its environment and ecosystems and rapid depletion of its precious mineral resources, including fossil fuels and fresh water. We hope our international collaborative mission will act as a catalyst for a liveable planet, which will promote prosperity and peaceful relations within and between nations.

24

God Is the Source of the Universe

'Where your talents and the needs of the world cross, there lies your purpose.'

– Aristotle
Pre-Christian Greek philosopher and scientist

At some moment, all matter in the universe was contained in a single point, which is considered the genesis of the universe. A 'big bang' occurred, causing expansion of energy and converting it to matter. The majority of atoms that were produced by the big bang were hydrogen, along with helium and traces of lithium. Modern calculations place this moment at approximately 13.82 billion years ago. God is a unique force; God caused the big bang and created the universe for some purpose. God is not a religious idea but the supreme force beyond all that exists. We are nothing but a part of a dynamic universe beyond our comprehension, and there is a God even beyond the universe.

There is Hiranyagarbha, one of the creation hymns in the Rig Veda:

हिरण्यगर्भ समवर्तताग्रे: भूतस्य जतस्य जात: पतिरेक आसीत ।
स दाधार पृथिवीं ध्यामुतेमां कस्मै देवाय हविषा विधेम ।।

Born with fire in its womb
There was ocean here and there and up and below woken as the only life
Which God like that should we pray to with sacrifices?

There is a hadith on the authority of Abu Dharr, who asked Prophet Muhammad (peace be upon him):

'Did you see the God?'
The Prophet said, 'He is a Light; how could I see Him?'[84]

Scientifically speaking, after the initial expansion following the big bang—which would have been a burst of light—the universe cooled sufficiently to allow the formation of subatomic particles, including protons, neutrons and electrons. Stars evolved from cosmic gas clouds in a fierce and complex battle between gravity and internal gas pressure. In this maelstrom, the density of the gas increased due to its own gravitational pull. This caused the gas to heat up; as a consequence the pressure rose, and the compression process came to a halt. If the gas managed to shed the resulting thermal energy, compression could continue and a new star was born.[85]

The solar system began forming about 4.6 billion years ago, or about nine billion years after the big bang. A molecular cloud made mostly of hydrogen and traces of other elements began to collapse, forming a large sphere in the centre, which would become the sun, as well as a surrounding disc. This surrounding accretion disc would coalesce into a multitude of smaller objects that would later become planets, asteroids and comets. The sun is a late-generation star, and the solar system incorporates matter created by previous generations of stars. Indian-American astrophysicist Subrahmanyan Chandrasekhar won the 1983 Nobel Prize for physics for his mathematical theory that led to the currently accepted theory on the later evolutionary stages of massive stars.

Everything that starts must end—including our solar system, and indeed, the universe itself. What will happen to the universe? There is no single definitive model of the universe. I rest my belief in Albert Einstein's theory—that the universe is following an eternal series of oscillations, each beginning with a big bang and ending with a big crunch—till such time as a consensus to the contrary emerges on this issue. According to this theory, the universe will continue to expand until the gravitational attraction of matter causes it to collapse inwards and bounce back again. This would occur on a timescale which is almost unimaginable to us.

In contemplating the universe, it is very important to realize the smallness of our being. Our existence is ineffably minuscule and insignificant! What we see around us is but a small part of the colossal reality. Our place in the universe is like a speck of sand in the Thar Desert. Before we attempt to contemplate the grand design, let us get a sense of the vastness of the universe. Light would take less than the tenth of a second to go around the earth. But the approximate diameter of the universe is perhaps 500 billion light years!

The sun is a relatively small star, yet it can hold around 1.3 million earths. Betelgeuse, a red giant star about 640 light years from earth, could accommodate about 1,000 suns across its diameter. For the purpose of understanding, if the sun is the size of an orange, on that scale, the earth is a grain of sand circling in an orbit around it at a distance of about 10 metres. And on the same scale, the nearest star to the sun, a star called Alpha Centauri, is 2,000 kilometres away. And again in the same scale, a galaxy can be visualized as a cluster of oranges, (which is actually thirty million kilometres in diameter), where an average distance of 3,000 kilometres separates each orange.

In all major religious traditions the sun is seen as the source of all life. This is true in the sense that the earth exists because the sun exists. Every life form on earth derives its sustenance from the light energy radiated by the sun. The sun's core consists of plasma—gas so hot that it has become completely ionized, and its atoms stripped of their electrons. At these temperatures, the protons of hydrogen nuclei are moving so rapidly that they overcome their mutual repulsion and collide to form helium nuclei. This type of reaction is called nuclear fusion. In the sun, in every second, 600 million tonnes of hydrogen atoms are converted into helium, generating 4×10^{22} megawatts of energy emitted as light.

Extrapolating into the future, in 1.1 billion years from now, the sun will be 10 per cent brighter than it is today. The extra energy will cause a moist greenhouse effect. Eventually, the earth's atmosphere will dry out, as the water vapour is lost to space and would never return. In

3.5 billion years from now, the sun will be 40 per cent brighter than it is today. It will be so hot that the oceans would boil and the resulting water vapour would be lost to space as well. The ice caps would long have permanently melted, and snow would be ancient history; life would be unsustainable anywhere on the surface of the earth. The earth will resemble dry, hot Venus.[86]

In about six billion years, the sun's core will run out of hydrogen. The inert helium ash built up in the core will become unstable and collapse under its own weight. This will cause the core to heat up and get denser. The sun will grow in size and enter the red giant phase of its evolution. The expanding sun will consume the orbits of Mercury and Venus, and probably gulp up the earth as well. Even if the earth survives, the intense heat from the red giant sun will scorch our planet and make it absolutely impossible for any semblance of life to exist.

The burning helium of the sun will then form carbon. This phase will last for about 100 million years until this source of fuel is exhausted. Finally, the shell of helium will become unstable, causing the sun to pulse violently. It will blow off a large fraction of its atmosphere into space over the course of several pulses. When the sun has blasted off its outer layers, all that will remain will be the central core of carbon. In fact, it will be an earth-sized diamond with the mass of a star, slowly cooling down for trillions of years.

Subrahmanyan Chandrasekhar estimates the maximum size of a stable white dwarf to be approximately 3×10^{30} kilograms, which is about 1.4 times the mass of the sun. Stars with mass higher than the Chandrasekhar limit ultimately collapse under their own weight and become neutron stars or black holes. Stars with a mass below this limit are prevented from collapsing by the pressure of degeneracy of their electrons.

Studying the universe is an awe-inspiring experience as profound as studying God. For in studying the universe, we are contemplating God's work. And studying God is indeed a balancing act. At times the theologian has to hold his breath, as it were, and suspend his sense of the sacred in order to understand deep truths. But he should also spend time on his knees—perhaps both mentally and literally—

revelling in the presence of God as he studies God's attributes. It is fascinating to look at examples of fine-tuning in the universe. We can see in every detail of the universe, the evidence for the existence of God. Logical analysis of physical constants requires a good deal of spiritual breath holding.[87]

No one would know better the mystery of human life than Francis Collins, the first director of the National Human Genome Research Institute and now director of the National Institute of Health (NIH), USA. Collins has led the effort to decode human DNA, and has, in the process, developed a revolutionary method of screening genes for disease. He said so eloquently: 'That God is a God who both created the universe, and also had a plan that included me as an individual human being. The evidence supporting the idea that all living things are descended from a common ancestor is truly overwhelming.'[88]

Francis Collins writes in *The Language of God: A Scientist Presents Evidence for Belief*:

> If God chose to create you and me as natural and spiritual beings, and decided to use the mechanism of evolution to accomplish that goal, I think that's incredibly elegant. And because God is outside of space and time, He knew what the outcome was going to be right at the beginning. It's not as if there was a chance it wouldn't work. So where, then, is the discordance that causes so many people to see these views of science and of spirit as being incompatible? In me, they both exist. They both exist at the same moment in the day. They are not compartmentalized. They are entirely compatible. And they are part of who I am.[89]

Nonetheless, science is the only reliable way to understand the natural world, and its tools when properly utilized can generate dazzling insights into material existence. But science is powerless to answer questions such as 'Why did the universe come into being?', 'What is the meaning of human existence?', and 'What happens after we die?'. One of the strongest motivations of humankind is to seek answers to profound questions, and we need to bring all the power of both the scientific and spiritual perspectives to bear on understanding what is both seen and unseen.

There is indeed no conflict in being a rigorous scientist and a person who believes in a God who takes a personal interest in each one of us. Science's domain is to explore nature. God's domain is in the spiritual world, a realm inexplorable with the tools and language of science. It must be examined with the heart, the mind and the soul— and the mind must find a way to embrace both realms.

I have worked with many scientists, practising multiple faiths. Some of my colleagues have been atheists. I had a sense that if you are going to accept the existence of God, at some level you have to give up control, and you cannot just do what you want to because it feels good. And I liked very much being in control. When one recognizes the desire to have a relationship with God, one also has to come face-to-face with one's own massive imperfections. If you can see God in some way as a mirror to yourself, you realize just how far you fall short of anything that you could be really proud of. And this can initially be a terribly distressing experience for anybody.

God had a plan to create creatures with whom He could have fellowship: in whom He could inspire the moral law; in whose souls He could be infused, and whom He would give free will to make decisions about their own behaviour—a gift which is oftentimes misused. God is unique in giving His people ways for fellowship, to witness and to remember what a mighty and merciful God He is. My fellowship with Pramukh Swamiji is testimony to this.

In the fourth and concluding part of this book, I will discuss creative leadership as the engine of change. Creative leaders are not born. They are the product of particular circumstances and conditions; they evolve to bring change for the better. I have enumerated eight facets of creative leadership, namely—fearlessness, courage, ethical living, non-violence, forgiveness, compassion, vision and cooperation. I will also share the stories of Nachiketa, Abdul Qadir , Abraham Lincoln, Thiruvalluvar, Mahatma Gandhi, Nelson Mandela, the Dalai Lama, Vikram Sarabhai and Verghese Kurien, who epitomize these facets.

PART FOUR

EVOLUTION OF CREATIVE LEADERSHIP

'A leader is best when people barely know he exists, when his work is done, his aim fulfilled, they will say: we did it ourselves.'

– Lao Tzu
Philosopher and poet of ancient China

25

A Fearless Look into the Face of All Facts

'Be truthful, gentle, and fearless.'

– Mahatma Gandhi

In the fourth and concluding part of this book, I will be sharing what I learned during my fellowship with Pramukh Swamiji on leadership. He is a great spiritual leader, and while observing his actions in leading the BAPS across the world, I have developed certain insights into how a great leader evolves. Leadership has been defined in many ways, depending on the organizational context in which it exists. These contexts could be political, military, business, spiritual, intellectual, adventures, sports, the arts or other fields of human endeavour. Of all the definitions that can be found in literature, I would like to describe a creative leadership process, in its essence, as the capacity for getting people to follow you to accomplish a *shared* objective.

Whatever financial resources, technology or strategy we employ in conducting our business, the results are delivered ultimately by people. More and more, it is being recognized that leadership—the process of getting people to follow you and getting the job done—is a critical management function. The eight chapters in this part will help you to discover the essence of true leadership, and the qualities and skills that help you become an effective leader. I will start with the quality of fearlessness, which I consider to be the foundation of the edifice of leadership. If a leader is not fearless, his mission is bound to crumble during crises, as a building with weak foundations would collapse during storms, floods and earthquakes.

Nachiketa is the child protagonist in an ancient Hindu fable about the attributes of the soul and Brahman. The story is told in the *Katha Upanishad*. At the end of the yajna in Nachiketa's time, it was customary to donate cows to the temple. Nachiketa noticed that his father, a miser, was giving offerings of old, barren, blind and lame cows, none of which yielded any milk. This disturbed Nachiketa. He asked his father, 'I too am yours, to which god will you offer me?' This made his father angry, but he decided not to say anything. Nachiketa repeated his question. Stung by his son's reproach, his father answered in a rage, 'I give you to Yama'—the god of Death.

An obedient boy, Nachiketa followed his father's command and went to Yama's home, but the god was out. Nachiketa waited three days at his doorstep without food or water. When Yama returned, he was sorry to see that a child had been waiting for so long without hospitality. To compensate for his embarrassment, Yama granted Nachiketa three boons. Nachiketa first asked for peace for his father and himself. Yama agreed. Next, Nachiketa wished to learn the sacred fire sacrifice, to which Yama also consented. For his third boon, Nachiketa asked to learn the mystery of what comes after death.

Yama was most reluctant on this; after all, this mystery had not even been revealed to the gods. He asked Nachiketa to ask for some other boon, and offered many material inducements. Yama even offered him the happiness of heaven. But Nachiketa would not relent. He told Yama that material things would last only for a brief while. And he who has encountered death personally, how could he desire anything else? Yama was quietly pleased with Nachiketa's fearlessness and resolution in seeking spiritual knowledge, and elaborated on the soul, atma, which persists beyond death. He explained that the soul of each person, or the divine breath, is inseparable from Brahman, the supreme spirit, the vital force in the universe.

Swami Vivekananda famously said, 'If I get ten or twelve boys with the faith of Nachiketa, I can turn the thoughts and pursuits

of this country in a new channel.' Pramukh Swamiji considers the
fearlessness in Nachiketa as the biggest virtue in a child. Swaminarayan
Akshardham complex in Gandhinagar hosts the Sat-Chit-Anand
water-laser show on the Nachiketa story for its visitors every evening.
When I saw the show, I recalled the beautiful lines of Gurudev
Rabindranath Tagore:

> Let me not pray to be sheltered from dangers,
> but to be fearless in facing them.
> Let me not beg for the stilling of my pain, but
> for the heart to conquer it.[90]

Another brave young soul was nine-year-old Abdul Qadir, who
left his widowed mother in the hinterlands of fourteenth-century
Iraq to get an education, joining a caravan going to Baghdad. The
caravan reached a city in Hamdaan safely. When it left from there
and headed for a mountainous region, sixty bandits attacked, the
leader of whom was Ahmed Badwi. The people in the caravan did not
possess the strength to fight them, and the robbers snatched all their
valuables, and sat down to distribute the loot amongst themselves.
Abdul Qadir was standing peacefully on one side. One of the robbers
asked him if he had anything valuable with him. Abdul Qadir told
him fearlessly: 'Yes, I have forty dinars.' The robber did not believe
him and walked away. Another robber asked him the same question,
and Abdul Qadir gave the same reply. This robber also disbelieved
him, and walked off, laughing.

The second robber went to Ahmed Badwi and showed him the
looted articles. He mentioned the words of Abdul Qadir, and the
leader told him to bring the child before him. Abdul Qadir was
taken to the leader of the robbers. Ahmed Badwi asked him, 'Tell
me the truth, do you have anything valuable?' Abdul Qadir replied,
'Yes! I have already told your soldiers that I have forty dinars.' The
leader of the robbers asked, 'Where are they?' Abdul Qadir replied,
'They are stitched into my clothes under my armpits.' The leader of
the robbers checked and found the dinars there. He was shocked by
the boldness and bravery of this young boy, and was stunned to see

that the young boy was so fearless and confident in communicating the truth to him.

Ahmed Badwi asked Abdul Qadir, 'Who made you so brave?' Abdul Qadir said, 'When I was leaving home, my respected mother advised me to always speak the truth and not to lie. Why would I disregard the advice of my mother for forty dinars?' Ahmed Badwi felt the impact of these words. His hardened heart melted, and tears gushed forth from his eyes, cleansing the darkness and evil that was in his heart. He said, 'O child! You obeyed the advice and words of your mother so obediently, and I have been disobeying the commands of God for so long.' After saying this, he cried for so long that he was inconsolable. Ahmed Badwi fell at the feet of Abdul Qadir and repented from a life of robbery and torment. Upon seeing their leader, his men also fell at the feet of Abdul Qadir and said to their leader, 'You were our leader when we were robbing people, now you are our leader in repentance as well.' The courageous child Abdul Qadir later grew to become al-Qutb ar-Rabbani (Lordly Cardinal Pole), Hazrat Sheikh Abdul Qadir Jilani, may God be well pleased with him.[91]

Nothing in life is to be feared. It is only to be understood. In his classic 1937 book *Think and Grow Rich*, Napoleon Hill identified six basic fears, of which—either singly or in a combination—every human suffers at one time or another. Most people are fortunate if they do not suffer from the entire six. Named in the order of their most common appearance, they are: the fear of poverty, the fear of criticism, the fear of ill health, the fear of loss of love of someone, the fear of old age, and the fear of death. Napoleon Hill said, 'All other fears are of minor importance; they can be grouped under these six headings.'[92]

The six fears by themselves are self-explanatory. They follow a common thread in terms of consequences. Let us take the fear of poverty, which Napoleon Hill believes to be the most destructive of the six basic fears, as an example. He spells out that this fear hinders the faculty of reason, destroys imagination, undermines enthusiasm, leads to uncertainty of purpose, encourages procrastination, and diverts effort. It also kills love and other finer emotions, destroys friendship and leads to sleeplessness, misery and much unhappiness.

Fears are nothing more than states of mind. One's state of mind is subject to control and direction. Man can create nothing which he does not first conceive in the form of an impulse of thought. Following this statement is another of still greater importance—namely, man's thought impulses begin immediately to translate themselves into their physical equivalent, whether those thoughts are voluntary or involuntary. Thought impulses which are picked up my mere chance and thoughts which have been released by other minds, may determine one's financial, business, professional or social destiny, just as surely as do the thought impulses which one creates by intent and design.

We need to make some conscious decisions to overcome our fears. Fear of poverty can be handled by being at peace with whatever wealth you can accumulate without worry. This does not mean that you shun hard work, but that you no longer grasp, hoard and cling senselessly to money. Fear of criticism can be handled by deciding for yourself that you will not fear what others have to say about your decisions. Do what your intuition tells you; be guided by your higher purpose. Refuse to treat old age as a handicap. Instead, leverage your wisdom, experience and insight for success. Concentrate your mind on being well. And do not be reckless about your health; actively care for your body. Be comfortable even if you are without a partner. Be at peace even if you do not have love. You may be alone, but you are not lonely. Fill your days productively. And above all, accept that death is inevitable. If you are merely transiting from one form to another in death, then what is there to fear? Rabindranath Tagore summed it up so nicely, 'Death is not extinguishing the light; it is only putting out the lamp because the dawn has come.'[93]

In addressing your fears, you should ask yourself: 'What kind of leader will I be? The kind who can rally the troops and take an organization forward in uncertain times, or the kind who, paralysed by fear and uncertainty, lets opportunities go by and allows threats to manifest?' How can you tell which kind of leader you are? Ask yourself these three questions. The first question is: Do you have a reliable reality check? Fearless leaders need someone or something to force them to avoid denial. Often, people pretend they do not know something, and sometimes they create a story that explains away or rationalizes an unpleasant reality. Such people do not go very far in their missions. Once you face the truth, you should be able to take some action in response. Your reality check should not only show you what the truth is but ask, 'What are you going to do about it?'

The second question is: Can you take quick and decisive action, even if it is uncomfortable? Good leaders move very quickly. You need to learn to act despite any discomfort. Though many leaders take a sense of comfort as an indication that everything is okay, we suggest it to be the exact opposite. If you are completely comfortable, you should start asking, 'Where are the areas that I can move out of the comfort zone to advance the project?'

The third question is: Can you accept responsibility when things go wrong without self-recrimination or blame? There are leaders who lob every problem over the wall to make it someone else's fault—it is the employees' fault, it is operations' fault, it is the market's fault, and so on. And there are those who even do not blame others for their missteps, but get hopelessly caught up in self-recrimination. Shame can result in a self-critical paralysis. The right way is neither blaming nor self-recriminatory. Fearless leaders can recognize a problem without blaming themselves or anyone else. Instead, they look in the mirror and say, 'I have contributed to this in some way. So now I am going to do this to fix it.'

There is a prayer in Atharva Veda (XIX, 15:6) that defines fearlessness most comprehensively:

अभयं मित्रादभयममित्रादभयं ज्ञातादभयं परो यः ।
अभयं नक्तमभयं दिवा नः सर्वा आशा मम मित्रं भवन्तु ।।

May we be fearless, from friends and enemies, from known and
    unknown.
From night and day, may all the directions be our allies.

A good leader knows that suffering acute temporary fear while speaking the truth is easier to overcome than enduring the perpetual fear of the unspoken truth. When I reflect upon the life of

Pramukh Swamiji, I feel that he has been a captain of his heart, mind and soul. He has hurled himself off the shores of apparent truth to venture deep into the realms of his inner truth, to be genuine and at peace with who he really is. He had abandoned the pretence of living up to the expectations of others, and personified what it means to be truly and completely Gunatit.

26

What Prevented You from Prostrating When I Commanded You?

'It was pride that changed angels into devils; it is humility that makes men as angels.'

– Saint Augustine
Fourth-century Christian theologian and philosopher

In the interlocking civilizations of ancient Greece and ancient Rome in the classical period of antiquity, a person would be chosen to make predictions or utter divine revelations of the future, inspired by the gods. This person, called the oracle, was thought to be a portal through which the gods spoke directly to people. Any priestess throughout the history of the Temple of Apollo at Delphi, was given the name Pythia.

Delphi is a sacred place on the south-western spur of Mount Parnassus in the valley of Phocis in Greece. The legend is that Zeus determined the site of Delphi when he sought to find the centre of his Gaia, the Grandmother Earth. He sent two eagles flying from the eastern and western extremities, and the path of the eagles crossed over Delphi, where the navel of Gaia was found.

When Chaerephon, the friend of Socrates, visited the temple of Apollo, he asked the oracle at Delphi if anyone were wiser than Socrates. The oracle responded that no one was wiser. Chaerephon, upon his return to Athens, told this to everyone. Socrates, however, considered the oracle's response a paradox, as he believed he possessed no wisdom whatsoever. But it was not easy to brush aside the oracle's proclamation.

Socrates therefore proceeded to test the riddle by approaching men considered wise by the people of Athens—statesmen, poets and artisans—in order to refute the pronouncement made by the oracle. Questioning them, Socrates concluded that while each man thought he knew a great deal and was wise, in fact they all knew very little and were not wise at all. Socrates realized the oracle was correct: while so-called wise men thought themselves wise and yet were not, he himself knew he was not wise at all. Paradoxically, this made him the wisest, since he was the only person aware of his own ignorance. Socrates then declared that moral excellence was more a matter of divine bequest.[94]

Pramukh Swamiji is a living example of Socratic wisdom. I learnt from him that while our bodies have five senses—touch, smell, taste, sight and hearing—not to be overlooked are the qualities of our souls: intuition, peace, foresight, trust and empathy. The differences between people lie in their use of these qualities; most people barely know anything about the inner qualities, while a few people rely on them just as they rely on their physical senses; and in fact, probably even more.

I learned early in my life the importance of walking the path of truth. There are only two mistakes one can make along the path of truth: not going all the way, and not starting. During my Arabic classes as a child I learned about Iblis or Satan. What is Satan's role vis-à-vis man? Does Satan have overwhelming power over man, so much so that the latter cannot walk the path of submission to, and harmony with, the will of God?

The Holy Quran talks about Iblis as a physical being made of fire. He is portrayed as a rebellious creature, basking in the glory of the matter he was made of and showing arrogance to man, who was made of clay. Iblis held this grudge against man. He asked God to grant him immortality in this life, so that he could concentrate on his vendetta against man. His objective in this is to topple man from the lofty station that God has put him in and rouse in him the struggle between good and evil. He spares no effort in tempting man to incline

towards doing what would in the end spell disaster for his being, by
dampening down man's spirit and weakening his position with God.

While God granted Iblis his wish, it was made abundantly clear
to him and to us, the human beings, that the power of Iblis does not
go beyond luring us towards disobedience to God and committing
vile acts. There is, by no means, any direct authority that empowers
Iblis to exercise force, coercion and repression on man. Indeed, it is
the type of man who chooses to embark on unbelief, waywardness,
cheapening his faith and not experiencing a sense of enmity to Iblis,
who gives Iblis sway over him. In contrast, the person who chooses the
path of belief does not usually give Iblis any chance to manipulate him
because of the strength of his belief.

إِنَّ عِبَادِي لَيْسَ لَكَ عَلَيْهِمْ سُلْطَانٌ وَكَفَى بِرَبِّكَ وَكِيلاً

As for My servants, no authority shall you have over them: Enough is
your Lord for a Disposer of affairs (Holy Quran: 17.65).

Iblis is a matter of the unseen, which we have come to know about
from God through what He revealed to His prophets. Iblis has no
power to exert on man, apart from trying to mislead him by way
of devilish insinuations and creating tempting conditions for man
to commit what is vile. Man, on the other hand, has been endowed
with a conscious intellect that can draw the line between good and
evil and perceive divine messages with clarity. This clears all the roads
to acquiring the necessary knowledge leading to God's way. Man has
also been graced with a strong will that helps in the process of sound
decision making and walking with firm steps on the right path.

This is what makes the struggle between man and Iblis an equal
contest. In this fight, man has the freedom to make correct choices
amidst evil inclinations, tempting scenarios and infernal suggestions.
And he has the means of willpower, intellect and conviction to emerge
victorious from this stand-off, without giving in to weakness or
failure. Moreover, the Holy Quran arouses in the minds of believers
the strength of conviction that is capable of defeating all the forces of

evil. As for those who fall victim to Iblis's temptations, their failure is not due to any intrinsic weakness but rather, it is because they have contributed to paralysing—and eventually neutralizing—the powers at their disposal.

In this light, we should now know that lengthening Satan's reign till the Day of Judgement, and giving him the freedom to seduce man—who is armed with all the weapons necessary to put up a determined fight—are a sign of God's confidence in man. This is so that man should be able to choose his destiny on account of his will and capability, and not because of coercion and repression, because that could weaken his resolve and make him buckle. Furthermore, allowing man to exercise his will and capability makes him stronger. And the judicious expression of will and capability are the hallmarks of one who is the master of his own destiny and who makes events subservient to his willpower and choice.

The life of Abraham Lincoln exemplifies a judicious will inspired by God in times of moral crisis. Abraham Lincoln was a deeply spiritual man who never embraced organized religion. Dogma repelled him; he preferred to embody his beliefs rather than recite them. I saw, in the National Cathedral in Washington DC, a statue of a genuflecting Abraham Lincoln. The statue's kneeling posture is a moving and apt depiction of genuine piety; its pose represents the truest form of moral leadership.

In 1862, Lincoln's life took a dramatic turn. The civil war was not going well for the Union, and Lincoln was being savaged in both the Yankee and the Confederate press. His son Willie died suddenly. His wife was suffering from mental instability and chronic depression. All this, and yet another devastating Union defeat, at the second Battle of Manassas, were more than any lesser mortal could have endured. There were no easy answers. He became convinced that blame for the war lay on both sides. What kept him from disengaging or capitulating was the godly foundation of his inherent pragmatism. This endowed his life with purpose. He told a friend:'When everyone seemed panic-stricken, I got down on my knees before Almighty God and prayed. Soon a sweet comfort crept into my soul.'95

Lincoln took no joy in his own innate scepticism. He wrote, 'I was more devout than I am.' His absence of belief did not lead to irreverence. Lincoln's struggle with the mystery of the unseen gave ballast to his outlook. While alienated by confessional church life, Lincoln steadfastly believed that a divine purpose was at work, shaping human events. The Bible was his favourite book, and his speeches and letters were sprinkled with biblical allusions and phrases.

In his second inaugural address, delivered on 4 March 1865, a weary but resolute Lincoln longed for peace. 'Fondly do we hope, fervently do we pray, that this mighty scourge of war may speedily pass away.' He wondered aloud why the war had lasted so long and been so brutal. Lincoln noted the paradoxical irony of both sides in the civil war praying to God and appealing for divine support against the other. The God of judgement, however, would not be misled or denied. Lincoln declared:

> If God willed that the war continue until every drop of blood drawn with the lash, shall be paid with another drawn by the sword, as was said 3,000 years ago, so still it must be said the judgments of God are true and righteous altogether.[96]

Ralph Waldo Emerson expressed this so beautifully:

> If the red slayer thinks he slays,
> Or if the slain think he is slain,
> They know not well the subtle ways
> I keep, and pass, and turn again.[97]

Just like Abraham Lincoln, we suffer scepticism and spiritual qualms; we are beset by doubts and inner and outer troubles. And we are constantly building and demolishing our own mental house. But instead of making and breaking our house in distress, perhaps—just as Abraham Lincoln did in his most trying moments—we should get down on our knees and pray to the Almighty. If we can empty our minds—make them calm and quiet—then God's path will emerge before us. The easiest way for us to know God's will is to become the instrument and not the artisan. If we become only the instrument for carrying out God's plans, God's will can start acting in and through us. God does the acting and He is the action. He is everything. We only observe. A failure here will bring us to the same question on the Day of Judgement that Iblis faced on the day of creation, 'What Prevented You From Prostrating When I Commanded You?'

How do you know if you are executing God's will or if you are fulfilling your own ego? When you are fulfilling the demands of the ego, you are bloated with pride. Always, there will be a feeling of superiority when the ego is fulfilled. But when you execute the will of God, the question of superiority or inferiority does not arise. At that time, you feel only your oneness. You feel that God has appointed you or that God has accepted you as His chosen instrument, and that He is acting in and through you. No matter what you achieve, even if it is something very grand, extraordinary or unusual, you will not have any sense of personal pride. On the contrary, you will feel extremely grateful to God that He has chosen to fulfil Himself in and through you. There will be no pride; but only a feeling of expansion.

Self-giving to God's Will
Is, without fail,
A slow-ripening
But most delicious fruit.

The Irish author C.S. Lewis wrote in *The Problem of Pain,* 'For you will certainly carry out God's purpose, however you act, but it makes a difference to you whether you serve like Judas or like John.'[98] In the company of Pramukh Swamiji I have realized the transforming power of one's pious conduct upon others. Swamiji seldom gives orders; he doesn't command, argue, reprimand or persuade. He lives immersed in the Divine. His millions of devotees and well-wishers believe in him, as we believe that the sun has risen—not only because we see it, but also because by it we see everything else.

27

Purity Is the Feminine, Truth the Masculine Forms of Divinity

'Purity of speech, of the mind, of the senses, and of a compassionate heart are needed by one who desires to rise to the divine platform.'

– Chanakya

Two seas and an ocean—the Bay of Bengal, the Arabian Sea and the Indian Ocean—meet at Kanyakumari, the southernmost tip of the Indian peninsula. Atop a small island there stands a 40-metre-tall stone sculpture of the Tamil poet and philosopher Thiruvalluvar, author of the *Thirukkural*. In the Tamil language, Thiru is an honorific prefix; it is given to the author Valluvar and his book, which was composed in the second century BC.

Nothing, except folklore, is known about the life of Thiruvalluvar. He was reputed to have been a righteous saintly householder. Valluvar was a name associated with those engaged in the weaving profession. It was also a term applied to an officer proclaiming the king's orders, riding on an elephant and beating a proclamation drum. Regardless of the incongruous origins of his name, Thiruvalluvar diagnosed the intricacies of human nature with perspicacity, literary mastery and exceptional skill, exploring the subjective concepts of human psychology.

The *Thirukkural* is one of the most important works in the Tamil language. This is reflected in some of the other names by which the text is known: *Tamil Marai*, Tamil Vedas; *Poyyamozhi* (words that never fail); and *Deiva Nool* (divine text). There are 1,330 couplets organized into 133 chapters, which are grouped into three sections: Aram (righteousness), Porul (wealth) and Inbam (love). While Aram and Inbam discuss ethical living in human life, Porul deals with public affairs. It preaches simplicity and truth throughout its verses.

The ethics propounded by the *Thirukkural* are eminently practical and universal. Its concern is primarily the world of all of us. It is realistic in its approach to human life, and Valluvar makes no distinction between men on the basis of caste or creed. According to him, there are indeed two classes of people: the noble and the ignoble. But birth, he says, has nothing to do with either. The noble man, he says, will help others even with his bones, whereas the ignoble, governed by fear and greed, is completely worthless, and in a crisis will only sell himself (Kural 1080).

எற்றிற் குறியர் கயபரொன்று உற்றக்கால்
விற்றற்கு உரியர் விரைந்து

Valluvar gives supreme importance to virtue. He affirms that all aspects and all stages of human life should be governed by virtue. He deals with a wide range of virtues or positive qualities to be cultivated and negative qualities to be eschewed. Valluvar is particularly harsh on two things. The first is ingratitude. He says, 'All other sins may be redeemed, but never ingratitude.' The second thing is meat eating. 'How could anyone,' he says, 'wish to fatten himself by eating fat of other beings? Butchering is disgrace; and eating meat is senseless' (Kural 254).

அருளல்ல தியாதெனிற் கொல்லாமை கோறல்
பொருளல்ல தவ்வூன் தினல்

Valluvar is equally harsh on consuming alcohol. He says, 'Liquor does not differ from poison' (Kural 926).

துஞ்சினார் செத்தாரின் வேறல்லர் எஞ்ஞான்றும்
நஞ்சுண்பார் கள்ளுண் பவர்

Valluvar places a strong emphasis on righteousness. He states that good conduct and character is the pathway to perfection. It earns the appreciation and respect of people. It also leads to purification of heart, which is an indispensable requirement for higher spiritual attainment. On the other hand, bad conduct leads to disgrace, because it is a source of all evils and spells endless miseries and ruin (Kural 137).

ஒழுக்கத்தின் எய்துவர் மேன்மை இழுக்கத்தின்
எய்துவர் எய்தாப் பழி

Ethics, virtues, righteousness and purity indeed make a human different from the beast. Pramukh Swamiji says, 'We must be pure. I do not speak merely of the purity of the senses. We must observe great purity in our wills, in our intentions—in all our actions.' When I am in the company of Pramukh Swamiji, I wonder if the eighteenth-century English poet Lord Byron wrote these famous lines for him:

The light of love, the purity of grace,
The mind, the Music breathing from (his) face,
The heart whose softness harmonised the whole—
And, oh! that eye was in itself a Soul![99]

Pramukh Swamiji promotes ethical living. He teaches the philosophy of making practical decisions for daily life which take into account ethics and moral values. His simple teachings naturally expand to encompass sustainability, environmentalism, wildlife preservation and animal welfare. He presents ethics and moral values as a personal choice, and not as some doctrine or creed. In his simple words, he describes morality as 'regular reflection on the day-to-day decisions that confront us'.

Ethical living is concerned primarily with the interpersonal dimension of our behaviour. How do we treat one another individually and in groups—and increasingly, other species and the environment? The key here is that morality brings us into contact with others and asks us to consider the quality of that contact. We start asking ourselves: 'Is that the way I should treat someone else?' 'Is that the way someone else should treat me?' Because we have the ability to be critical of our interpersonal behaviour and our interaction with animals, we have the ability to develop codes and norms to guide that behaviour and interaction. Those moral norms and codes, in addition to a set of virtuous character traits, are what we mean when we talk about ethics.

Ethics poses questions about how we ought to act in relationships and how we should live with one another. Ethics asks us to consider whether our actions are right or wrong. It also asks us how those character traits that help humans flourish (such as integrity, honesty, faithfulness and compassion) play out in everyday living. Ethical norms and principles have developed over time and across cultures, as rational people of goodwill consider human relationships and how human beings act when they are at their best.

When I revisited the *Thirukkural* after studying the work and methods of Pramukh Swamiji, a systematic approach emerged in my mind. There are five questions that—if posed daily—can help with the how-to of everyday righteousness.

First is the question: 'Did I practise any virtues today?' The virtues are indeed habits of the heart we learned from our parents and the primary-school teacher. They are indeed the best parts of us. Did I cross a line today that gave up one of those virtues? Or was I, at least some of the time, a person who showed integrity, trustworthiness, honesty, compassion or any of the other virtues I was taught as a child?

The second question is: 'Did I do more good than harm today? Or did I try to?' Consider the short-term and long-term consequences of your actions.

The third question is: 'Did I treat people with dignity and respect today?' All human beings should be treated with dignity simply because they are human. People have moral rights, especially the fundamental right to be treated as free and equal human beings, not as things to be manipulated, controlled or cast away. How did my actions today uphold the dignity and the moral rights to which every person is entitled?

The fourth question is: 'Was I fair and just today? Did I treat each person equally unless there was some relevant moral reason to treat him or her differently?' Justice requires that we be fair in the way we distribute benefits and burdens. Whom did I benefit and whom did I burden? How did I decide?

The fifth question is: 'Was my community better because I was in it? Was I better because I was in my community?' Consider your primary community, however you define it—neighbourhood, apartment building, family, company, etc. Was I able to go beyond my own interests to make that community stronger? Was I able to draw on my community's strengths to help me in my own process of becoming a better human being?

This everyday ethical reflection must occur before we can effectively confront the larger moral questions. A person who wants to take moral leadership on global issues must take special responsibility for what is going on inside his or her own self—inside his or her own consciousness—lest the act of leadership create more harm than good. All of us can be leaders for good; the choice is ours. We share a responsibility for creating the external world, because we project either a spirit of light or a spirit of shadow on that which is other than us. We project either a spirit of hope or a spirit of despair. We have a choice about what we are going to project, and in that choice we help create the world that is.

Aristotle wrote that virtue not only makes good works, 'but the one doing the work becomes good as well'.[100] Becoming good, through repeated virtuous acts, is the very reason and order of our human nature, for it is only in goodness that we penetrate mysteries of our existence and behold a full human life. The pure man, with his well-formed conscience, understands that truth obligates him to pursue it at all costs. We are truth seekers, as Pramukh Swamiji says, because this is precisely the way that God has lovingly created us.

What exactly is meant by seeking truth? How can one become a truth seeker? We must all join together to bring peace. Let us say that this is the search for the truth. It will not be an easy task in any way. We have lived in darkness and fear for so long that mistrust has become second nature to us. Violence is everywhere: crime is expected, evil is tolerated. But this must change. Slowly, and with conscious effort, we can find the truth; we can lose our fears, and each of us can walk in the light of our own perfection. This is what Pramukh Swamiji has done and is doing through his disciples and devotees. This is what I found unique in Pramukh Swamiji. And this is the foundation of our fellowship.

We believe that for the world to be a better place, the change must start with each individual. This is the one true way. Each one of us can choose right over wrong: do good simply for good's sake, choose love over hate, see the potential good in all things, oppose that which is evil and destructive, avoid hurting any living thing, and so on. If we can learn to live life the one true way, there is nothing that cannot be achieved, and nothing in life that will be denied to us—unfailing health, fertility, joy, a sure defence and wealth (Kural 738).

பிணியின்மை செல்வம் விளைவின்பம் ஏமம்
அணியென்ப நாட்டிவ் வைந்து

There is a lie that acts like a virus within the mind of humanity. And that lie is that there is not enough good to go around. There is scarcity and there is limitation and there is just not enough. The truth is that there is more than enough good to go around. There are more than enough creative ideas. There is more than enough power. There is more than enough love. There is more than enough joy. All of this begins to come through a mind that is aware of its own infinite nature. There is enough for everyone. If you believe it, if you can see it, if you act from it—it will show up for you. That is the truth.

28

There Is No Such Thing As Defeat in Non-violence

'Non-violence leads to the highest ethics, which is the goal of all evolution. Until we stop harming all other living beings, we are still savages.'

– Thomas A. Edison
Prolific nineteenth-century inventor

Is spirituality confined to temples and monasteries, or can a spiritual approach be taken in day-to-day life, and can it be a formula for worldly living? Many young people ask me this question. I normally used to give them the example of Mahatma Gandhi, who made the Indian freedom movement a spiritual pursuit of ordinary people. He waged a non-violent campaign against a mighty empire, which is unique in the history of humanity. I, like many others, have practised non-violence throughout my life, and express it by not eating any form of meat. But I could comprehend its true meaning only after meeting Pramukh Swamiji. I have found Pramukh Swamiji to be the embodiment of non-violence. He is full of compassion and steadfast in his conviction—both hallmarks of higher consciousness. I have understood, through his fellowship, that access to higher consciousness is the purpose of human evolution, and non-violence is the means to access the higher consciousness. I would like to explain non-violence with a poetic example:

A Gunatit sadhu goes about
Like a bee, which, not harming
Flower, colour or scent,
Flies off with the nectar
And produces honey.

In this chapter, I will try to present the ideal of non-violence as the most powerful strategy to maximize the meaning of our lives. Let us start with the Buddha. The Buddha's path begins with a vow to not kill, but it culminates in identification with non-violence as the essence of what liberates the mind and heart from hate, fear and self-promoting delusion. Non-violence is the essence of what the Buddha taught. Non-violence is liberating, because in each and every moment that it suffuses one's mind, the mind feels compassion, identification and empathy with other beings. For the Buddha, non-violence is a precept that enables the journey to experience the fundamental meaning of itself. Initially, the student obeys the precept of non-violence. Eventually, he or she comes to embody non-violence as the cherished quintessence of life.

Vardhaman Mahaveer, the twenty-fourth and last tirthankara (lit. 'ford-maker' or a spiritual pioneer who is able to ford the river to cross the perpetual flow of earthy life) of Jainism, suggested eight measures for self-realization. Three of them are related to one's approach, while the other five are about one's actual conduct in life. The three appropriate approaches advocated by Mahaveer are appropriate knowledge, appropriate philosophy and appropriate conduct. Appropriate knowledge—samyak gyan—is a duty bestowed upon a person in life to obtain appropriate knowledge about the world and humanity. Appropriate philosophy—samyak darshan—requires a proper philosophy to ensure a healthy outlook and a meaningful life. Appropriate conduct—samyak charitra—demands care about one's conduct and that it is ethical and salutary. For ensuring appropriate conduct, samyak charitra, Mahaveer recommended five great vows to his followers. These are ahimsa (non-violence), satya (truthfulness); asteya (not stealing), brahmacharya (abstinence), and aparigriha (no possessions).[101]

The widespread promulgation of non-violence in ancient India eventuated nearly three centuries after Vardhaman Mahaveer's time, in the aftermath of one of the bloodiest conquests in recorded history. The great Mauryan Empire was the subcontinent's most geographically extensive empire. In 300 BC, it held sway throughout almost the entire Indian subcontinent, save for parts of present-day Tamil Nadu and Kerala—and the feudal republic of Kalinga, which was situated on the Bay of Bengal in present-day Odisha and northern Andhra Pradesh. Emperor Ashoka's forebears had coveted Kalinga's rich lands, and with an overwhelmingly large army which he personally commanded, Ashoka invaded it around 260 BC to fulfil these long-standing Mauryan territorial ambitions.

The ensuing war was bloody in the extreme, and the casualties were especially appalling, given that the instruments of warfare at that time were swords, spears and arrows. The number of fallen soldiers—perhaps as many as 250,000 Kalingan and Mauryan warriors—rivalled the scale of many of the twentieth centuries' great battles. Vastly outnumbered, the Kalingan army fought valiantly but were annihilated in this gory encounter, which legend tells left the River Daya running red with blood. Seeing the destruction, and the havoc wreaked on life and property by the war, Ashoka was overwhelmed by grief and remorse, and repented of his military aggression. He turned to non-violence (ahimsa) and spread the message of non-violence to the remotest corners of his kingdom by engravings on rocks and pillars.

This turned out to be a political masterstroke. In embracing non-violence, Ashoka forestalled the possibility of any rebellion in his vast and diverse empire. Subjugated kings, princes, aristocrats, bureaucrats, commanders and others imbibed the virtue of non-violence and non-aggression. His purported virtuousness also helped in establishing peace with neighbouring lands on the extensive borders of the Mauryan Empire. Non-violence strengthened the foundations of his highly centralized empire, which he then governed with relative ease.

More than two millennia later, Gandhiji's emphasis on non-violence did not initially impress his British and Indian critics. British

rulers saw non-violence as a camouflage; political opponents saw
it as sentimentalism. To the British, who tended to see the Indian
freedom struggle through the prism of Europe's turbulent history,
the remarkably peaceful tenor of Gandhi's campaigns was beyond
comprehension. To the radical Indian politicians—who were more
than somewhat acquainted with the history of the French and Russian
Revolutions or the Italian and Irish nationalist struggles—it seemed
foolish to miss opportunities and sacrifice tactical gains, for reasons
more relevant to ethics than to politics.

British religious teacher Horace Alexander was a good friend of
Gandhiji. He saw him in action, and graphically described the attitude
of the non-violent resister to his opponent:

> On your side you have all the mighty forces of the modern state—
> arms, money, a controlled press, and all the rest. On my side, I have
> nothing but my conviction of right and truth, the unquenchable spirit
> of man, who is prepared to die for his convictions than submit to your
> brute force. I have my armless comrades. Here we stand; and here if
> need be, we fall.[102]

Far from being a craven retreat from difficulty and danger, non-
violent resistance demands courage of a high order—the courage to
resist injustice without rancour, to unite the utmost firmness with the
utmost gentleness, to invite suffering but not to inflict it, to die but
not to kill.[103]

Gandhiji did not make the facile division of mankind into 'good'
and 'bad'. He was convinced that every human being—even the
'enemy'—had a kernel of decency: there were only evil acts, no wholly
evil men. His modus operandi of satyagraha was designed not to
coerce the opponent, but to set into motion forces which could lead
to his conversion. Relying as it did on persuasion and compromise,
Gandhi's methods were not always quick in producing results, but the
results were likely to be more durable for having been brought about
peacefully. 'It is my firm conviction,' Gandhi affirmed, 'that nothing
enduring can be built upon violence.' The rate of social change through
non-violent methods was not, in fact, likely to be much slower than

that achieved by violent methods; it was definitely faster than that expected from the normal functioning of institutions, which tended to fossilize and preserve the status quo.[104]

Gandhiji did not think it possible to bring about radical changes in the structure of society overnight. Nor did he succumb to the illusion that the road to a new order of things could be paved merely with pious wishes and fine words. And it was unsatisfactory to blame the opponent or bewail the times in which one's lot was cast. However heavy the odds, it was the satyagrahi's duty never to feel helpless. The least he could do was to make a beginning—with himself.

If he was crusading for a new deal for peasantry, the Mahatma would go to a village and live there. If he wanted to bring peace to a disturbed district, he would walk through it, entering into the minds and hearts of those who were going through the ordeal. If an age-old evil like untouchability was to be fought, what could be a more effective symbol of defiance for a reformer than to adopt an untouchable child? If the object was to challenge foreign rule, why not act on the assumption that the country was already free, ignore the alien government and build alternative institutions to harness the spontaneous, constructive and cooperative effort of the people? If the goal was world peace, why not begin today by acting peacefully towards your immediate neighbour, going more than halfway to understanding him, and win him over?

Though he may have appeared a starry-eyed idealist to some, Gandhiji's attitude to social and political problems was immensely practical. There was a deep mystical streak in him, but even his mysticism seemed to have little of the ethereal about it. He did not dream heavenly dreams or see things unutterable in trances; when 'the still, small voice'[105] spoke to him, it was often to tell how he could fight a social evil or heal a rift between two warring communities. Far from distracting him from his role in public affairs, Gandhiji's religious quest gave him the stamina to play it more effectively. To him, true religion was not merely the reading of scriptures, the dissection of ancient texts, or even the practice of cloistered virtue—it had to be lived in the challenging context of political and social life.

Gandhiji utilized his non-violent methods on behalf of his compatriots in South Africa and India, but he did not conceive non-violent opposition only as a weapon in the armoury of Indian nationalism. On the contrary, he fashioned it as an instrument for righting wrongs and resolving conflicts between opposing groups, races and nations. As early as 1924, he had declared that 'the better mind of the world desires today, not absolutely independent states, warring one against another, but a federation of independent, of friendly interdependent states'. He envisioned the world as one big family.[106]

The pastor and leader in the African-American civil rights movement, Martin Luther King Jr, received the Nobel Peace Prize in 1964 for combating racial inequality through non-violence. He famously declared: 'Christ furnished the spirit and motivation while Gandhi furnished the method.' In February 1968, barely two months before he was assassinated, speaking about how he wished to be remembered after his death, King stated:

> I would like somebody to mention that day that Martin Luther King Jr. tried to give his life serving others. I would like for somebody to say that day that Martin Luther King Jr tried to love somebody. I was a drum major for righteousness. And all of the other shallow things will not matter. I would not have any money to leave behind. I would not have the fine and luxurious things of life to leave behind. But I just want to leave a committed life behind.[107]

This is the true essence of non-violence. Everything you do has an impact on other people, on the planet and on the animals with whom you share the world. Living non-violence as a way of life involves making the right connections. It involves making the right choices so that your actions align with your moral values. Nearly all of the problems in the world today stem from the fact that people have forgotten who they really are. Non-violence offers direction, so you can remember who you are and act in a reconnected way. It is a win-win way of living. You will build a better life for yourself and a better world for everyone. Being aware and aligned with your values makes you conscious, complete and more powerful. And when millions of conscious, empowered people join together through non-violence, it will create a movement the likes of which the world has never seen.

'Vasudhaiva kutumbakam' is a Sanskrit phrase that means that the whole world is one single family. The same concept is to be found in the Sangam period, 300–100 BC, in the Tamil purananuru poem as 'யாதும் ஊரே யாவரும் கேளீர்', which means, 'every country is my own and all the people are my kinsmen'. The Ahmadiya Muslim community elaborates the doctrine of unity (tawhid), with three categories, namely the unity of God, the unity of religion and the unity of mankind. Baha'ullah, the founder of the Bahai Faith, wrote in his *Tablet of Maqsud*, '... the earth is but one country, and mankind its citizens'. The word 'Ubuntu', which is the name of a prominent philosophy in South Africa, means literally 'humanness'. It is often translated as 'humanity towards others', and means 'the belief in a universal bond of sharing that connects all humanity'.[108]

This humanity towards others—regardless of their race or creed— is abundant in Pramukh Swamiji. When I sit with Pramukh Swamiji, I feel that through his eyes the universe perceives itself, and through his ears the universe is listening to its harmonies. Pramukh Swamiji is indeed the witness through which the universe becomes conscious of its glory, of its magnificence. When I sit with him, I feel that everything is connected. In a nutshell, non-violence is an expression of this interconnection. The leaves of a tree affect the direction of the wind and the way the pollen drifts. The way the light reflects in Swamiji's eyes illuminates reality. Everything is a part of a totality, and in this totality I have realized that non-violence is an active and powerful way to build a better world. It involves this fundamental understanding: everything and we are connected. Non-violence means living your life sincerely, supporting these connections. There is no defeat as there is no fight; there is only the victory of becoming one with all that truly is.

29

Forgiveness Forces Us to Grow Beyond What We Are

'Darkness cannot drive out darkness; only light can do that.
Hate cannot drive out hate; only love can do that.'

– Martin Luther King Jr
Leader in the African-American civil rights movement

We all know that lives are not calmly flowing rivers. Relating to others, whether it be friends, strangers or family members, is always accompanied by the risk of being hurt, and such hurts happen all the time. Our parents may have been too tough on us; our teachers at school or university may have been unpleasant; colleagues could have created problems for projects we were working on. Getting hurt is part and parcel of the human condition. The most common reaction to being hurt is to get angry, coupled with a desire to get back at the transgressors. We want to hurt them the way they have hurt us. We want them to feel pain. Unfortunately, many of us have been in this dark place. This is like a prison.

Individuals, teams, organizations, institutions and societies can only move forward when people are not preoccupied with past hurts. And one of the factors that truly differentiates transformational leaders from the run-of-the-mill kind, is the ability to turn feelings of resentment, bitterness and blame into something constructive and reparative. When leaders forgive, they dissipate built-up anger, bitterness and animosity, thereby releasing an enormous amount of stored energy that can be used in much more constructive ways. Forgiveness offers people the chance to take risks, to be creative, to learn and to develop their own leadership capabilities. Through forgiveness, truly transformational leaders instil a sense of pride, respect and trust in their followers, thus creating heightened levels of commitment, self-sacrifice, motivation and performance. Are there any role models? Who is the best example?

I consider Nelson Mandela as one of the most remarkable figures of our era. Mandela was born on 18 July 1918, in a small village in a region on the east coast of South Africa. His father was a chief who was dispossessed of his tribal authority by a white magistrate, on the grounds of insubordination. He was nine when his father died. He was taken into the household of the tribal regent of the Xhosa people, who instilled in him the diplomacy and authority which was necessary to hold together the various factions of his people. It was a crucial part of his upbringing, indelible on his leadership style and in his regal manner.

Mandela joined the African National Congress (ANC) as a student. Initially, the party believed in a Gandhian, non-violent struggle for equality. But after the massacre of sixty-nine demonstrators by security forces at Sharpeville in 1960, the ANC decided that an armed struggle was the only feasible solution. In 1963, Mandela and his colleagues targeted military and government institutions, and he was eventually arrested for his role in the armed group. During the Rivonia trial, he garnered widespread attention for setting out his vision for democracy and equal rights for all South African citizens. Mandela was convicted of conspiracy to overthrow the state and sentenced to life imprisonment.

Mandela served twenty-seven years in prison, initially on Robben Island and later in Pollsmoor Prison and Victor Verster Prison. At the Robben Island prison, Mandela was tasked with manual labour and broke stones with the other prisoners. Campaigners in London and around the world marched for his release and for an end to apartheid. The song 'Free Nelson Mandela' became the anthem of a generation. Mandela walked out of prison in 1990.

Almost immediately after his release, he called for South Africans to 'let bygones be bygones', leading South Africa away from violence and towards peaceful democracy. With this vision and benevolence, he entered the next phase of his life as a statesman. Mandela's power as a politician stemmed from a steely will; but this was combined with a kindly heart and a deep desire for people to respect each other and live harmoniously. These facets of his character were evident in the speech he made when he was facing a possible death sentence in 1964. He told the court:

> During my lifetime I have dedicated myself to this struggle of the African people. I have fought against white domination, and I have fought against black domination. I have cherished the ideal of a democratic and free society in which all persons live together in harmony with equal opportunities. It is an ideal which I hope to live for and achieve. But if need be, it is an ideal for which I am prepared to die.[109]

It was this declaration that set him apart from other black leaders of his generation, and identified his special brand of leadership of the resistance to apartheid. Black South Africans can attribute much of his legacy to his and his companions being spared the death sentence. Instead of execution, they were shackled and carted off to an island prison. You would imagine that a man emerging from twenty-seven years in prison would be consumed with anger, bitterness and a thirst for revenge. But Mandela instead preached reconciliation, forgiveness and tolerance, disarming those who sought to undermine the transition from apartheid to full and equal franchise.

I travelled to South Africa in September 2004, and while I was there, I visited Nelson Mandela. When I entered his house, I found him a bundle of cheerfulness. I was awed by this frail but towering luminary: this great man who had peacefully won freedom for South Africa over the tyranny of apartheid. When I was leaving his home, he came to the portico to give me a send-off. He discarded his walking stick and I became his support. I asked him, 'Dr Mandela, how did you feel when you walked out of prison after twenty-seven years?' He said, 'As I walked out of the door towards the gate that would lead to my freedom, I knew if I didn't leave my bitterness and hatred behind, I'd still be in prison.'

When I asked him for a message, he said, 'What can I tell you, Mr President? You come from the country of Mahatma Gandhi. He was one of the great pioneers of South Africa's freedom movement. What we learnt from him is that the first thing is to be honest with yourself. You can never have an impact on society if you have not changed yourself ... Great peacemakers are all people of integrity, of honesty, and of humility.'

It is quite an eye-opener to compare Nelson Mandela's philosophy of leadership and forgiveness with that of the leadership in the neighbouring country Zimbabwe. Instead of generosity, restraint and forgiveness, the leaders there have fostered bitterness, vindictiveness, anger and hatred. Vindictiveness has been expressed not only towards the erstwhile white ruling class, but also to large segments of the indigenous population, comprising black compatriots who hold views opposing those of the government. Zimbabwe today is a land with a ruined economy, populated by citizens living miserable and fearful lives.

Mahatma Gandhi warned that 'The weak can never forgive. Forgiveness is the attribute of the strong.'[110] We cannot change what has happened to us; there is no delete button for the past. Whatever transgressions there may have been, it is something that is going to be with us forever. So the crucial questions are how we choose to deal with these trespasses, and how we metabolize our feelings of hurt.

For most people, the memories of hurt become like permanent video recordings implanted in their heads, and every time these recordings are played, they feel the pain all over again. How can one stop them playing? How can one end this suffering? The answer lies in self-reflection, self-understanding and self-expression. I learned this from Pramukh Swamiji, who showed exemplary calmness and forgiveness in the aftermath of the terrorist attack on Akshardham Temple. While the world learns from such expansive acts of large-heartedness, individuals are inspired by the smaller, invisible actions of Pramukh Swamiji. The hundreds of thousands who have personally met him for confession or guidance have experienced his all-encompassing and unconditional forgiveness and acceptance. He has a heart wherein the whole world can live and forgive.

Forgiveness is a five-step process. The first step on a journey of forgiveness is to remind ourselves how the energy required to keep a grudge alive will ultimately sap our vitality. We must be cognizant of how a desire for revenge may defile our inner space, and even turn us into a person as cruel as the one who has hurt us. And we need to acknowledge that forgiveness is a much healthier option than carrying old wounds, which becomes a burden that steals pleasure from our lives. The capability for self-reflection is important for promoting positive behaviours towards others and facilitating social interactions and relationships. Thiruvalluvar wrote so beautifully (Kural 156):

ஒறுத்தார்க்கு ஒருநாளை இன்பம் பொறுத்தார்க்கு
பொன்றுந் துணையும் புகழ்

Who wreak their wrath have pleasure for a day;
Who bear have praise till earth shall pass away!

Second, while going through the self-reflection process, it is imperative to understand why a transgression has occurred in the first instance. Again, for reasons of mental health, we need to find explanations. Here, the capacity to be truly transcendent comes into play. The ability to put ourselves in the transgressor's shoes is a sine qua non to understanding what has really happened. While doing so, we will most probably not agree with the rationale that led to the wrongful act against us, but we will surely penetrate a deep understanding of why this event has occurred.

Third, it will be necessary to express the emotions attached to the hurt. Without expressing these emotions, it will be very difficult to let go. If the transgression elicits anger or sadness, these feelings need to be deeply felt and expressed. Naturally, the best option is to express these feelings towards your transgressors, particularly as they may not even be aware of the hurt that they have caused. If you want to maintain a relationship with the person you are trying to forgive, you need to find ways to communicate why you are angry and what needs to be done to find a resolution. Whatever the transgression may have been, the forgiver needs to fully express how it made him or her feel. It is not enough simply for you to try to forget, because merely bypassing the emotion does not allow true forgiveness.

Fourth, for true forgiveness to occur, the forgiver needs to have a reasonable understanding that the transgression was conditional. Forgiveness is not always easy. At times, it may feel more painful to forgive the one that inflicted a wrong, than it did to suffer the wrong itself. And yet, there is no peace without forgiveness. Therefore, this forgiveness should be unconditional.

Finally, the step that completes the forgiveness cycle is letting go, and this may be the most difficult step to take. It is never easy to promise not to hold a grudge—letting go of a grudge means ending rumination on the matter, stopping oneself from dwelling on the injustice and affirming that the transgression will not be referred to in the future. Being able to do this, however, also means letting go of a position of power; only when forgivers surrender the dominant role, can they and their transgressors relate to one another again on an equal basis. For many people, this step is what makes forgiveness such a challenge.

The road to forgiveness is not easy to take. Too many get stuck on the journey, finding it hard to let go of negative rumination and their bitterness. But these people should be reminded that they have a choice. They can choose to carry on regretting things. Or they can take the view that things have happened for a reason, and that they may benefit from learning from their experience. Such understanding will tell them what they could have done differently to prevent the transgression in the first place. They also need to realize that life is not only about learning to forgive those who have hurt us. It is also about the recognition that all of us are human, and that all humans make mistakes. It is essential to realize that forgiveness is ultimately a gift to ourselves. Only through forgiveness can wounds heal. And as we let go of grudges, we no longer define our lives by how we have been hurt. The truth is, unless you let go—unless you forgive yourself, unless you forgive the situation, unless you realize that the situation is over— you cannot move forward.

30

The Best Name for God Is Compassion

'The purpose of human life is to serve, and to show compassion
and the will to help others.'

– Albert Schweitzer
Philosopher and Nobel Peace Laureate

The fourteenth Dalai Lama, whose religious name is Tenzin
Gyatso, lives in Dharamshala, in Himachal Pradesh, India. He
has resided there since his denunciation of the People's Republic of
China and his establishment of a Tibetan government in exile in 1959.
He has travelled the world in the intervening years, advocating the
welfare of Tibetans, teaching Tibetan Buddhism and talking about
the importance of compassion as the source of a happy life. Pramukh
Swamiji and I have met him several times, though not together, and
we both admire the importance he gives to peace of mind. The Dalai
Lama famously said:

> Warm-heartedness is a key factor for healthy individuals, healthy
> families and healthy communities. Scientists say that a healthy mind
> is a major factor for a healthy body. If you are serious about your
> health, think and take most concern for your peace of mind. That's
> very, very important.[111]

On 6 October 1950, The People's Liberation Army (PLA) crossed
the River Jinsha and defeated the Tibetan army. Instead of continuing
with the military campaign, China asked Tibet to send representatives

to Beijing to negotiate a truce. The members of the Tibetan delegation signed an agreement under duress in 1951, which affirmed Chinese sovereignty over Tibet. The Chinese government did not allow the Tibetan representatives to communicate with the Dalai Lama in Lhasa. China annexed Tibet by military force and deployed its army around the Dalai Lama's palace and other monasteries.[112]

In March 1959, artillery shelling by the People's Liberation Army seriously damaged Lhasa's three major monasteries, namely Sera, Ganden and Drepung. Members of the Dalai Lama's bodyguard were disarmed and publicly executed. Thousands of Tibetan monks were executed or arrested, and monasteries and temples around the city were looted or destroyed. In mortal danger, and braving capture by Chinese troops and border guards, the Dalai Lama undertook a perilous fifteen-day trek through the Himalayas from Lhasa into Indian territory. On 18 April 1959, he and his retinue of twenty men, including six cabinet ministers, reached Tezpur in Assam.

Within a period of months, the Dalai Lama set up the Government of Tibet in exile in Dharamshala. He re-established the approximately 80,000 Tibetan refugees who followed him into exile in agricultural settlements. He created a Tibetan educational system in order to teach the Tibetan children their language, history, religion and culture. The Tibetan Institute of Performing Arts was established in 1959, and the Central Institute of Higher Tibetan Studies became the primary university for Tibetans in India. The Dalai Lama supported more than 200 monasteries and nunneries in an attempt to preserve Tibetan Buddhist teachings and the Tibetan way of life.[113]

In the ensuing decades, the Dalai Lama has been very active in spreading India's message of non-violence and religious harmony throughout the world, stating, 'I am the messenger of India's ancient thoughts the world over.' He has said that democracy has deep roots in India, and that he considers India the master and Tibet its disciple, as great scholars like Nagarjuna went from Nalanda to Tibet to preach Buddhism in the eighth century. He has noted that millions of people have lost their lives in violence, and the economies of many countries have been ruined due to conflicts in the twentieth century.

He declares, 'Let the twenty-first century be a century of tolerance and dialogue.'[114]

It is unimaginable that tolerance and dialogue would prevail in this century without compassion. In the classical literature of Hinduism, compassion is a virtue with many shades, each shade explained by different terms. Four most common terms are daya, karuna, kripa and anukampa. Some of these words are used interchangeably to explain the concept of compassion, its sources, its consequences and its nature. Karuna means placing one's mind in another's favour, thereby seeking to understand the other from their perspective. Kripa is pity, or feeling sorry for the sufferer; it is marred with condescension. Anukampa refers to one's state after one has observed and understood the pain and suffering in the other. Daya, the virtue of compassion to all living beings, is a central concept in Hindu philosophy.

Daya is the virtuous desire to mitigate the sorrow and difficulties of others by exerting whatever effort is necessary for this. It is the value that treats all living beings as one's own self; the welfare and the good of other living beings are paramount. Such compassion is one of the necessary paths to being happy. Daya is treating a stranger, a relative, a friend and a foe as one's own self; it is the state of existence in which one sees all living beings as part of one's own self, and when everyone's suffering is seen as one's own suffering. Daya is contrasted with abhiman, which is arrogance and contempt for others. While compassion is the source of dharmic life, arrogance is the root of sin.

Thiruvalluvar declares that one must pursue one's life path with compassion; all life deserves one's love, and that charity without compassion is empty and inconceivable (Kural 243).

அருள்சேர்ந்த நெஞ்சினார்க் கில்லை இருள்சேர்ந்த
இன்னா உலகம் புகல்

Those whose hearts are drawn towards mercy
will never be drawn into the dark and woeful world.

In the Muslim tradition, foremost among God's attributes are mercy and compassion, Rahman and Rahim in Arabic. All chapters of the Quran begin with the verse:

بِسْمِ ٱللهِ ٱلرَّحْمَـٰنِ ٱلرَّحِيمِ

In the name of Allah the Compassionate, the Merciful.

Eminent Tibetan scholar Thupten Jinpa, who is also the long-serving English translator for the Dalai Lama, defines compassion as 'a mental state endowed with a sense of concern for the suffering of others and aspiration to see that suffering relieved'. Specifically, he defines compassion as having three components: a cognitive component: 'I understand you;' an affective component: 'I feel for you;' and a motivational component: 'I want to help you.'

The most compelling benefit of compassion in the context of work is that compassion creates highly effective leaders. To become a highly effective leader, you need to go through an important transformation. Good leaders must shift from 'I' to 'We'. The practice of compassion is about going from self to others. In a way, compassion is about going from 'I' to 'We'. So, if switching from 'I' to 'We' is the most important process of becoming an authentic leader, those who practise compassion will already know this, and will have a head start.[115]

Pramukh Swamiji is a living example of compassion-directed leadership. He is a leader, who in addition to being highly capable, possesses a paradoxical mix of two important and seemingly conflicting qualities: great inspiration and personal humility. He is highly determined, but the focus of his aspiration is not his own self; instead, it is his vision for the greater good of humanity. Because his attention is focused on the greater good, he feels no need to inflate his own self-image. That makes Pramukh Swamiji highly effective and inspiring.

The following was expressed by His Holiness the Dalai Lama, in an address during his official visit to the bicentenary celebration of Aksharbrahman Gunatitanand Swami in 1985 in Ahmedabad:

Your Organization is doing great service to mankind by spreading the message of goodness and joy. It is indeed commendable that the Swaminarayan movement has not limited its work to the movement alone, but has gone out in society and conducted a door-to-door crusade against the evils of society, to promote peace and harmony. I am deeply impressed by the fact that the youths are so actively involved in the activities of this movement.

If we look at the two distinguishing qualities of Pramukh Swamiji—great inspiration and personal humility—in the context of the three components of compassion (cognitive, affective and motivational), we can find that the cognitive and affective components of compassion, which entail understanding people and empathizing with them, tone down the excessive self-obsession within us and thereby create the conditions for humility. The motivational component of compassion—wanting to help people—creates ambition for greater good. In other words, the three components of compassion can be used to train the two distinguishing qualities of compassion-directed leadership.

While I worked in two very large organizations—ISRO and DRDO—and then as president of India, I had many opportunities to interact with leaders at different levels. I have thus developed certain insights into the process of leadership. And I can confidently say that on our best days—when we feel in control, rested and hopeful—most of us are effective leaders, able to sustain resonance and the relationships we need to do our jobs well. But too often, this equilibrium is lost. Our relationships are not what we want them to be: our bodies suffer from fatigue, illness or neglect, and our judgement becomes impaired.

What is going on, and what can we do to help ourselves be at our best most of the time? Leadership is stressful, and stress increases the electrical activity in the right prefrontal cortex of our brains, releasing hormones that activate the 'fight or flight' response. Our bodies go on high alert and respond accordingly. Ideally, our bodies need time to rest and assimilate these stress hormones and physiological responses. But in today's leadership environment, stress is ever present, and we don't get a break from it. For this reason, leaders need to consciously manage themselves and get to grips with stress—and create ways of renewing themselves.

Renewal occurs as different parts of the limbic system of the brain are activated to offset those parts aroused under stress. When

I was guiding Father John for his PhD work at Anna University on neuroplasticity, to aid mentally challenged children to better perform their everyday tasks, I learned that when activity in the parasympathetic nervous system (PSNS) increases, activity in the sympathetic nervous system (SNS) subsides. The PSNS activates a set of hormones that lower blood pressure and strengthen the immune system. Given the demands and pressures of leadership, it is only through balancing stress with renewal that resonant leadership can be sustained. And this renewal inevitably activates and bolsters the functioning of the PSNS.

True renewal relies on three key elements that may initially sound too 'soft' to be part of the hard work of leadership, but are, in fact, absolutely essential if a leader is to sustain resonance. The first element is mindfulness, or living in a state of full, conscious awareness of one's whole self, other people and the context in which we live and work. In effect, mindfulness means being awake, aware and constantly attending to ourselves and to the world around us. The second element, hope, enables us to believe that our vision of the future is attainable, and to move towards our goals while inspiring others to reach for their dreams as well. When we experience the third critical element for renewal, compassion, we understand people's wants and needs and feel motivated to act on our concern.

Mindfulness starts with self-awareness: knowing yourself enables you to make choices about how you respond to people and situations. Deep knowledge about yourself enables you to be consistent; to present yourself authentically. Just as importantly, mindfulness allows you to notice the subtle clues that tell you to attend carefully to yourself, others or your surroundings. Pramukh Swamiji did just that—he noticed small but important changes in the way he felt and in people's responses to him. Noticing these small changes allowed some fine-tuning, helping the progress of his mission.

I should note here that Pramukh Swamiji is not driven to change by any sort of fear of impending failure; he builds on his strengths. And knowing when to change and fine-tune is the essence of building on your strengths as a leader. Moreover, the spark that ignites

Pramukh Swamiji's commitment to change is the desire to be good and to do good works for others. He prays and perseveres for the good and growth of not just BAPS and his devotees, but also for the welfare of the whole world. This is the cornerstone of his successful leadership.

Though he is the head, he functions like the heart. Pramukh Swamiji has generated an environment of love and freedom, where anyone and everyone can approach him and talk to him. He listens, understands and encourages others to think. He is not opinionated, but open to suggestions. And he appreciates new ideas. No wonder he has created a generation of young leaders, dedicated teams and committed volunteers. Pramukh Swamiji is a leader of leaders, who welcomes change without changing the core of spirituality.

There is a famous Buddhist saying about the need to leave the boat after crossing the stream. The boat was useful only to cross the stream; the path ahead we must walk after leaving the boat in the water. In this way, Pramukh Swamiji has moved swiftly from one goal to the next, and sometimes consciously slowed himself to carry the people with him. He has never lost sight of both his purpose and the people he leads. Such an unbroken connection with your inner and outer environment is essential to cultivate mindfulness as a habit, a lifelong practice.

Hope, like other positive emotions and mindfulness, has a positive impact on our brains and hormones. It affects our perceptions of the events around us, so that we tend to see things more positively. Such contemplation then slows the breathing, lowers the blood pressure, strengthens the immune system and engages the parasympathetic nervous system. We feel calm, happy, amused and optimistic. We are poised for the challenges ahead.

And hope is contagious: leaders who believe in the future will inspire their co-workers, thus creating a resonant environment even when things are tough. This is especially important in times of crisis, as hopeful people are better able—both physically and mentally—to cope with challenges. Pramukh Swamiji inspires hope in a deeply spiritual way: not just by words, emotions or actions, but by providing insights into the all-doership of God. He who falls from God's hands lands in his lap. The idea that God is always with us and never deserts us keeps hope alive in times of crises. This is why BAPS has overcome many seen and unseen challenges and continues to renew and evolve, providing hope and direction to other charitable organizations.

Engaging with a positive, hopeful attitude and attending to the self and others are two ways to physiological and psychological renewal. And there is one more element of renewal: compassion. This third element is not often considered to be a critical component of leadership; but in fact, it has everything to do with business and leadership. Compassion is a fundamental human experience that sparks both personal renewal and organizational resonance.

The journey to renewal is available to anyone willing to embark upon it. But personal change of this order is not easy. Many people unthinkingly respond to the pressure inherent in leadership by working harder and doing more of the same. This is like turning up the heat on a kettle in danger of boiling over. The real solution lies in renewal, which is a function of our individual capacity for mindfulness, hope and compassion.

Furthermore, being honest with oneself is the first—and hardest—step towards renewal. Through mindfulness, we learn to reflect, and to attend to both the quiet voice inside and the subtle clues from others and our environment, which can steer us in the right direction. Through hope, we reinvigorate ourselves and inspire others. Through compassion, we spark physiological and psychological renewal, while building strong, trusting and meaningful relationships. Consciously attending to ourselves and to those around us—including the communities where we work and play—can pay important dividends to ourselves, our relationships, and the organizations we serve. Pramukh Swamiji told me once, 'I have just three things to teach: simplicity, patience and compassion. These three are your greatest treasures.' What more could anyone need, I wondered.

31

Vision with Action Can Change the World

'Your vision will become clear only when you can look into your own heart. Who looks outside, dreams; who looks inside, awakes.'

– Carl Jung
Psychiatrist and author

In 1962, I was selected for the job of rocket engineer at the Indian Committee for Space Research (INCOSPAR). INCOSPAR was established from the talent pool at the Tata Institute of Fundamental Research (TIFR), Bombay (now Mumbai), to organize space research in India. A board chaired by Dr Vikram Sarabhai interviewed me. As I entered the room, I sensed the positive energy emanating from Dr Sarabhai—there was a benign aura around him. He was an icon by then, but I was seeing him for the first time. Dr Sarabhai's questions did not probe my existing knowledge or skills. Rather, they appeared to be an exploration of my possibilities. He was looking at me as if in reference to a large whole. The entire encounter seemed to me to be a total moment of truth, in which my dream was enveloped by a larger dream.

I once read in a newspaper a quote from the African-American sprinter Wilma Rudolph. She won three gold medals in athletics in the 1960 Olympic Games in Rome, and was considered the fastest woman in the world at the time. Her statement made a deep impression on me: 'Never underestimate the power of dreams and the influence of the human spirit. We are all the same in this notion: the potential for greatness lives within each of us.' I decided to follow the bold Indian dream of space research seen by a great visionary, Dr Vikram Sarabhai. With the passage of time, INCOSPAR transformed itself into the Indian Space Research Organization (ISRO). Dr Vikram Sarabhai launched the Indian Space Programme, and I was appointed as the project director of India's first satellite launch vehicle that would later send the Rohini satellite into orbit.

Dr Vikram Sarabhai was born on 12 August 1919 in Ahmedabad. The Sarabhai family was an influential and wealthy Jain business family. His father, Ambalal Sarabhai, was an affluent industrialist who owned many textile mills in Gujarat. As a child, Vikram Sarabhai saw luminaries such as Gurudev Rabindranath Tagore, Jiddu Krishnamurti, Jawaharlal Nehru and Maulana Abul Kalam Azad visit his house. But it never distracted him from his studies and he excelled academically. Vikram Sarabhai worked under the Nobel laureate C.V. Raman at the Indian Institute of Science, Bangalore (now Bengaluru), before he got his PhD in physics from Cambridge University in 1947. While Vikram Sarabhai was himself a man of indefatigable energy and versatile personality, he could also spot the best minds and nurture them to work on his vision.[116]

Vikram Sarabhai enjoyed a global stature. While he secured the cooperation of the National Aeronautical and Space Administration (NASA) in the Satellite Instructional Television Experiment (SITE) programme, the first Indian satellite, Aryabhata, was put into orbit in 1975 from a Russian cosmodrome.

The establishment of the Indian Space Research Organization emerged out of Vikram Sarabhai's great vision. He successfully lobbied the government after the Russian Sputnik launch on 4 October 1957, convincing the authorities concerned to institute a space programme. Dr Sarabhai emphasized the importance of a space programme with these persuasive words:

> There are some who question the relevance of space activities in a developing nation. To us, there is no ambiguity of purpose. We do not have the fantasy of competing with the economically advanced nations in the exploration of the moon or the planets or manned space

flight. But we are convinced that if we are to play a meaningful role nationally, and in the community of nations, we must be second to none in the application of advanced technologies to the real problems of man and society.[117]

A true visionary, Vikram Sarabhai was ahead of his time. He was perhaps the first Indian to realize that in the fast-changing world driven by even faster technological changes, learning how to balance the needs of individuals with the no-less-real needs of an institution was of paramount importance. The way Indian higher education was then designed and our universities structured, there was no place where future business leaders could be groomed. It is fine to be on the side of theory, but all theories will ultimately prove irrelevant if they are not applied to the greater body of business. With this in mind, Vikram Sarabhai founded the Indian Institute of Management (IIM) in Ahmedabad, and was its first director from 1961 to 1964. He anointed the young Ravi Mathai, then only thirty-eight years old and with a qualification of BA (Hons) from Oxford, to succeed him. The rest is a glorious history of institutional excellence.

Why is the legacy of Vikram Sarabhai ever more important today? The modern world needs visionaries like him. The globalized and Internet-connected world is witnessing an increasing interdependence between all countries. Both businesses' and people's fates are more closely connected, so it has become the development trend of international relationships to establish peace, seek cooperation and promote development.

Pramukh Swamiji shared with me many times his wish for peace, development, security and prosperity in the world. He feels that Indian people's kindness, openness, tolerance for people of other countries and willingness to engage in dialogue is indeed inbuilt in our civilizational heritage. Moreover, he firmly believes in the potential of the Indian people to co-build a harmonious world—where there is permanent peace and shared prosperity under a condition of mutual benefits, cooperation and a 'win-win'—with all other countries. This is significant for BAPS, which has a role in helping the world to understand the true spirit of Indian civilization—that nurtures an ethos of peace and prosperity—and the attitude of Indians, who overwhelmingly wish for the global good.

सर्वे भवन्तु सुखिनः सर्वे सन्तु निरामया ।
सर्वे भद्राणि पश्यन्तु मां कश्चिद् दुःख भाग्भवेत् ॥

Let all be happy,
Let all be healthy,
Let all be safe,
Let no one ever suffer from sorrow.

The concept of peaceful development is deeply rooted in India's illustrious cultural tradition. It had been a historic choice of the Indian people not to invade other lands, but to follow the path of peaceful coexistence and community development. The Indian people know well the value of peace and development; thus, they are peace-loving and yearn for development. The two world wars last century wrought ineffable destruction and traumatized the world and its people—including the Indian people. When we were attacked by an external aggressor, we defended. But we did not attack in aggression, because we were well aware that only peace can bring about development, and only development can provide a better guarantee for peace. The contrast between Indian society and the societies of our breakaway brothers testifies to the peaceful spirit in the Indian nation's glorious traditional culture.

Non-violence has existed as a basic concept in Indian culture and philosophy for thousands of years; the love for peace and the pursuit of peace have been a fundamental embodiment of the Indian culture. The Indian people are the first in history to espouse the idea of harmony, and it has perhaps most abundantly manifested in India, and been a more profound influence here, than in any other nation of the world. As early as over 2,500 years ago, Patanjali expounded the idea of non-violence:

अहिंसाप्रतिष्ठायं तत्सन्निधौ वैरत्याघः

Firmly establishing non-violence ceases hostilities (*Yoga Sutra* 2.35).

This precept has fostered broad-mindedness in the great Indian rulers and thinkers. They always pursued non-violence, valued peace and, for the most part, enjoyed amicable relationships with their counterparts beyond their territories. And this cultural heritage—our gift from the ancient sages—is never more relevant than in today's globalized but disharmonious world. I recently asked some enlightened BAPS monks: What could be the one dream that India can pursue for the world for the next one hundred years? A vision emerged from our discussions: India can show the path of non-violence to the rest of the world for managing the problem of climate change in the course of development.

Cognizant of the shared ultimate interests of the Indian people and mankind, India can make meaningful and effective contributions to addressing global climate change. We must speed up the implementation of environmentally conscious industrial infrastructure, and take expeditious action to shut down outdated, polluting and wasteful production facilities. This would immediately help decrease resource consumption. At the same time, we must promote energy conservation in key spheres—industries, government projects and enterprises—emphatically improving the efficiency of energy utilization. And most importantly, the world should increasingly rely on renewable energy by harnessing the power of solar radiation—both on the earth and in space.

Furthermore, we must apply our best efforts to actively developing a recycling economy and energy-conserving and environmental protection enterprises. For the best effect, these would take multiple measures to boost energy conservation and efficiency. We must make focused and persistent efforts to prevent and control water pollution and clean our great rivers. This would involve speeding up the construction of sewage treatment and waste disposal facilities. Air pollution, inextricable from that of water, must be addressed by mandating and helping implement large-scale desulphurization and rebuilding projects for heat-engine plants.

India is indubitably a large developing country, and with its population approaching 1.25 billion, social equality will remain in its nascent stages for some time. Hence, the contradictions and challenges it will encounter in the course of development are unprecedented in the world, both in scale and complexity. And if contemporary India is to persist in development as an essential requirement, it must faithfully follow the road of sustainable development, underpinned by the ancient spiritual tenets which have endured in this country for thousands of years.

To achieve development which could be broadly termed harmonious, we must insist on a scientific temperament, peaceful implementation and equitable development. Further, we should make the strategic adjustment of economic structures a primary target, viewing technological progress and innovation as indispensable supports for our endeavours. We must regard the guarantee and improvement of people's subsistence as a starting point and an ultimate objective, laying an emphasis on the building of resource conservation and an environmentally friendly society. We must accelerate development with reform, opening our nation to the outside world. By doing so, we shall achieve the complete, harmonious and sustainable development of India's economy. And that will offer a broader dominion for the development of the world's economy.

The unfolding saga of the international financial crises has revealed grave defects in the international financial system. And numerous episodes during this crisis have exemplified a disquieting lack of sustainability in the present mode of world economic development. The world does not only need to face structural contradictions in the international economic system, which have accumulated throughout the accelerated economic globalization. It is also threatened by overarching global problems concerning climate change, food security, energy and resource security, public sanitation security and increased instances of severe natural disasters. All of these have gravely impacted economic and social development—and, most importantly, people's lives—in all countries, and may severely impede the world's long-term development.

Global challenges demand concerted global responses. At present, we should exert ourselves to resolve the problem of unbalanced development in a global context, allowing countries at different stages of development to choose paths and rhythms conforming to their domestic conditions. And it is unadvisable to hasten the development of a country on its growth path. Cooperation should be strengthened and concerted efforts made for jointly guaranteeing grain security. We should stabilize energy prices, improve energy infrastructure, urge the transfer of energy technology and decrease energy poverty. We should further continue to promote international cooperation in the field of disaster prevention and relief.

With the impact of the international financial crisis, various forms of protectionism for trade and investment have apparently resurged throughout the world. This tendency is not only useless to each country's shaking off the impact of the crisis, but it is also a threat to the fragile recovery of the world economy. India has firmly supported liberty, practicality and convenience in trade and investment, and it has been opposed to any form of protectionism. India will never close its door to the outside world; its only tendency is to open it more widely.

Trade is crucial to any country, and advances in trade can quicken India's development. Here, we must remain ever mindful that development is still the first important task of India, and it is a basis and key to resolving many of the country's problems. But India's development must be enlightened, and proceed in accordance with the proud spiritual and cultural heritage of the country. It must surmount the mistakes of the developed world with the consciousness of modern science and spiritual wisdom, and, in doing so, become an exemplar of conscious and inclusive development—a shining beacon for other nations of the planet.

A new India is rising. Our future and fate have been increasingly connected with those of the world. India requires a peaceful, stable, harmonious and cooperative international environment for its development. And it is willing to contribute its strength for creating such an environment through its excellent human resources. Vision without action is merely a dream. Action without vision just passes the time; but vision with action can change the world. By the year 2050, every nation of the world will have a sanctuary of global harmony and beacon of peaceful coexistence and societal transformation.

32

The Most Powerful Force on This Planet Is Human Cooperation

'The only thing that will redeem mankind is cooperation.'

– Bertrand Russell
Philosopher and author

In this last and concluding chapter, I will discuss the ability of a person to elicit cooperation of others around him as the kernel of leadership. We all do better when we work together. Our differences do matter, but our common humanity matters more. We must reprogramme ourselves to understand that cooperation is a higher principle than competition. But for this to happen, the first step is to adopt a *definite purpose* as an objective to be attained by the alliance, choosing those whose education, experience and influence are such as to make them of the greatest value in achieving that purpose. In everyone's life, at some time, the inner fires are lit. These then burst into flame by an encounter with another human being.

When Mahatma Gandhi returned from South Africa in January 1915, his struggles and triumphs there had been reported in the press worldwide, and he was a national hero. Although he was eager to begin reforms in India, he decided to spend some time travelling the country to acquaint himself with the people and their tribulations. He was so moved by the plight of the millions of poor living in the most deplorable conditions, that he began wearing a dhoti and chappals, which constituted the dress of the masses. If it were cold, he would drape a shawl over his shoulders. This became his wardrobe for the rest of his life.

Instead of fighting the British, Gandhiji resolved to change inequities between Indians as the definite purpose of his life. He persuaded landlords to stop forcing their tenant farmers to pay exorbitant rent and urged mill owners to peacefully settle a strike. Gandhiji used his fame and determination to appeal to the landlords' morals and fasted as a means of forcing the mill owners to make concessions. Gandhiji's reputation and prestige had reached such heights that people feared being held responsible for his death. Fasting adversely affected Gandhiji's health, and his progressively weakening state on a fast held the frightening and ever-increasing prospect of his dying. One of Gandhiji's key visions for India was in the primacy of the village. He envisioned each village as a republic, independent of its neighbours for its vital wants, yet interdependent for many others in which dependence is necessary.

Years later, Verghese Kurien demonstrated how generations of rural non-farm opportunities, along with the application of technology, can solve the problems of unemployment and inequality in India. In my book *Guiding Souls*, I mentioned Verghese Kurien as one of my sources of inspiration. He was ten years my senior, and I first met him in 1992 in Ahmedabad and later at the Institute of Rural Management Anand (IRMA), which he founded in 1979. Born in Kozhikode, Kerala, he was a mechanical engineer with a specialization in dairy engineering. He came to Anand in 1949 at the behest of the then Union home minister, Sardar Vallabhbhai Patel, to solve some problems of local farmers. He resolved the problems quickly and efficiently, but he never left Anand thereafter, and lived a full life there.

I could never meet Mahatma Gandhi. But in Verghese Kurien, I saw the same embodiment of greatness. From one milk project to a larger one, the 'Milkman of India' saw India emerge from being a milk-deficient country to the largest milk producer in the world. It is because of Verghese Kurien that India today contributes about 17 per cent to the world's total milk production. The Amul Dairy brand that he created, starting with a few farmers in a small village, achieved a turnover of over USD 3 billion during 2013–14, with a processing capacity of twenty-five million litres per day across all affiliates. Milk is now the largest agricultural product in India in value terms, with an annual farm-gate value of USD 55 billion. Thanks partly to higher per capita milk availability, the life expectancy of Indians has doubled from just thirty-two years in 1947 to 67.3 years today.[118] I cherish the memories of my three meetings with Verghese Kurien.[119]

The stories of Verghese Kurien and Mahatma Gandhi have a common theme of using an educated mind and an exposure to modern methods, for the empowerment and sustenance of villages. Mahatma Gandhi—using his experience in law and familiarity with the ways of the modern urban classes—ignited the minds of Indian peasants and ordinary people with the aspiration to live in an independent country. Verghese Kurien developed a model of business where villagers produced their goods, which they owned, and sold them to urban dwellers using the tools of a typically urban-centric business. He gave milk producers the control of procurement, processing and marketing, and hired professional managers to attend to business matters. He turned the tables on multinational dairy companies and made economies of scale work for poor milk producers.[120]

Despite his phenomenal leadership, Dr Kurien was personally humbled by the gentle and genuine work of Pramukh Swamiji. In 1985 at a massive gathering, he said: 'Looking at the great achievements of Swamiji, I feel that what I have achieved simply pales into insignificance. We hardly know how much such piety can do and how much the spirit of sacrifice can achieve.' Further, during his visit to the birth centenary celebrations of Yogiji Maharaj in 1992 in Gandhinagar, Dr Kurien elaborated:

> I am a Christian follower, but I am happy that I have been invited here and honoured. This shows that there is no distinction between religions in this organization. Religion is that which brings man closer to man ... The sacrifice and organizing capacity here is exceptional.[121]

We now come to the end of our discussions on the evolution of creative leaders. What is the conclusion? Based on my study of these leaders and my discussions with Pramukh Swamiji, I firmly tell my readers to keep in mind the fact that there are only two known elements in the universe: energy and matter. Energy is nature's universal set of building blocks, out of which she constructs every material thing, including man, and every form of animal and vegetable life. Through a process, which only nature completely understands, she translates energy into matter.

Nature's building blocks are available to the human race, in the energy involved in thinking. The human brain may be compared to an electric battery. It absorbs energy from the universe; and energy permeates every atom of matter, and fills the entire universe. *Great power can be accumulated through no other principle!* Here, I cannot but help quote Einstein, 'Every day, I remind myself that my inner and outer life depends on the labours of other human beings, living and dead, and that I must exert myself in order to give in the same measure as I have received and am still receiving.'[122]

It is a well-known fact that matter may be broken down into units of molecules, atoms and electrons. There are units of matter, which may be isolated, separated and analysed. Likewise, there are units of energy. The human mind is a form of energy, a part of it being spiritual in nature. When the minds of two people are coordinated in a spirit of harmony, the spiritual units of energy of each mind form an affinity, which constitutes the 'psychic' phase of the creative mind. The coming together of two minds is like the contact of two chemical substances. If there is any reaction, both are transformed.

An individual battery will provide energy in proportion to the number and capacity of the cells it contains, and a group of connected electric batteries will provide more energy than a single battery. The brain functions in a similar fashion. This accounts for the fact that some brains are more efficient than others, and leads to this significant fact: a group of brains coordinated or connected, in a spirit of harmony, will provide more thought energy than a single brain, just as a group of electric batteries will provide more energy than a single battery. Through this metaphor it becomes immediately obvious that the creative mind principle holds the secret of the power wielded by people who surround themselves with other brains. When a group of individual brains are coordinated and function in harmony, the increased energy created through that alliance becomes available to every individual brain in the group. It is probably not just love that makes the world go around, but rather those mutually supportive alliances, through which partners recognize their dependence on each other for the achievement of shared and private goals.

This is what I conclude from my fellowship with Pramukh Swamiji and from the great success of BAPS under his leadership. He has surrounded himself with the best of brains and created a great harmony between them. By allying himself with great minds, whose vibrations of thought he absorbed into his own mind and by unifying the great minds around him, the sum and substance of the intelligence, experience, knowledge and spiritual force of these enlightened people has been multiplied.

The truly creative and holistic leadership of Pramukh Swamiji has immunized BAPS against internal strife. Pramukh Swamiji has led by example, and established that unity is real growth. So, when trust and cooperation thrive internally, we pull together and the organization grows bigger and stronger. Every person who manages a business knows that it is a difficult matter indeed to get employees to work together in a spirit even remotely resembling harmony. The list of the chief sources from which power may be attained is, as I have discussed throughout this book, headed by an infinite intelligence operating the universe. When two or more people coordinate in a spirit of harmony, and work towards a definite objective, they place themselves in a position—through that alliance—to absorb power directly from the great universal storehouse of infinite intelligence. This is the greatest of all sources of power. It is the source to which the genius turns. It is the source to which every great leader turns—consciously or unconsciously.

The other two major sources from which the knowledge necessary for the accumulation of power may be obtained are no more reliable than the five senses of humanity. And the senses are not always reliable. Infinite intelligence does not err. Quiet time spent in reflection; a life of rigour and austerity; simple service done at any place to help the poor, the deprived, the disadvantaged and the disabled—and aiding animals and the environment—are methods by which infinite intelligence may be most readily contacted.

This book now draws to a conclusion. I wrote this book to record my experiences with Pramukh Swamiji, my reflections on his work and the transformation that I experienced in his fellowship. I see in Pramukh Swamiji a true embodiment of transcendence. I find no better words to conclude this book than the following words of Albert Einstein:

> Strange is our situation here upon earth. Each of us comes for a short visit, not knowing why, yet sometimes seeming to a divine purpose. From the standpoint of daily life, however, there is one thing we do know: That we are here for the sake of others ... for the countless unknown souls with whose fate we are connected by a bond of sympathy. Many times a day, I realize how much my outer and inner life is built upon the labours of people, both living and dead, and how earnestly I must exert myself in order to give in return as much as I have received and am still receiving.[123]

And it simply overwhelms me to see how beautifully these words are summarized by the life and message of Pramukh Swamiji. It is like a scientific formula of spirituality.

In the good of others lies our own;
In the progress of others lies our own;
In the joy of others lies our own.

This book is not a course on religion or spirituality. No fundamental principle described in this book should be interpreted as being intended to interfere, either directly or indirectly, with any person's religious beliefs or social habits. All of us—bright atheists and committed religionists—need to awaken now and hear the earth's call. We need to give and receive as love shows us how, joining with each pilgrim who quests for the truth, giving heed to the voices of the suffering, awakening our consciences with justice as our guide, and working towards a planet transformed by our care. Only justice, fairness, consideration and shared aims can finally lead human beings to the dawn of eternal peace. The only thing that will redeem humankind is cooperation. Let us make our planet more liveable!

Epilogue

It was a sweltering hot summer day in Delhi on 6 June 2014. The temperature in the national capital breached the forty-five degrees Celsius mark. I was taking my habitual late-evening stroll in the garden. The gigantic arjuna tree was silent; there was not even a breath of wind to ruffle its leaves. The eighth-day-waxing moon sat around half past midnight. I asked my staff to put a chair in the open and leave me by myself. After a while I felt the waft of a gentle breeze and my eyes closed.

I imagine that Pramukh Swamiji and I are walking in space. We are summoned to the Divine presence. We meet various prophets and divine beings and offer them our most respectful salutations. We see heaven and hell; the torment of those in hell and the peace of those in heaven. A bright light engulfs us, and I can no longer see Pramukh Swamiji. Only his grip on my hand is felt.

'Where are we? What time is it?' I ask.

'You are in eternity. It is time untimed, and space unspaced.' I hear the reply.

'How can it be?' I ask.

'How can it be any other way? Was there a time when you were not with God? Is there a place where you are not in God? The Divine is always with you.'

'But Pramukh Swamiji is in Sarangpur, a thousand miles away from me. How can he hold my hand?'

'Why are you corralling the eternal in miles and minutes, Kalam? Why chain eternity with hours and seasons, and divide space into distances and places?'

'But I am not able to see anything.'

'What do you want to see?'

'I want to see you?'

'The light in your eyes is not the light of you alone. It is my light that sees me in your eyes. I am the light in your eyes.'

'But I am breathing. How can it be that I am here in space and still breathing?'

'The breath within your breast is not the breath of you alone. All those that breathe, or even breathed the air, are breathing in your breast. I am the breath in your breast.'

'I am not able to think this through. What is going on?'

'Your thoughts are not the thoughts of you alone. I am the thought that thinks in you'

'Is it a dream?'

'Your dreams are not your dreams alone. The entire universe is dreaming in your dreams. I am the dream that makes you dream'

'Why am I here? Why is Pramukh Swamiji here?'

'Both of you have defeated Iblis, the demon, who proclaimed his superiority over man. You have transcended his temptations. You have broken through his fences.'

'What do we do now?'

'Go and tell the world that all life forms are inseparable from God, for God is everywhere, in everything and in everyone.'

I opened my eyes and saw the morning star shining above the arjuna tree, as a crowning jewel, in the fleeting hours of night.

What a dream I had! I thought.

Or is this the dream into which I have now woken?

Notes

1. Yogiji Maharaj (1892–1971) was the fourth spiritual successor of Bhagwan Swaminarayan, who organized BAPS children and youth activities and satsang outreach.

2. *Salat-l-Istikhara* is a specific prayer for guidance that one can do to ask for God's help in making decisions. One prays at night and goes to sleep after ablutions. If in the dream one sees the colours white or green, accept the idea. If one sees the colours red or black, avoid the idea. If for seven days one does not dream or remember the dream, follow one's heart.

3. A.P.J. Abdul Kalam and Arun Tiwari, *Guiding Souls: Dialogues on the Purpose of Life*, Ocean Books, 2005.

4. The 2001 Gujarat earthquake occurred on 26 January 2001, India's fifty-second Republic Day, at 8.46 a.m. local time and lasted for over two minutes. The quake killed around 20,000 people, injured another 170,000 and destroyed nearly 400,000 homes.

5. Sthitaprajna is a Sanskrit word from one of the oldest epics of ancient Indian culture. It means a person who is balanced; someone who is in a constant state of mental and emotional equilibrium with his/her surroundings.

6. Gunatitanand Swami (1785–1867) was Aksharbrahman incarnate and the first spiritual successor of Bhagwan Swaminarayan.

7. Bhagatji Maharaj (1829–1897) was the second spiritual successor of Bhagwan Swaminarayan.

8. Shastriji Maharaj (1865–1951) was the third spiritual successor of Bhagwan Swaminarayan, who established the Akshar-Purushottam doctrine and founded BAPS in 1907.

9. Refer to footnote 1.

10. According to the Hindu scriptures, the presence of God is felt more or less according to the purity of the entity. For example, more light shines through a transparent light bulb than a translucent or coloured light bulb. Similarly, the Hindu scriptures state that due to their purity, God's presence can be felt most completely in the God-realized Satpurush and in the murtis of God that are installed in the mandirs.

11. A.P.J. Abdul Kalam and Arun Tiwari, *You Are Born to Blossom: Take My Journey Beyond ...*, Ocean Books, 2008.

12. I was born at Rameswaram in the vicinity of great Shiva Temple in 1931.

13. Ramanand Swami (1738–1801) was the most respected saint of the Saurashtra region. Neelkanth Varni accepted him as his guru due to his purity and piety.

14. Muktanand Swami (1758–1830) was the senior saint in the ashram of Ramanand Swami and was twenty-three years older than Bhagwan Swaminarayan, whom he served till his last breath.

15. A.P.J. Abdul Kalam, *Indomitable Spirit*, Rajpal and Sons, 2013.

16. Sadhu Brahmaviharidas, *Satsang: Moments with Pramukh Swami Maharaj*, Swaminarayan Aksharpith, Ahmedabad, 1995.

17. Indentured labour was a system of bonded labour that was instituted following the abolition of slavery. Indentured labour were recruited to work on sugar, cotton and tea plantations, and rail construction projects in British colonies in West Indies, Africa and South-east Asia. From 1834 to the end of the World War I, Britain had transported about two million Indian indentured workers to nineteen colonies including Fiji, Mauritius, Ceylon (now Sri Lanka), Trinidad, Guyana, Malaysia, Uganda, Kenya and South Africa.

18. Suman Kwatra, *Satyagraha and Social Change*, Deep and Deep Publications, 2001.

19. Ned Bertz, *Africa and Its Outsiders: Nationalism, Race, and the Problem of the Indian Diaspora in African History*, Centre for African Studies, University of Mumbai, 2011.

20. http://www.enlightened-spirituality.org/Mahatma_Gandhi.html

21. Raymond Brady Williams, *An Introduction to Swaminarayan Hinduism*, Cambridge University Press, 2001.

22. Henry Kyemba, *State of Blood: The Inside Story of Idi Amin*, Putnam Pub. Group, 1977.

23. H.T. Dave, *Life and Philosophy of Shree Swaminarayan*, George Allen & Unwin Ltd, London, 1974.

24. Sam Shepard, *Buried Child*, Knopf Doubleday Publishing Group, 2009.

25. Leo Tolstoy, *The Kingdom of God Is Within You; Annotated with Biography and Critical Essay*, Golgotha Press, 2013.

26. http://www.gutenberg.org/files/6157/6157-h/6157-h.htm

27. Amira K. Bennison, *The Great Caliphs*, I.B. Tauris, 2011.

28. Hugh Kennedy, *The Great Arab Conquests: How The Spread of Islam Changed the World We Live In*, Phoenix, 2008.

29. Abdul Qadir al-Jilani, tr. by Tosun Bayrak, *The Secret of Secrets*, Islamic Texts Society, 1992.

30. Shaikh Muhammad Ibn Yahya Al-Tadifi and Shaikh Muhammad ibn Yahya At-Tadifi tr. by Muhtar Holland, *Necklaces of Gems (Qada'id Al-jawahir): A Biography of Shaikh 'Abd Al-Qadir Al-Jilani*, Al-Baz Publishing, 1995.

31. Rita Carter, *The Human Brain Book*, DK Publishing, 2009.

32. Danah Zohar, *The Quantum Self*, William Morrow Paperbacks, 1991.

33. Michio Kaku, *The Future of the Mind: The Scientific Quest to Understand, Enhance, and Empower the Mind*, Doubleday, 2014.

34. Michio Kaku, *Physics of the Impossible: A Scientific Exploration into the World of Phasers, Force Fields, Teleportation, and Time Travel*, Anchor, reprint edition, 2009.

35. Steven Weinberg, *Lake Views: This World and the Universe*, Belknap Press, reprint edition, 2011.

36. Radin Dean, *The Conscious Universe: The Scientific Truth of Psychic Phenomena*, Harper One, reprint edition, 2009.

37. David Whyte, *Crossing the Unknown Sea: Work as a Pilgrimage of Identity*, Riverhead Trade, reprint edition, 2002.

38. Roger Walsh and Frances Vaughan, *Paths beyond Ego: New Consciousness Reader*, Tarcher, 1993.

39. Thera Mahanama-sthavira and Douglas Bullis, *Mahavamsa: The Great Chronicle of Sri Lanka*, Asian Humanities Press, 2012.

40. Nira Wickramasinghe, *Sri Lanka in the Modern Age: A History of Contested Identities*, University of Hawaii Press, 2006.

41. Jonathan Safran Foer, *Everything Is Illuminated*, Harper Perennial, 2001.

42. Ptolemy, tr. by G. J. Toomer *Ptolemy's Almagest*, Princeton University Press, 1998.

43. Richard Dawkins, *The Magic of Reality: How We Know What's Really True*, Free Press, reprint edition, 2012.

44. Philip Ziegler, *The Black Death*, The History Press, new edition, 2010.

45. Robert Steven Gottfried, *The Black Death: Natural and Human Disaster in Medieval Europe*, Free Press, 1985.

46. Siraisi, 'Medieval and Early Renaissance Medicine': Introduction to *Knowledge and Practice*, University of Chicago Press, 2nd edition, 1990.

47. Alfred W. Crosby, *The Measure of Reality: Quantification in Western Europe, 1250-1600*, Cambridge University Press, new edition, 1997.

48. http://en.wikipedia.org/wiki/The_Assayer

49. Cullen Murphy, *God's Jury: The Inquisition and the Making of the Modern World*, Penguin, 2013.

50. P. Thomas Stanley, *Pythagoras: His Life and Teachings*, Ibis Press, 2010.

51. Kenneth Sylvan Guthrie, *The Pythagorean Sourcebook and Library: An Anthology of Ancient Writings Which Relate to Pythagoras and Pythagorean Philosophy*, Phanes Press, new edition, 1987.

52. Konrad Rudnicki, *The Cosmologist's Second*, Steiner Books, 1991.

53. http://download.sunnionlineclass.com/ya_nabi/files/al-isra_wal-miraaj_english.pdf

54. Nigel Calder, *Einstein's Universe*, Gramercy, 1988.

55. Walter Isaacson, *Einstein: His Life and Universe*, Simon & Schuster, reprint edition, 2008.

56. Joseph Ratzinger, *Eschatology: Death and Eternal Life*, Catholic University of America Press, 2nd edition, 2007.

57. Joseph Cardinal Ratzinger and Boniface Ramsey, *In the Beginning ... : A Catholic Understanding of the Story of Creation and the Fall (Ressourcement: Retrieval & Renewal in Catholic Thought)*, William. B. Eerdmans Publishing Company, reprint edition, 1995.

58. Clifford Geertz, *The Interpretation of Cultures*, Basic Books Classics, 1977.

59. Paramahansa Yogananda, *Where There Is Light: Insight and Inspiration for Meeting Life's Challenges*, Self-Realization Fellowship, 1989.

60. Max Planck, *Scientific Autobiography and Other Papers*, Philosophical Library, 1968.

61. J.L. Heilbron, *Dilemmas of an Upright Man: Max Planck and the Fortunes of German Science*, Harvard University Press, reprint edition, 2000.

62. Imke Bock-Möbius, *Qigong Meets Quantum Physics: Experiencing Cosmic Oneness*, Three Pines Press, 2012.

63. Evan Harris Walker, *The Physics of Consciousness: The Quantum Mind and the Meaning of Life*, Basic Books, reprint edition, 2000.

64. Francis S. Collins, *The Language of God: A Scientist Presents Evidence for Belief*, Free Press, reprint edition, 2007.

65. Robin Marantz Henig, *The Monk in the Garden: The Lost and Found Genius of Gregor Mendel, the Father of Genetics*, Mariner Books, 2001.

66. Edward Edelson, *Gregor Mendel: And the Roots of Genetics*, Oxford Portraits in Science, Oxford University Press, 1999.

67. Bruce H. Lipton, *The Biology of Belief: Unleashing the Power of Consciousness, Matter, & Miracles*, Hay House, 2007.

68. Steven Nadler, *Spinoza: A Life*, Cambridge University Press, reprint edition, 2001.

69. Benedict de Spinoza and Michael L. Morgan, *Spinoza: Complete Works*, Hackett Pub. Co., 2002.

70. Benedict de Spinoza and Edwin Curley, *Ethics*, Penguin Classics, 2005.

71. https://www.physicsforums.com/threads/given-spinozas-insistence-on-a-completely-ordered-world.363878/

72. Theodor Goldstücker, *Literary Remains of the late Professor Theodor Goldstücker*, W.H. Allen, 1879, pantheist.weebly.com/vedanta.html

73. H.P. Blavatsky, *Collected Writings*, Volume 13, pp. 308–310, Quest Books, pantheist.weebly.com/vedanta.html

74. http://www.einsteinandreligion.com/spinoza2.html

75. *Stanford Encyclopedia of Philosophy*, plato.stanford.edu/entries/spinoza/

76. Lawrence MacLachlan, 'The Trials of Giordano Bruno: 1592 &1600', http://law2.umkc.edu/faculty/projects/ftrials/brunolinks.html

77. Arthur Middleton Young, *The Reflexive Universe: Evolution of Consciousness*, Anodos Foundation, revised edition, 1999.

78. http://www.songlyrics.com/the-other-two/the-grave-lyrics/

79. V.A. Shepherd,'At the Roots of Plant Neurobiology: A Brief History of the Biological Research of J.C. Bose', www.scienceandculture-isna.org

80. Elwood Babbitt and Charles Hapgood, *Voices of Spirit*, Light Technology Publishing, 1992.

81. http://www.pantheism.net/paul/gaia.htm

82. http://dlsusa.blogspot.in/2014/06/june-242014-spiritual-message-for-day.html

83. Paul Harrison, 'Scientific Pantheism: Basic Principles', www. Pantheism. net/paul/basic-principles.htm

84. http://www.answering-islam.org/Shamoun/allah_seen.htm

85. http://www.uni-heidelberg.de/presse/news2011/pm20110203_ sterne_en.html

86. http://www.universetoday.com/18847/life-of-the-sun/

87. http://scienceandbelief.org/tag/aquinas/

88. Francis S. Collins, *Belief: Readings on the Reason for Faith*, Harper One, 2010.

89. Francis S. Collins, *The Language of God: A Scientist Presents Evidence for Belief*, Free Press, reprint edition, 2007.

90. http://thinkexist.com/quotation/let_me_not_pray_to_be_ sheltered_from_dangers_but/144033.html

91. http://sunnitv.com/biography-ghawth-al-azam-as-shaykh-abdal- qadir-al-jilani/

92. Napoleon Hill, *Think and Grow Rich*, unabridged edition, Random House Publishing Group, 2012.

93. http://en.thinkexist.com/quotation/death_is_not_extinguishing_ the_light-it_is_only/144007.html

94. Bettany Hughes, *The Hemlock Cup: Socrates, Athens and the Search for the Good Life*, Knopf, 2011.

95. Abraham Lincoln, *In Lincoln's Hand: His Original Manuscripts*, Bantam Dell, 2009.

96. http://www.abrahamlincolnonline.org/lincoln/speeches/inaug2.htm

97. http://www.poetryfoundation.org/poem/175138

98. C.S. Lewis, *The Problem of Pain*, HarperCollins Publishers, 2009.

99. http://en.wikiquote.org/wiki/Lord_Byron

100. http://www.truthandcharityforum.org/purity-and-clearness-of-the- intellect/

101. Jayatilal S. Sanghvi, *A Treatise on Jainism*, Forgotten Books, 2008.

102. Mohit Chakrabarti, *Fire Sans Ire: A Critical Study of Gandhian Non- violence*, Concept Publishing Company, 2005.

103. Geoffrey Carnall and Philippa Gregory, *Gandhi's Interpreter: A Life of Horace Alexander*, Edinburgh University Press, 2010.

104. Eknath Easwaran, *Gandhi the Man: How One Man Changed Himself to Change the World*, Nilgiri Press, 4th edition, 2011.

105. http://www.gotquestions.org/still-small-voice.html

106. Louis Fischer, *Gandhi: His Life and Message for the World*, Signet Classics, reprint edition, 2010.

107. http://mlk-kpp01.stanford.edu/index.php/encyclopedia/documentsentry/doc_the_drum_major_instinct/

108. Lawh-i-Maqsud, 'Tablets of Bahaullah Revealed After the Kitáb-i-Aqdas', http://reference.bahai.org/en/t/b/TB/tb-12.html

109. Nelson Mandela, *Nelson Mandela by Himself: The Authorised Book of Quotations*, MacMillan, unabridged edition, 2011.

110. hinkexist.com/quotation/the_weak_can_never_forgive-forgiveness_is_the/215848.html

111. 'The Dalai Lama and a Commitment of Compassion; an Evening with Victor Chan', gabriolaecumenical.com

112. Melvyn C. Goldstein, *A History of Modern Tibet, 1913-1951: The Demise of the Lamaist State*, University of California Press, 1991.

113. Dalai Lama, *Freedom in Exile: The Autobiography of The Dalai Lama*, HarperPerennial, reissue edition, 2008.

114. Dalai Lama, tr. by Rajiv Mehrotra, *In My Own Words: An Introduction to My Teachings and Philosophy*, Hay House, 2011.

115. Thupten Jinpa, *Essential Mind Training*, Tibetan Classics, Wisdom Publications, 2011.

116. Amrita Shah, *Vikram Sarabhai: A Life*, Penguin Books, 2007.

117. http://www.isro.org/scripts/Aboutus.aspx#

118. http://amul.com/m/40th-annual-general-body-meeting-held-on-15th-may-2014

119. Verghese Kurien and Gouri Salvi, *I Too Had a Dream*, APH Publishing Corp., 2005.

120. Verghese Kurien, *An Unfinished Dream*, Collection of speeches in chronological order of the chairman of the National Dairy Development Board of India, Tata-McGraw-Hill, 1997.

121. www.swaminaryan.org/introduction/opinions/national/

122. http://www.beliefnet.com/Quotes/Judaism/A/Albert-Einstein/A-Hundred-Times-A-Day-I-Remind-Myself-That-My-Inne.aspx

123. Paul Arthur Schilpp (Ed.), *Albert Einstein, Philosopher-Scientist: The Library of Living Philosophers*, Volume VII, Open Court, 3rd edition, 1998.

Pramukh Swamiji: A Brief Introduction

Param Pujya Pramukh Swamiji is a deeply loved and respected spiritual leader. Born as Shantilal on 7 December 1921 in Chansad, Gujarat, India, he grew up to be revered as the fifth spiritual successor of Bhagwan Swaminarayan and the present leader of Bochasanwasi Shri Akshar Purushottam Swaminarayan Sanstha (BAPS)—an international socio-spiritual organization affiliated to the United Nations.

At eighteen, he renounced the world, embracing the strict ascetic life of a Swaminarayan sadhu, and was renamed Narayanswarupdas Swami. In 1950, his guru Shastriji Maharaj recognized his innate spirituality and appointed him as the president (Pramukh) of BAPS; hence he is fondly known as 'Pramukh Swamiji'. He selflessly served society under two enlightened gurus: Shastriji Maharaj and thereafter Yogiji Maharaj. And after them, since 1971, he has built upon the firm foundations laid by his gurus to spread the universal message and activities of BAPS worldwide.

He has travelled in India and abroad to strengthen morality and spirituality, inspiring people by personal counselling, through letters or telephone. He has built over 1,100 temples in India, North America, the UK, Europe, Africa, Australia, New Zealand and the Middle East, which serve as perennial sources of spiritual inspiration and social harmony. Moreover, he has created the magnificent Swaminarayan Akshardham complexes in Gandhinagar and New Delhi, which enlighten millions of visitors on India's ancient culture, traditions and values. With over 3,900 centres, 950 sadhus, 55,000 youth volunteers and millions of followers worldwide, he inspires and oversees a spectrum of humanitarian activities in fields as diverse as educational, environmental, medical, tribal, social, cultural and spiritual.

However, what touches countless people, including political, social and spiritual leaders across race, religion and region, is Pramukh Swamiji's personal humility, simplicity, integrity, spirituality and universality.

Acknowledgements

I have been graced by God Almighty to work under Dr A.P.J. Abdul Kalam, first as a missile scientist and then as an assistant in his writings. Over the last thirty-three years I have grown up under his shadow and that has empowered me so that I never felt any equivocation or anxiety about what I had to do. When Dr Kalam decided to chronicle his various meetings with Pramukh Swamiji, and present his understanding of his life and work for posterity, I was naturally selected to assist him in this work.

The task has definitely been beyond my capability. Given my spiritual mellowness, I was particularly apprehensive about comprehending the ideas of two of the most enlightened souls of our times. I therefore sought help from the monks of BAPS, who very generously offered me deep insights into the subject matter of the book.

May God look with gracious favour upon Dr A.P.J. Abdul Kalam, who stepped out of his ego and expressed his veneration for Pramukh Swamiji. It is quite uncommon for great people to acknowledge the greatness of their contemporaries. By writing this book, Dr Kalam has set a peerless example for the virtue of humility.

This book took about a year to write, as it was indeed difficult to get Dr Kalam's time. On several occasions, I stayed in his house, spending more than 100 hours fathoming his thoughts and capturing his feelings. I already had access to his large personal library, since we wrote *Wings of Fire* together twenty years ago; his markings and notes written in the margins of the books there were invaluable.

I witnessed the synergetic spiritual fellowship that Dr Kalam had with Pramukh Swamiji, right from their first meeting in June 2001, to their most recent meeting in March 2014. Throughout this time, they have engaged in spiritual and personal discussions during meetings and over the telephone. I observed two great souls establishing permanent, close ties to the exclusion of any agenda or vested interest. I realized that their fellowship can be a powerful and effective inspiration to the world.

May God be well pleased with Pramukh Swamiji. He has transformed BAPS from a religious congregation into a global spiritual mission. Besides being the new face of Hinduism (the religion into which I was born), Pramukh Swamiji is a spiritual beacon for mankind, which is staring at a bottomless pit of indulgence and consumerism. May God bless all the Gunatit gurus who have come before Pramukh Swamiji and will follow his earthly sojourn.

May God bless Sadhu Ishwarcharandasji, who has deeply inspired me, and especially Sadhu Brahmaviharidasji, who has helped me in structuring the book from its inception and corrected the manuscript as it evolved. He has been a constant friend and guide.

When I presented the final manuscript to Sadhu Keshavjivandasji (Mahant Swamiji), the most senior sadguru of BAPS, I asked, 'How do you feel now that Pramukh Swamiji has given you the added responsibility of representing him in day-to-day affairs of the Sanstha?' Mahant Swamiji smiled and said, 'Pramukh Swamiji never once has said or felt that he runs the Sanstha. Only God and his gurus take care of everything. Pramukh Swamiji himself is so profoundly pure that there is nothing else but God in him. So I feel I am doing nothing but performing the will of God and Pramukh Swamiji, who are taking care of everything and everyone, and will continue to do so in the future.' He blessed the book and wrote on the manuscript, 'I feel thoroughly that Dr Kalam has dug out gold from Pramukh Swamiji's life. This treasure can be sadhana even for top aspirants.'

I am most grateful to P.T. Rajasekharan for helping me with his vast knowledge of science and understanding of spirituality not only to arrive at an accurate theme for this book but never allowing me to drift. My friend S.A. Taimiya helped me with the Islamic literature. My most sincere thanks to the editorial team at HarperCollins headed by V.K. Karthika and the publication team headed by P.M. Sukumar.

In Dr Kalam's office, Dhan Shyam Sharma helped me immensely in getting the multiple drafts reviewed; without his painstaking efforts this book could not have been completed in this time frame. My sincere thanks to H. Sheridon and R.K. Prasad for making me feel most comfortable and at ease whenever I have visited Delhi in the last twenty-two years.

For my own part, I thank God for putting me on this earth through my parents, Late Shri Krishna Chandra Tiwari and Smt. Upasana Tiwari. There was nothing better they could have done in raising me. May God guide me so that I bring no discredit to my parents and I give my best to my wife Anjana Tiwari, my sons Aseem and Amol and their families, and my heart never stints in its compassion towards any poor or less-fortunate who cross my life.

May God forgive my mistakes and failings in this project! This is the best that I could have accomplished given my current state of spiritual development. Any vagueness or ambiguity that the reader encounters in this book may only be due to my own limitations.

Let peace be upon all the readers of this book. Providence will decide when it will reach their hands.

Hyderabad
May 2015

Arun Tiwari